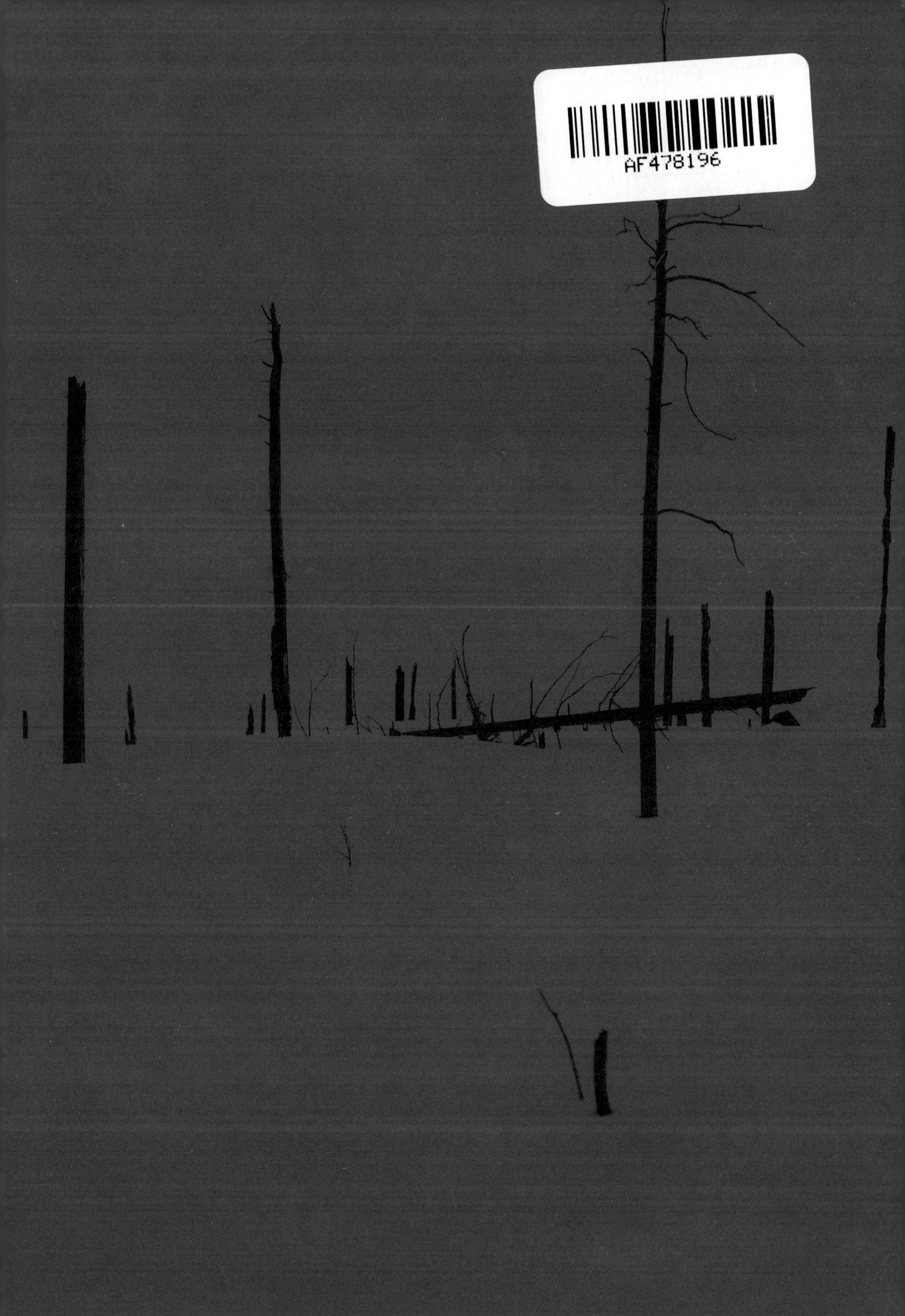
AF478196

Darren
Almond

Index

Darren Almond

Index

Parasol unit / Koenig Books, London

Part I
Fire Under Snow

Part II
Selected Works 1995–2007

Foreword

Seldom does an artist's work encompass such a variety of topics with the ease and high degree of aestheticism as that of Darren Almond. Since the beginning of his career in the early 1990s Almond has been dealing with both the private and collective human experience, with global and intimate concerns, in modes that are both analytical and emotional.

For his solo exhibition at Parasol unit foundation for contemporary art Almond has opted to engage with issues related to the human condition in our global world. Whether the stages on which the human tragedies he depicts are the remote labour camps of the Gulag[1] in Siberia, the vast and inaccessible mountain regions of Tibet, or even the sulphur deposits in Indonesia, Almond's work acts as a magnifying glass to highlight some of the unscrupulous causes of human tragedy in our world.

The realisation of the exhibition *Fire Under Snow* was an extraordinary endeavour that required Almond's total commitment. Through the entire process I looked on with admiration at Almond's enthusiasm and sense of responsibility towards the project. As is only befitting, I now express to him my deepest gratitude.

No acknowledgement would be complete without thanking Darren Almond's young family who so gracefully accepted his many trips to far distant lands to film works for this exhibition.

We at Parasol unit are proud to provide in this publication a comprehensive overview of Almond's body of works. We have had the great privilege of being able to reprint a previously published text by Simon Ertz, and to have remarkably insightful essays contributed by Robert Thurman and Julian Heynen, for which I cannot thank them enough.

For their constant efforts I am very pleased to thank Bridget Chew, Connor Linskey and Kathleen Madden at Darren Almond's studio. They could not have been more helpful throughout the preparation of this exhibition and its publication.

1   Gulag is an acronym for *Glavnoye Upravleniye Ispravitelno-trudovykh Lagerey i kolonii,* that is the Chief Directorate of Corrective Labour Camps and Colonies, formerly the main administrative department of the Soviet security service. Established 1930, it was responsible for prisons and forced labour camps in the USSR.

As usual many people contributed to the realisation of this project. It is once more my pleasure to thank Helen Wire for her acute editing skills, Marc Kappeler and Markus Reichenbach for their imaginative book design, Sam Forster for building an attractive exhibition space, and Anna Nesbit and Simeon Corless for their expert installation of the exhibition.

The team at Parasol unit seems to thrive on challenges; the more complex the project the more motivated they become. For their assistance in realising this exhibition I am grateful to Melanie Ahmed, Cliodhna Murphy, Nick Sanders, Miwa Takamura, Peter Turner and Emma Williams.

Finally, Parasol unit is thrilled to acknowledge the financial support of both the Arts Council of England and the Stanley Thomas Johnson Foundation, Bern, Switzerland. As a predominantly privately funded cultural institution with a public focus, Parasol unit regards such generous support to be highly encouraging. Private initiatives have become increasingly important and it is surely by supporting them that we can make a better world.

Ziba de Weck Ardalan
Director/Curator

Part I
Fire Under Snow

Tide

2008

600 digital wall clocks, Perspex, electro-mechanics, steel, vinyl, computerized
electronic control system and components
Each clock: 31.2 x 18.2 x 14.2 cm (12¼ x 7¼ x 5½ in)

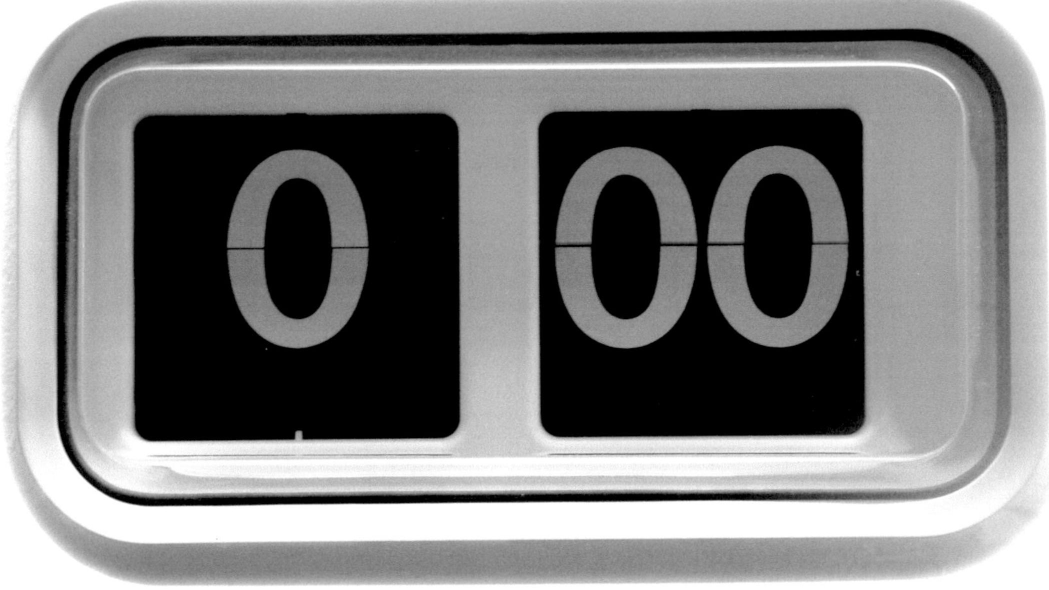

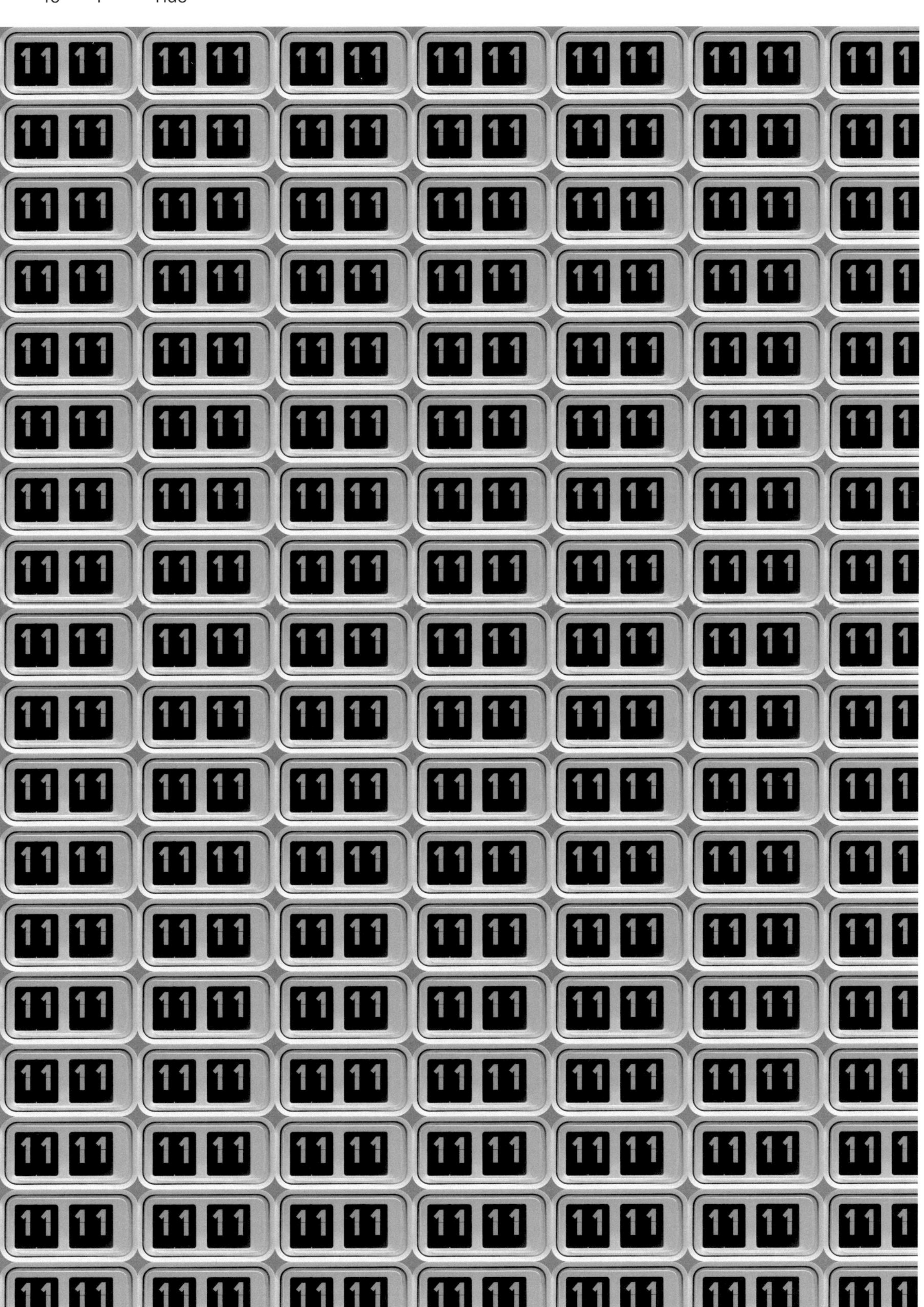

Don't be surprised ... all of this is life.[1]

Life as Carnival

Ziba de Weck Ardalan

Schwebebahn: A train glides along without stopping in an almost vertiginous manner to the hypnotic sound of techno music. And what a calamity, it is upside-down! Worse even, it's running backwards. The passengers seem to be standing or sitting with their feet resting on the ceiling of the train, something that defies our notion of gravity. Paradoxically, no one seems to mind; it looks as if they consider it a perfectly normal way to ride in a train. Darren Almond's 12-minute video *Schwebebahn* [p.132], 1995, is named after the world's first suspended monorail train, built in Wuppertal, Germany. The film has many peculiarities; it moves from black-and-white to colour and the frenzy stemming from the work clearly alludes to different worlds as well as to the past and present. In some ways watching it is not dissimilar to sitting in a rollercoaster at the mercy of whatever happens, with no control whatsoever over one's destiny.

If I Had You: An aging and dignified woman looks with some emotion at the various scenes projected around her, but for the most part she is looking at them with a degree of impatience, as if she already knows these scenes and having to see them over and over again is unnecessary and potentially painful for her. The scenes show a slowly revolving windmill lit by colourful lights in hues of pink and purple as if to indicate the passage of time in a sentimental way; a fountain in a park projecting water in sporadic bursts of energy, this time showing the passage of time in a festive way; and, finally,

1   Gabriel García Márquez, *In Evil Hour,* Harper & Row, Publishers, Inc., 1979, p.181.

in a partial view of a ballroom a couple glide gracefully around a parquet floor, dancing to a beautiful piano melody. The almost motionless quality of the aging woman is in strong contrast to the vitality and movement so evident in the other scenes. Yet clearly she is the protagonist of this work. *If I Had You* [p.170], 2003, is a four-screen projection about Almond's widowed grandmother as she reflects on her youth, remembering her late husband, their romance and the happy moments they'd had together. The impatience expressed on her face may also be an indication of her readiness to be reunited with her beloved. The eloquent juxtaposition of memories and emotion in this piece make it a powerful expression of the human condition.

In The Between: A high-speed train charges through a barren and mountainous landscape, its dizzying speed proof of its state-of-the-art technology, its hustling and uncompromising allure contrasting dramatically to a serene interior view of a monastery where Buddhist monks, oblivious to the outside world, are peacefully chanting prayers. The film *In The Between* [p.44], 2006, is a three-screen projection which takes as its subject the high-speed Qinghai–Tibet rail track that was completed in 2006 and now connects major Chinese cities to Lhasa and other destinations in Tibet. Almond's film can be seen as a metaphor for the intrusion of a superpower into the territories of a peaceful culture that can only surrender to it. But the underlying reality here is the tale of the railway's construction. Indeed, it took almost 50 years to complete some 2000 kilometres of track, half of which had to be laid at an altitude 4000 metres above sea level, a process which took place under harsh conditions of low oxygen levels and low temperatures, and ultimately claimed countless lives.

Night + Fog: Dead and bleak-looking trees stand out in snow-covered landscapes. In these large black-and-white photographs there is no evidence of life whatsoever. With their heavy grey skies they seem to instil in us a deep sense of nostalgia for what has been destroyed in these oppressive environments where life is non-existent. Although far more uncompromising and direct, these photographs find a kindred spirit in the nineteenth-century paintings of Caspar David Friedrich (1774–1840). They, too, seem to emanate feelings of nostalgia for what had been before something went terribly wrong. Almond's series of photographs *Night + Fog* [p.76], 2007, depict the forests around the city of Norilsk, Siberia, once at the centre of the former Soviet Gulag system of labour camps, a region where nickel mining remains the main activity. Norilsk is rated among the most polluted cities in the world, and the life expectancy of its inhabitants is at least ten years less than that of people living in other Russian cities.

Oświęcim, March 1997: An old and somewhat dilapidated bus stop stands in front of a large building that at first glance seems unidentifiable. Numerous graffiti cover the structure of the shelter and among them the word *Muzeum* is apparent. The scene is in the Polish town Oświęcim or as we have come to know it, Auschwitz. The larger edifice is one of the former concentration camp buildings that now function as a museum. The bus stops of Oświęcim are the subject of several important works by Darren Almond, perhaps because they have such highly emotive associations for us. Also, bus stops are obviously significant places, or rather *non-places,* in the lives of many people. A bus stop is where one waits, hopes, becomes agitated, agonized and, finally, anxious. It can also be a meeting place or, all too often, where one is subject to voyeurism: people waiting at a bus stop are an easy target for the study of human reactions and emotions. One work, *Oświęcim, March 1997* [p.140], 1997, consists of two black-and-white 8-mm films projected side by side. One shows a bus stop full of people waiting for a bus that never comes; while the other shows an empty bus stop. The agonizing mood of the people waiting for the bus is further intensified by the film being shown in slow motion.

These are only summary descriptions of just a few of Almond's most poignant works, his real-life tableaux, which are often highly critical of our world, and in which he puts time, memory, labour, exploitation, and corruption centre stage. But at its best I like to think of Almond's work as successive tales in which the protagonist is invariably humanity itself, the human condition, its *Fortuna.* This brings to mind the works of Francisco Goya (1746–1828), but comparing the human fortunes and misfortunes more traditionally depicted in Goya's work to those so vividly portrayed in Almond's is like comparing a drama described in a conventional novel to one written about in the magical-realist literature of some Latin-American writers, such as Isabel Allende (1942–) and Gabriel García Márquez (1928–), or the literature that came and still comes about in response to the horrific events of World War II, such as *The Painted Bird* by Jerzy Kosinski (1933–1991).[2]

Human emotions and the human condition appear with such immediacy and frankness in Almond's work that they seem to simultaneously

2   Jerzy Kosinski, *The Painted Bird,* Boston: Houghton Mifflin, 1965.

penetrate our skin and consciousness, leaving us no room for manoeuvre, yet they are depicted in a highly sophisticated manner. While Almond is expert at vividly laying bare human misfortune, he is also capable of explicitly displaying the essence of life which is ultimately its affirmation. It is precisely this dichotomy that makes Almond's work intriguing beyond any reference and makes us think that in Almond's view nothing is lost forever and redemption may be possible. 'I hoped that despite an increment of melancholia produced in *If I Had You* [p.170], I also hoped that it would provide a certain optimism.'[3]

The mood in Almond's work and the diversity of situations he treats so daringly and straightforwardly have an interesting parallel in a view of carnival expressed by David K. Danow (1944–). In his book *The Spirit of Carnival,* Danow writes: 'There is indeed a life-affirming and life-enhancing "spirit" that pertains to Carnival in its varied and numerous manifestations. … For the spirit hovering over the spectacle of Carnival shares the stage with a lurking, less benevolent, even demonic twin, which, in a sometimes flirtatious manner that can have disastrous results, will smile upon and favour death rather than life.'[4]

Almond's work with all its emotional content does indeed manifest a delicate balance between life and death, good and evil, loss and redemption, all without ever becoming nihilistic. His work centres on an archetypal component of human life – *Fortuna*. It speaks of humanity's struggle in the face of challenging and demanding *reality* which, more often than we would like to accept, can be considerably more dramatic and overwhelming than anything the human imagination could invent. For example, it becomes clear that the film *In The Between* [p.44], 2006, does not speak solely of the domination of a superpower, China, over a peaceful culture, Tibet, but more importantly it discreetly makes us aware of the misfortune of the countless people who were forced to work under such difficult conditions and finally of those who lost their lives during the process. Almond's compassion for the destiny of forced labourers is evident in his series of black-and-white photographs, entitled *Minus 60,000,* 2005, which features various views of a desolate and abandoned railway. A devastating view of a broken timber bridge testifies to the misery of the 60,000 prisoners of the Stalinist era who died building it.

3   Darren Almond in conversation with Brad Barnes, *Kultureflash,* 30.11.2005.
4   David K. Danow, *The Spirit of Carnival: Magical Realism and the Grotesque,* The University Press of Kentucky, 1995, p.1.

As a young boy Almond took up train-spotting to escape the claustrophobia of Wigan, the small town where he was born in the north of England. 'I have done a lot of travelling and psychologically I need that attachment [to Wigan] to keep focused. But there is also a need to make yourself vulnerable through travel and exposure to different cultures. That was very much tied up with the notion of being a train-spotter as a kid: I am going to do something that nobody knows I am doing and I am going to get out of here and see something along the way.'[5] The image of a young boy, dependent and unable to flee at will, spotting trains as a way of diverting his longing for a wider world, revives in our mind the works of numerous artists of the past. Think of Caspar David Friedrich's nostalgic depiction of a domestic scene in which a home-confined nineteenth-century woman stands in front of an open window overlooking the sea, apparently longing to travel away with the sailing vessels leaving the harbour. In the paintings of Edvard Munch (1863–1944) the inability of people to unleash their feelings and desires is often metaphorically expressed in terms of landscape in transition. And the American artist Joseph Cornell (1903–72), whose artistic creativity was galvanized by his longing for far-distant places, was prompted to create his three-dimensional collage and assemblage boxes that clearly express a private melancholy and emotion. But Almond, as a man of the twenty-first century, has been able to realise his dream to travel extensively. Considering all this, it is interesting to observe how Almond's nostalgia for his childhood vision of travelling to remote places continues to inspire his work, albeit in a sophisticated form.

Almond considers emotional response to be an integral component of his works, whether they deal with the private sphere of family and friends, such as *If I Had You* [p.170], 2003, *Traction* [p.154], 1999, and *HMP Pentonville* [p.142], 1997, or relate to some collective experience, such as *Oświęcim, 1997,* 1997, *Terminus* [p.174], 2007, *Night + Fog* [p.76], 2007, and *In The Between* [p.44], 2006. 'There are definitely places beyond the ken of mathematics; personally, I refer to the passing away of my grandfather and how unbeknown at the time I isolated myself from my school class at the precise moment of his departure. I felt it very intensely at the time.'[6] This is equally true of Almond's well-known time pieces, often made with digital-clock technology, in which conceptual and scientific aspects must prevail. Here again

5   Darren Almond in an interview with John Slyce, 'Transport Medium', *Flash Art,* January–February 2002, pp. 71–72.
6   Darren Almond in conversation with Brad Barnes, *Kultureflash,* 30.11.2005.

human emotions are clearly perceptible, not only because the undisputed connection between the passage of time and the past inevitably engenders a certain state of melancholy, but also because each moment of time-change marked by a digital clock brutally reminds one that time is lapsing.

Considering Almond's emotion-rich works, it is no wonder he has found much inspiration for his artistic creativity in the life and work of the Nobel Prize winner, Russian poet Joseph Brodsky (1940–96) who, prior to being exiled in 1972, spent eighteen months in a Siberian labour camp. Even in his later days Brodsky continued to reflect upon the homeland he had left behind and to express his emotional response to all its beauty, richness, sadness, and mercilessness.

In taking the reality of daily life as the subject matter for his dramatic works, Almond convincingly demonstrates that there is more to be stunned and bewildered by in real life than in any spectacle invented through the toil of one's imagination. In this he shares the view of some great thinkers, such as Gabriel García Márquez, Joseph Brodsky, David K. Danow, and not least the Russian literary theorist and philosopher Mikhail Bakhtin (1895–1975), whose poignant statement, 'The sensitive ear will always catch even the most distant echoes of a carnival sense of the world',[7] can only sustain what has been said above.

7   Mikhail Bakhtin, 'Problems of Dostoevsky's poetics', *Theory and History of Literature,* vol. 8. Caryl Emerson, trans. And ed., 1984, p.107.

Bearing

2007

Single-channel HD video with audio
35 minutes

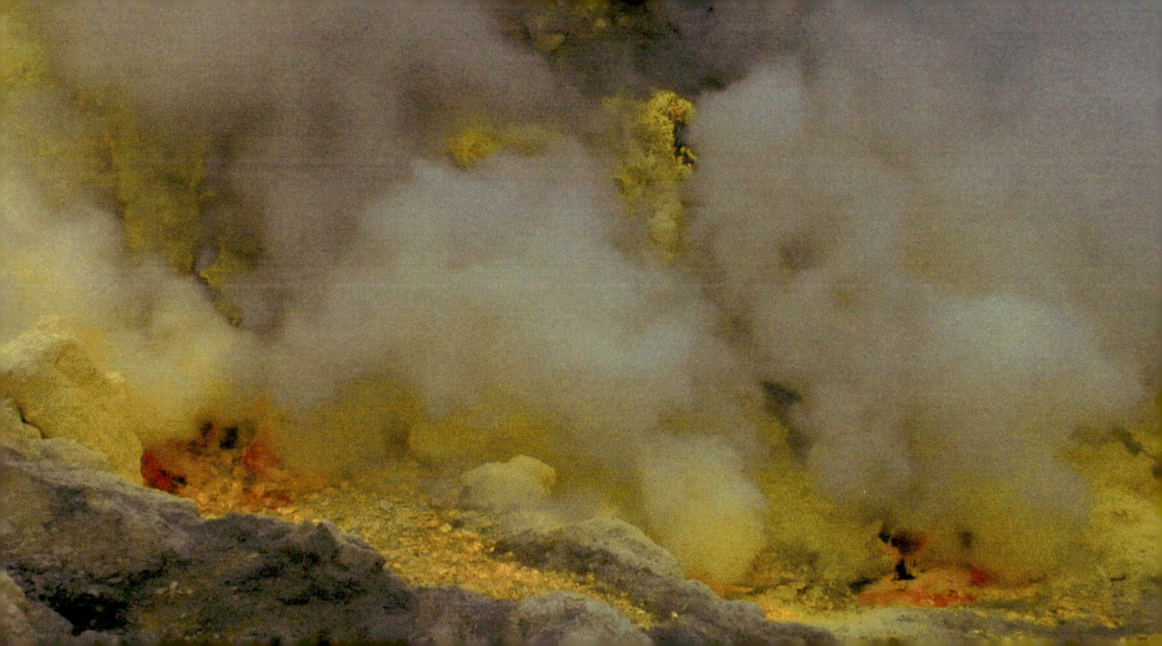

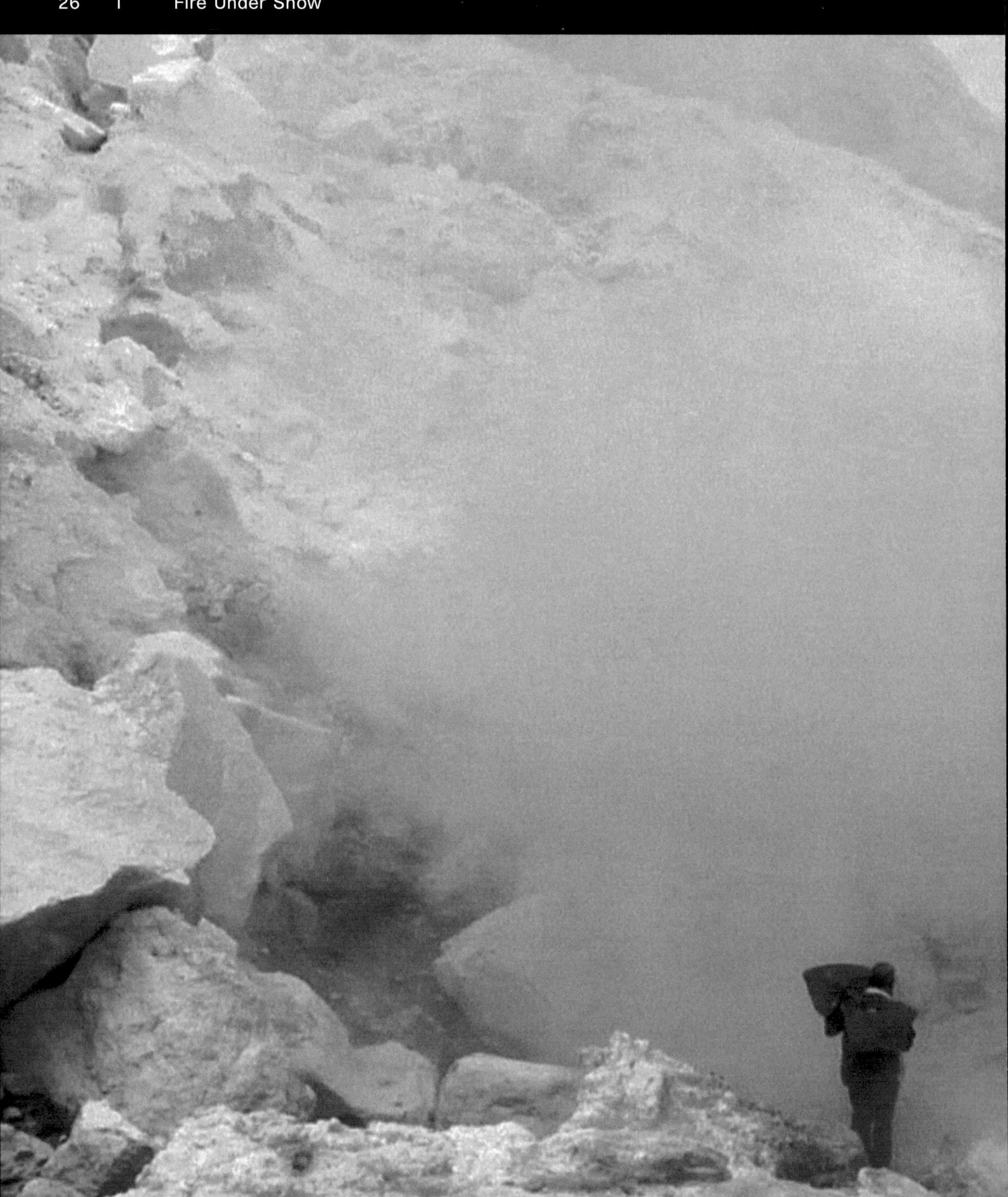

Bearing

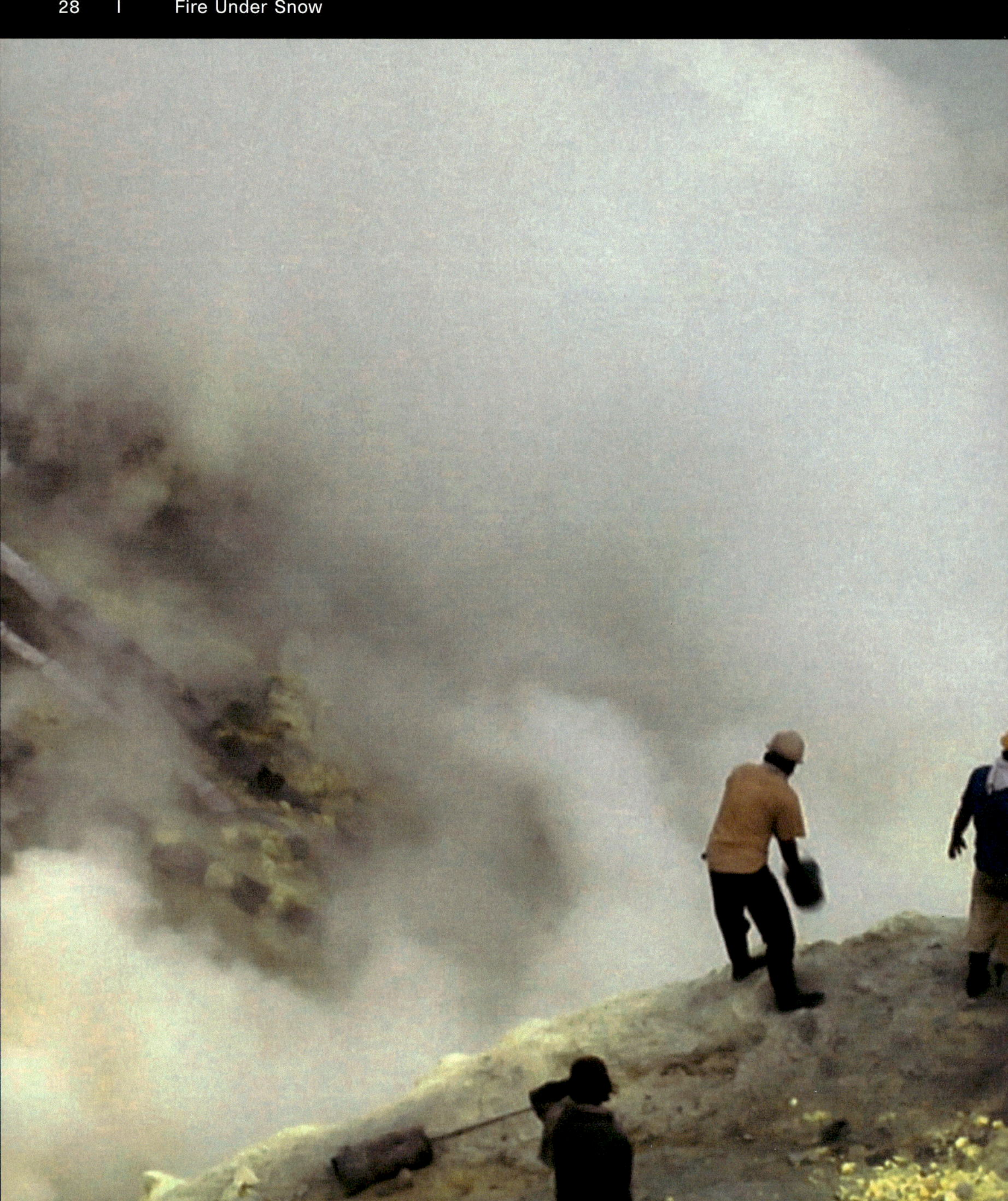

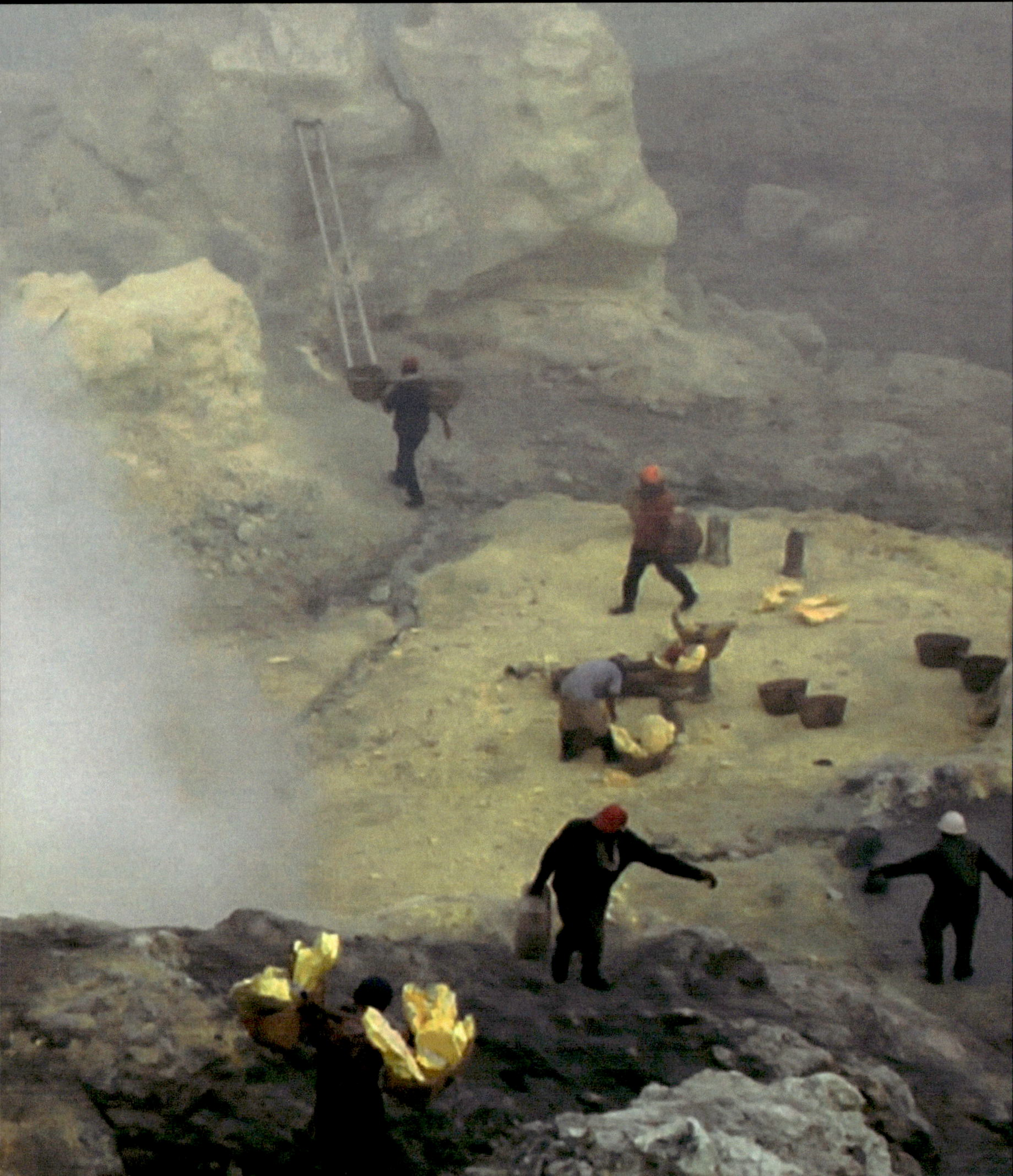

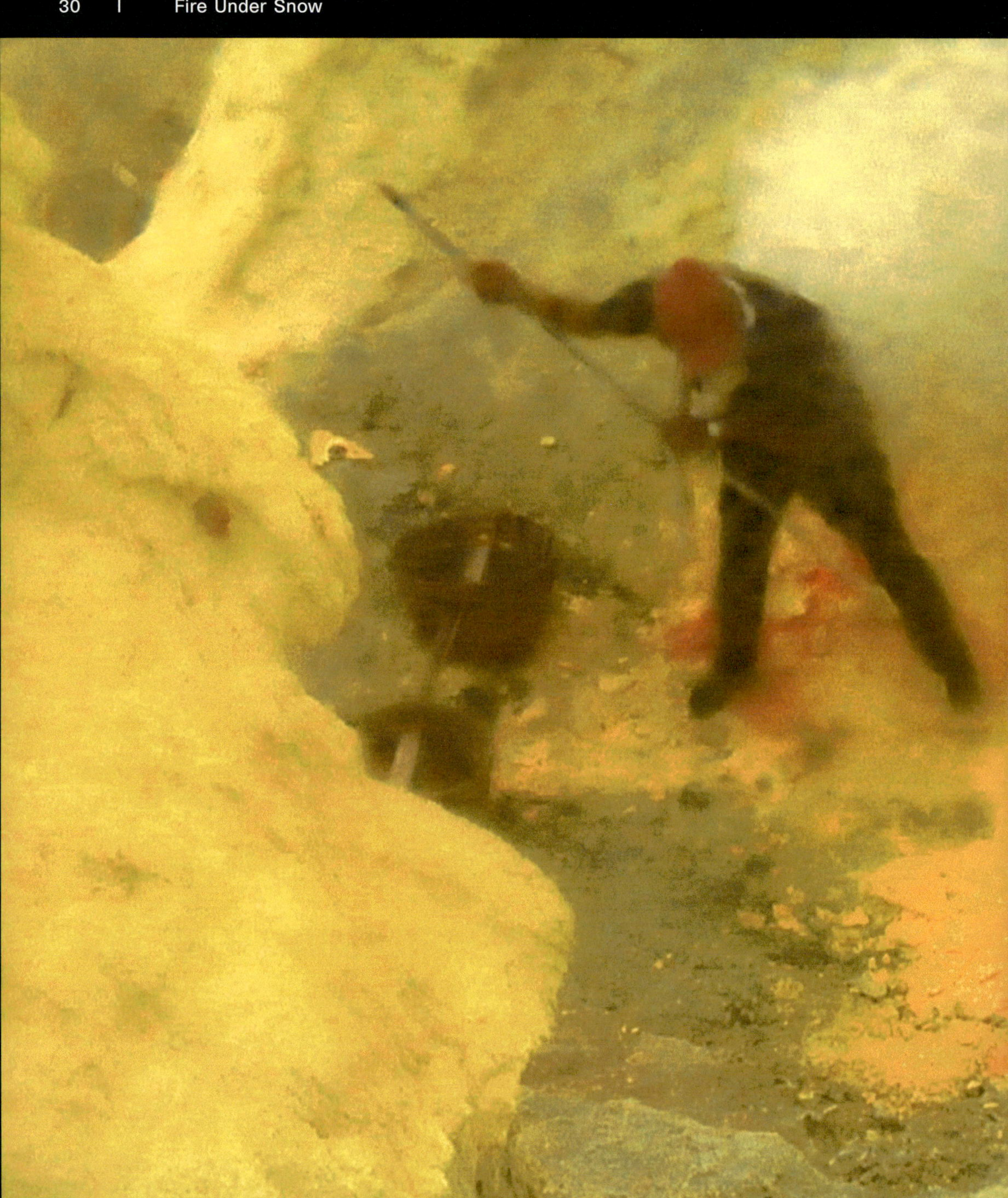

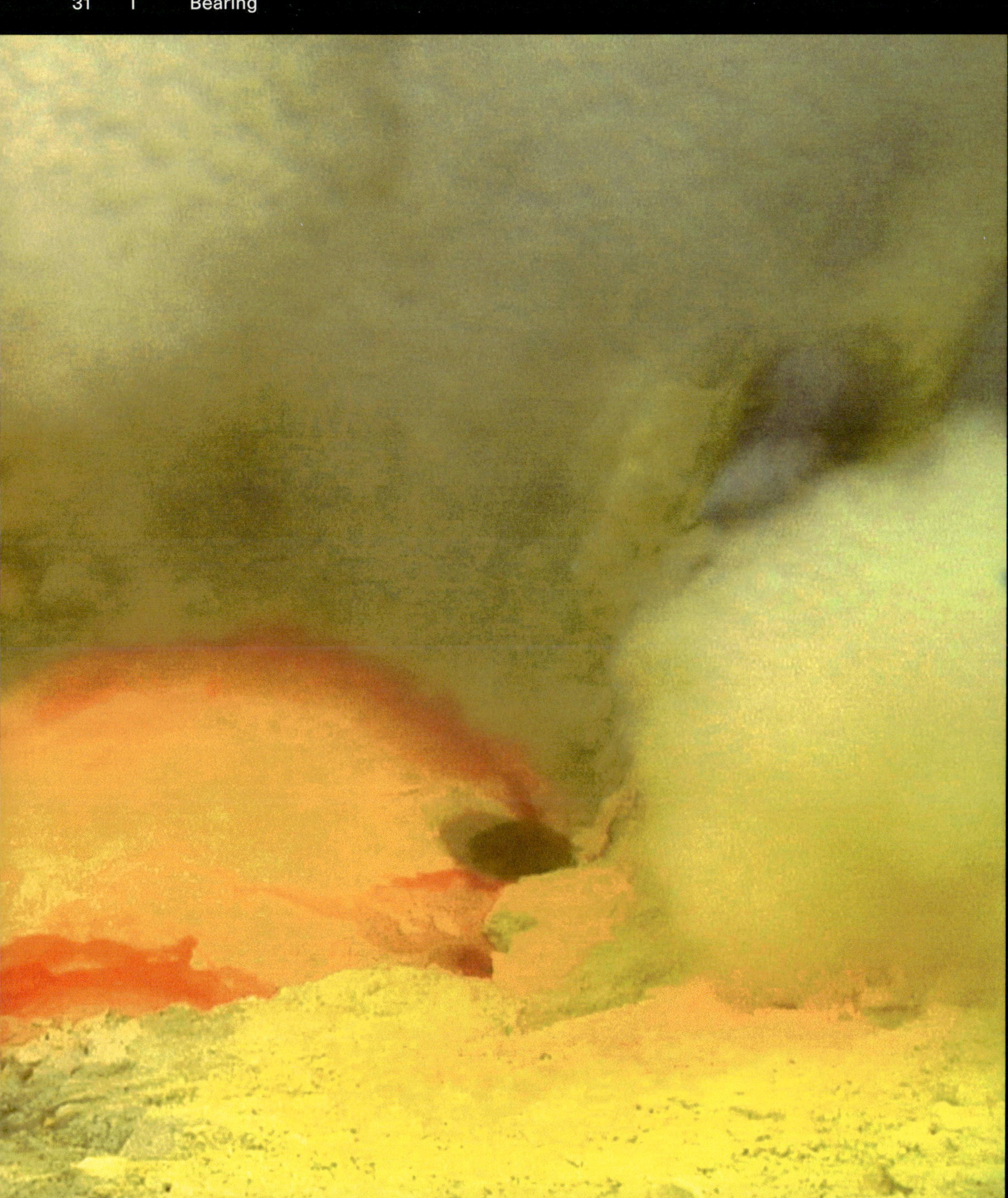

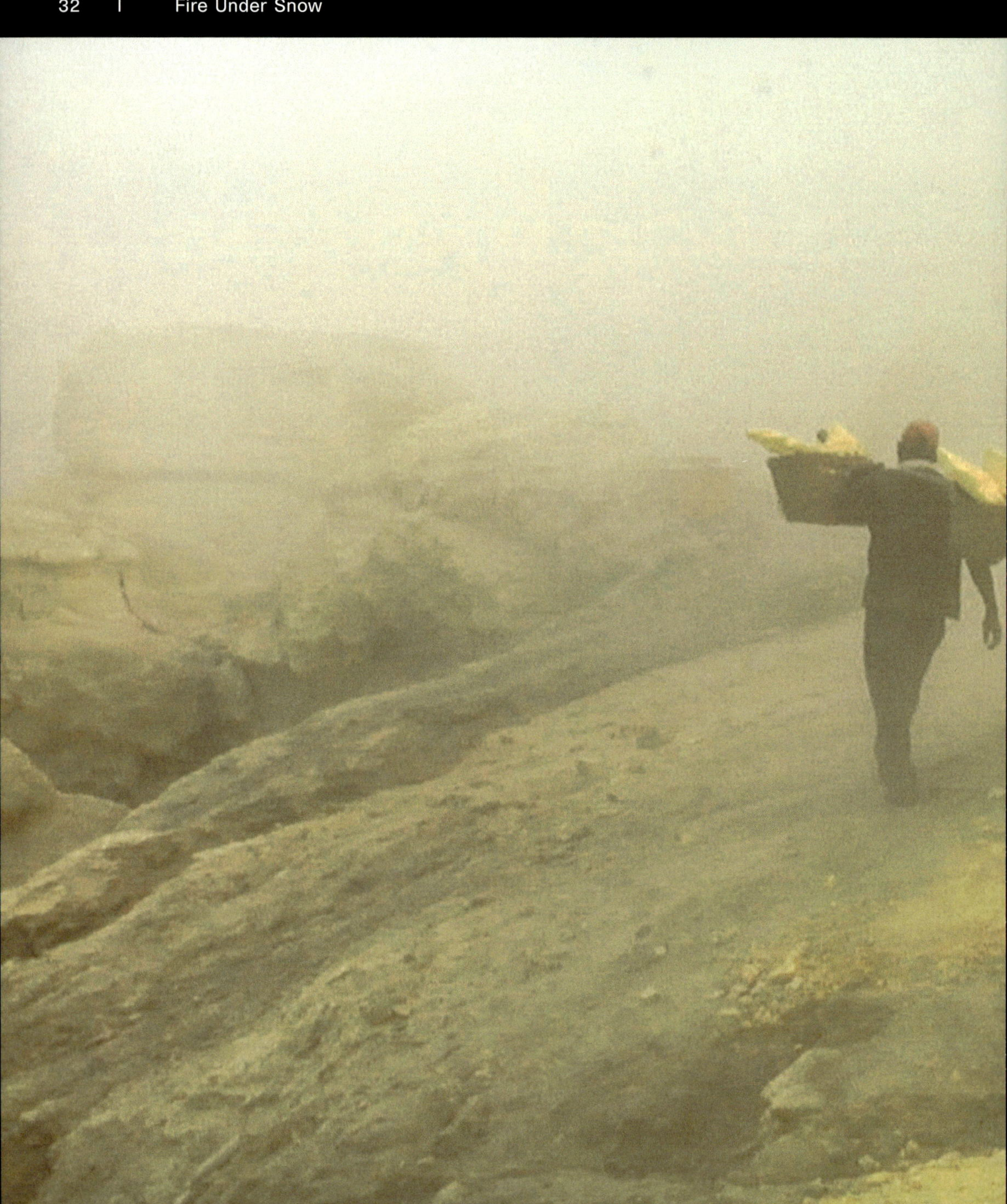

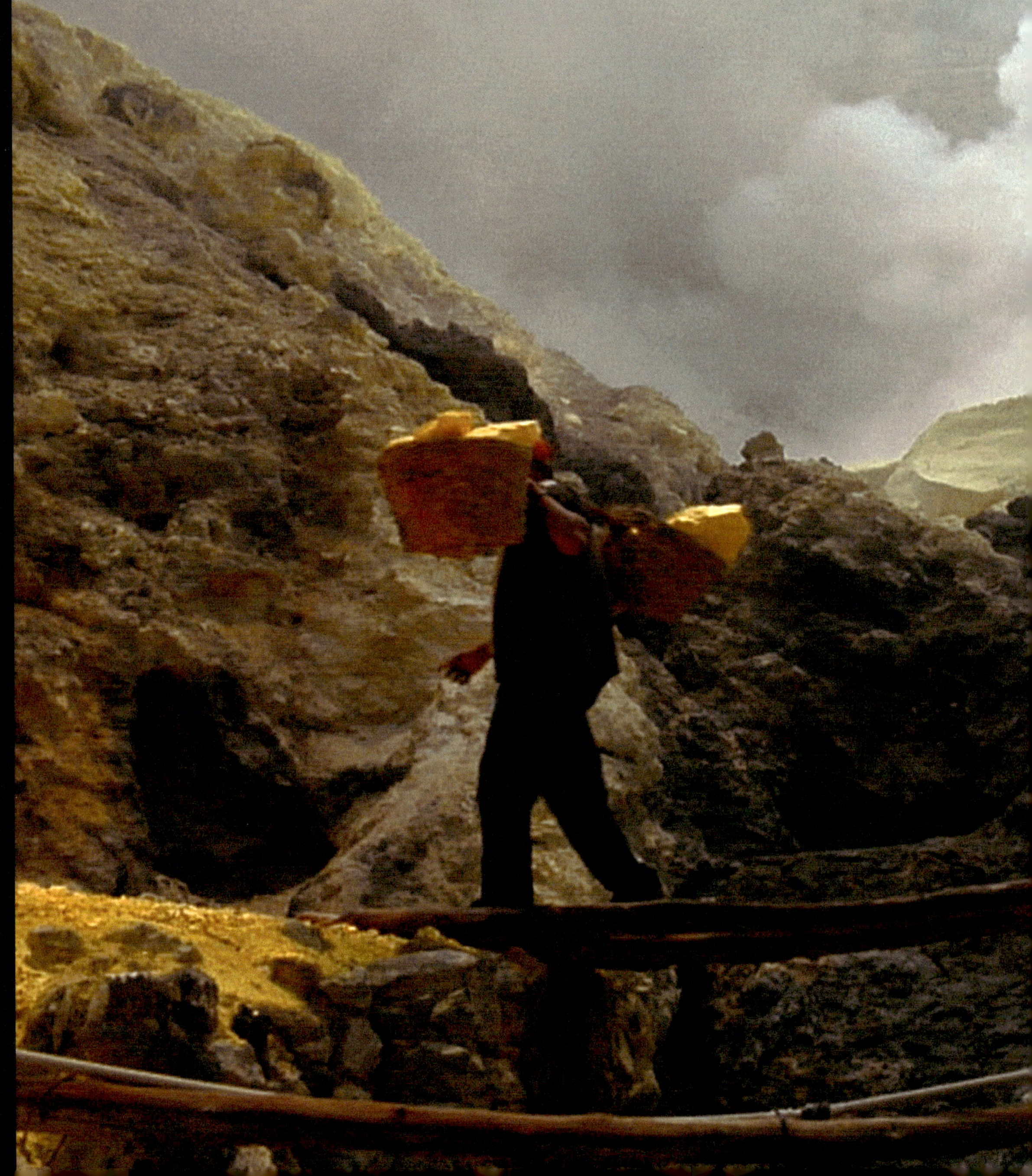

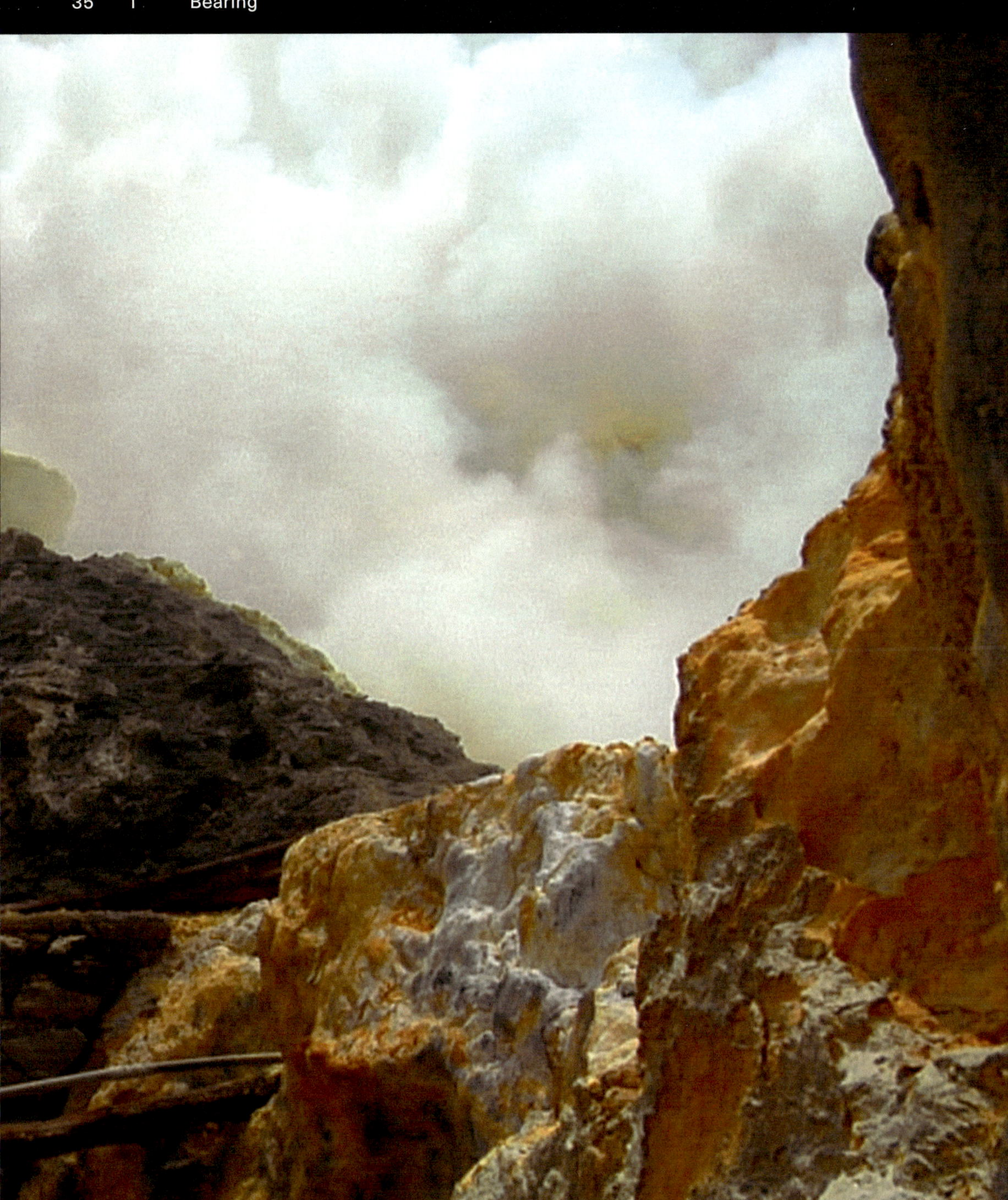

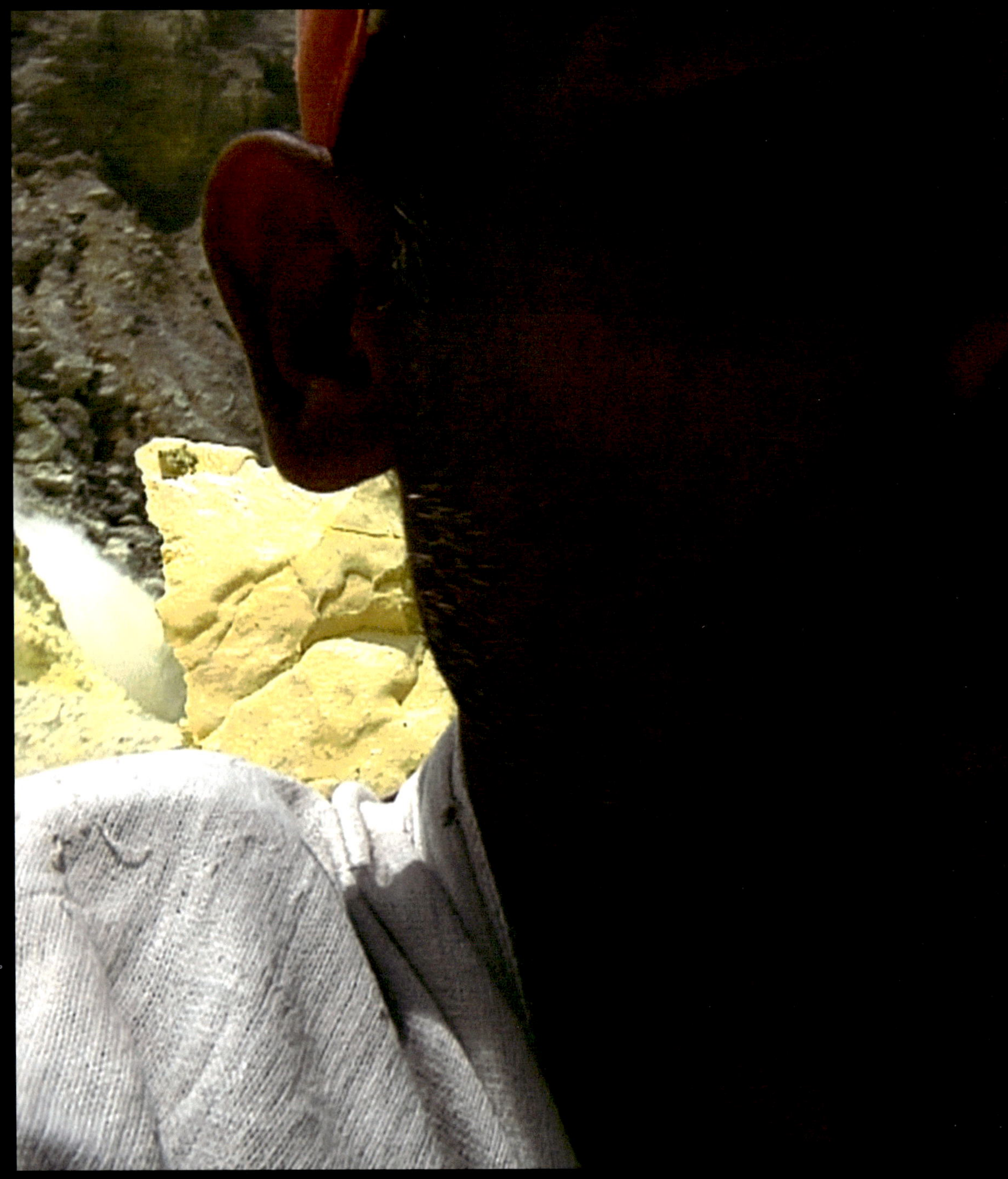

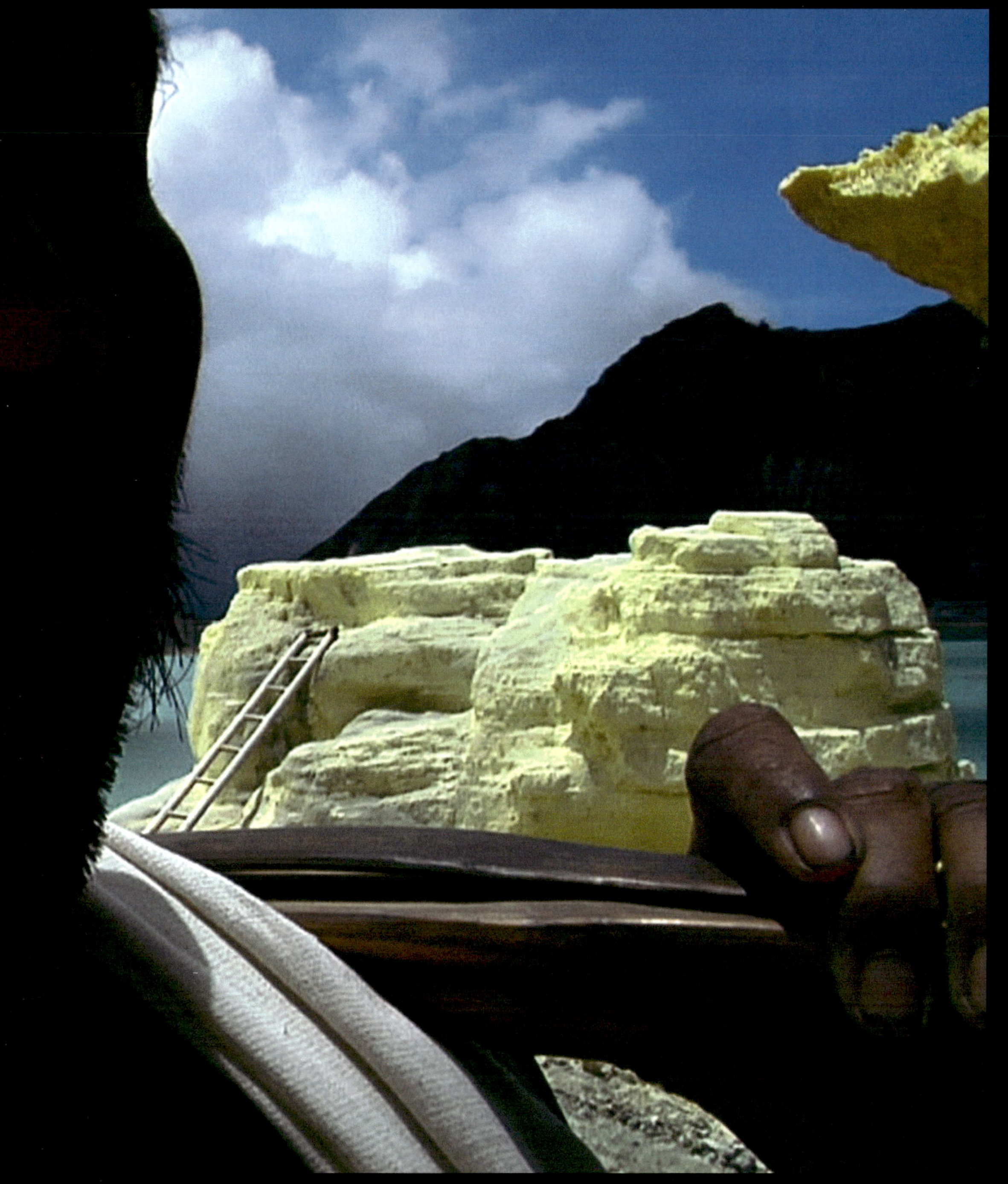

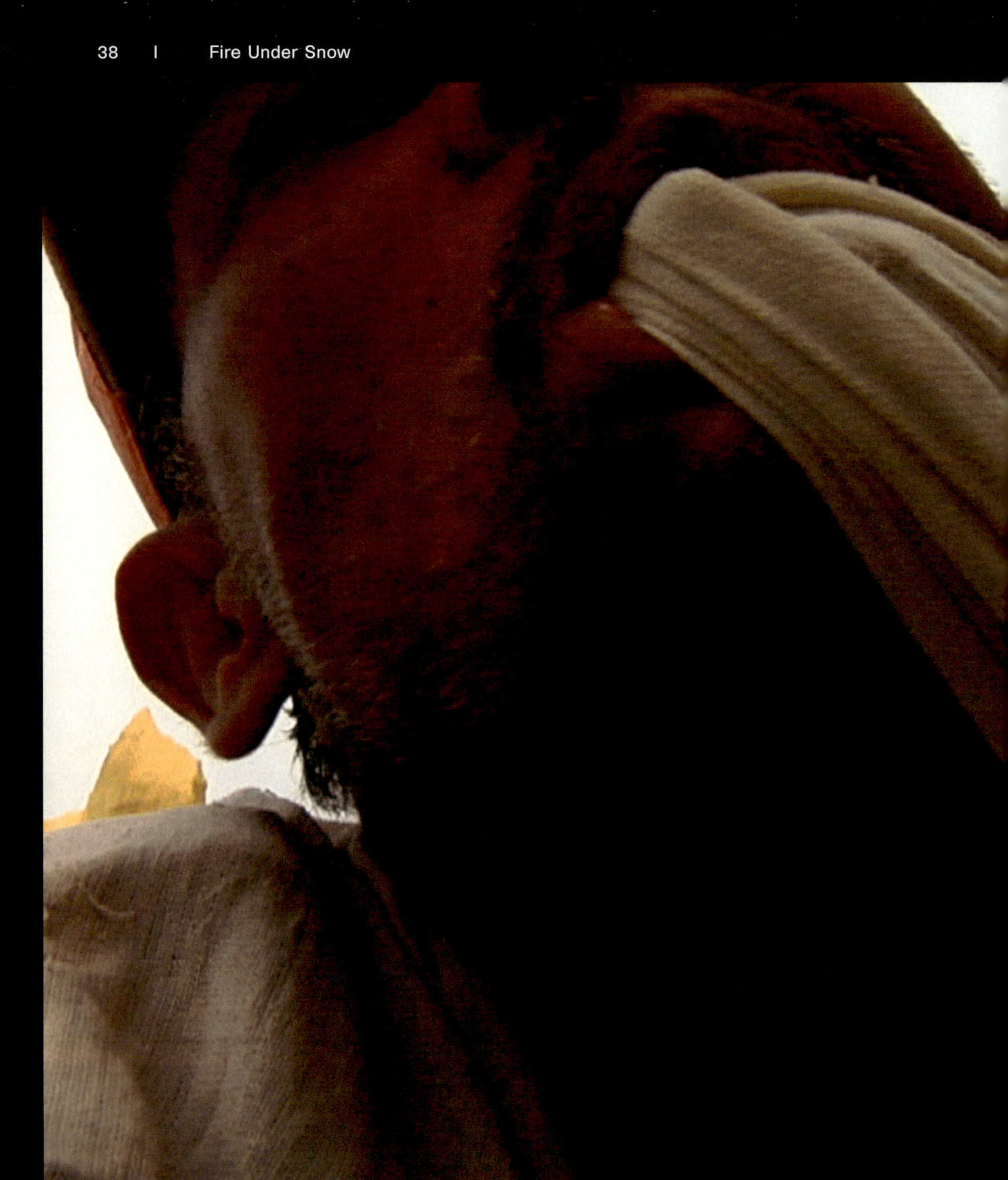

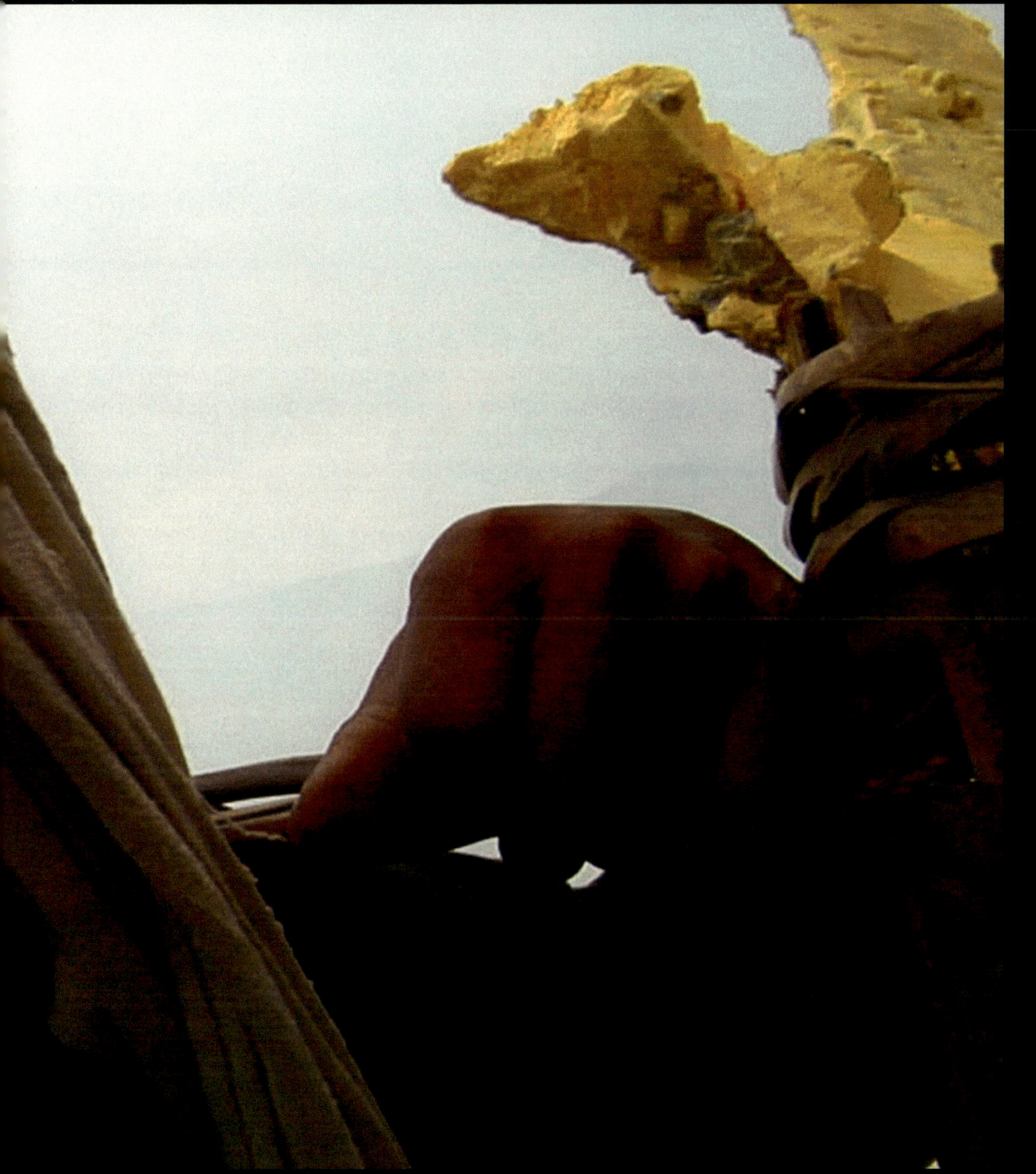

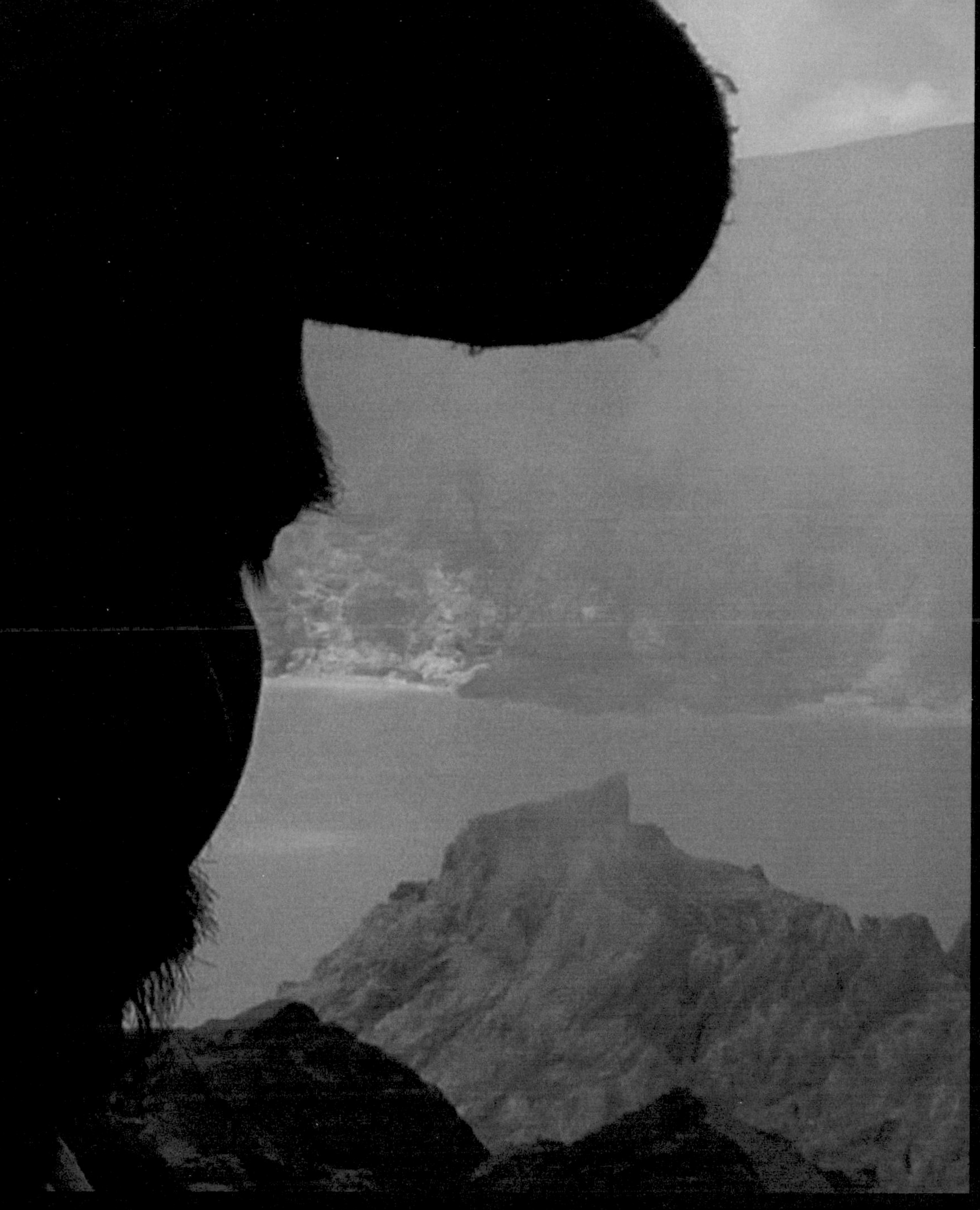

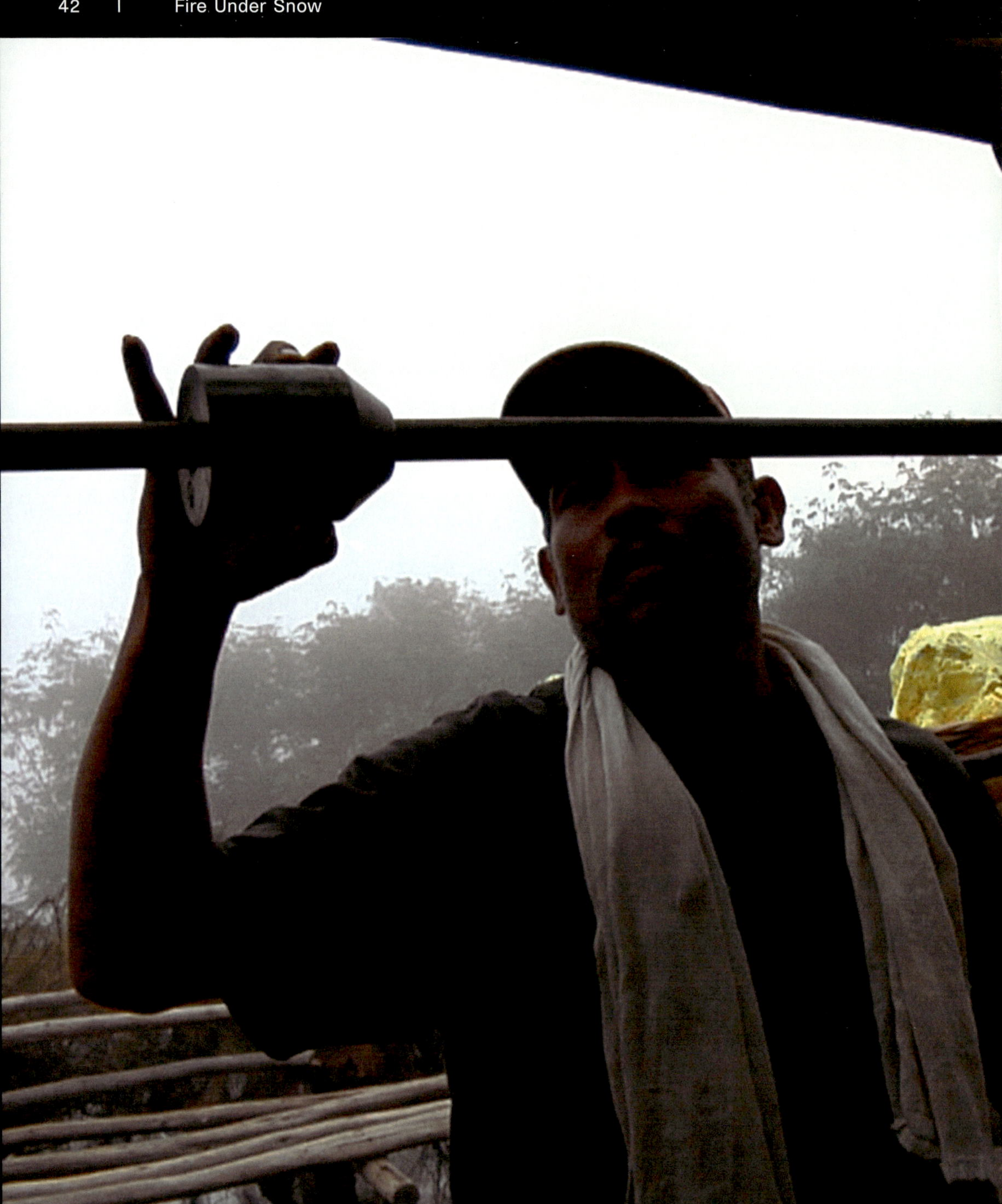

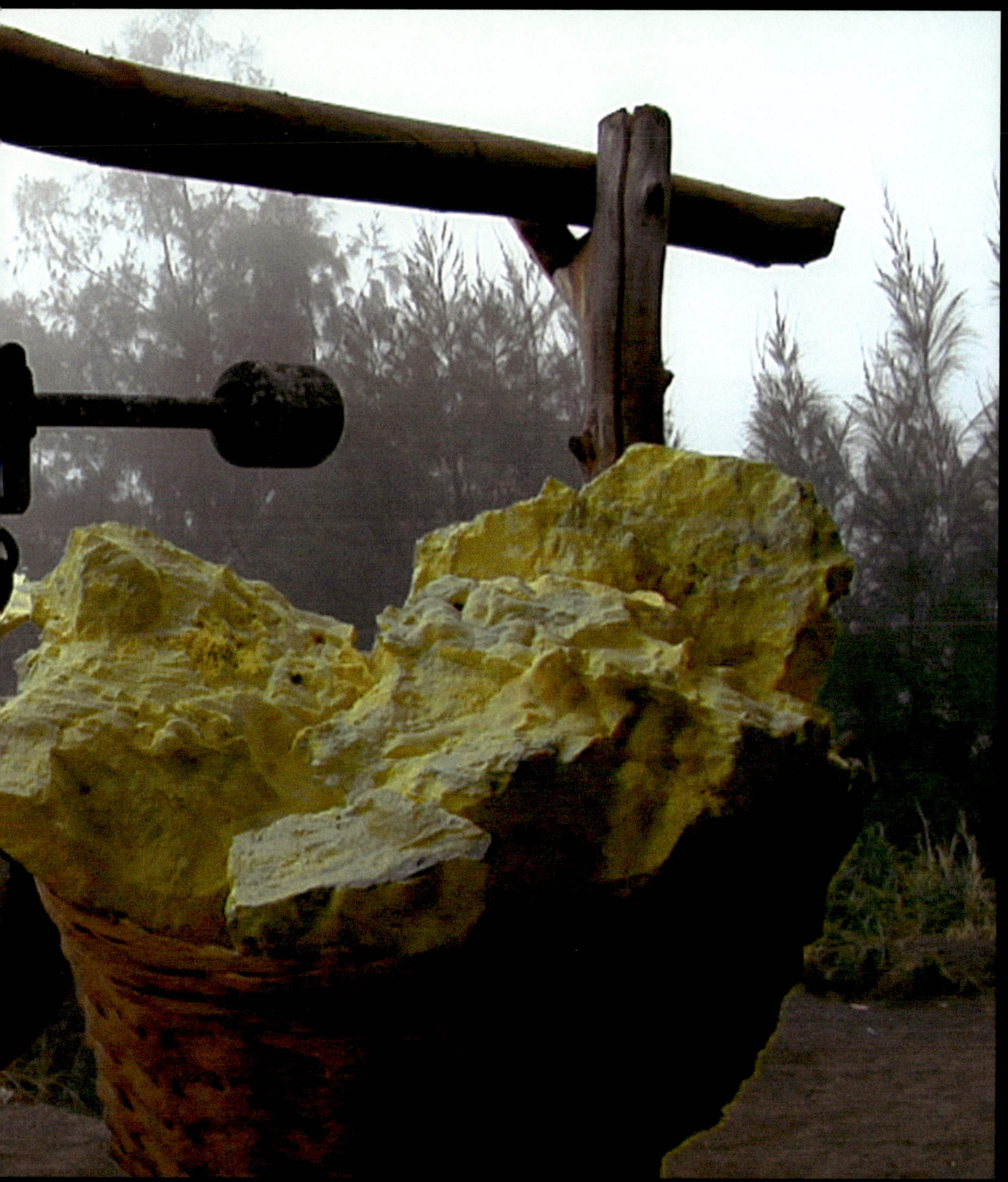

In The Between

2006

3-channel HD video with audio
14 minutes

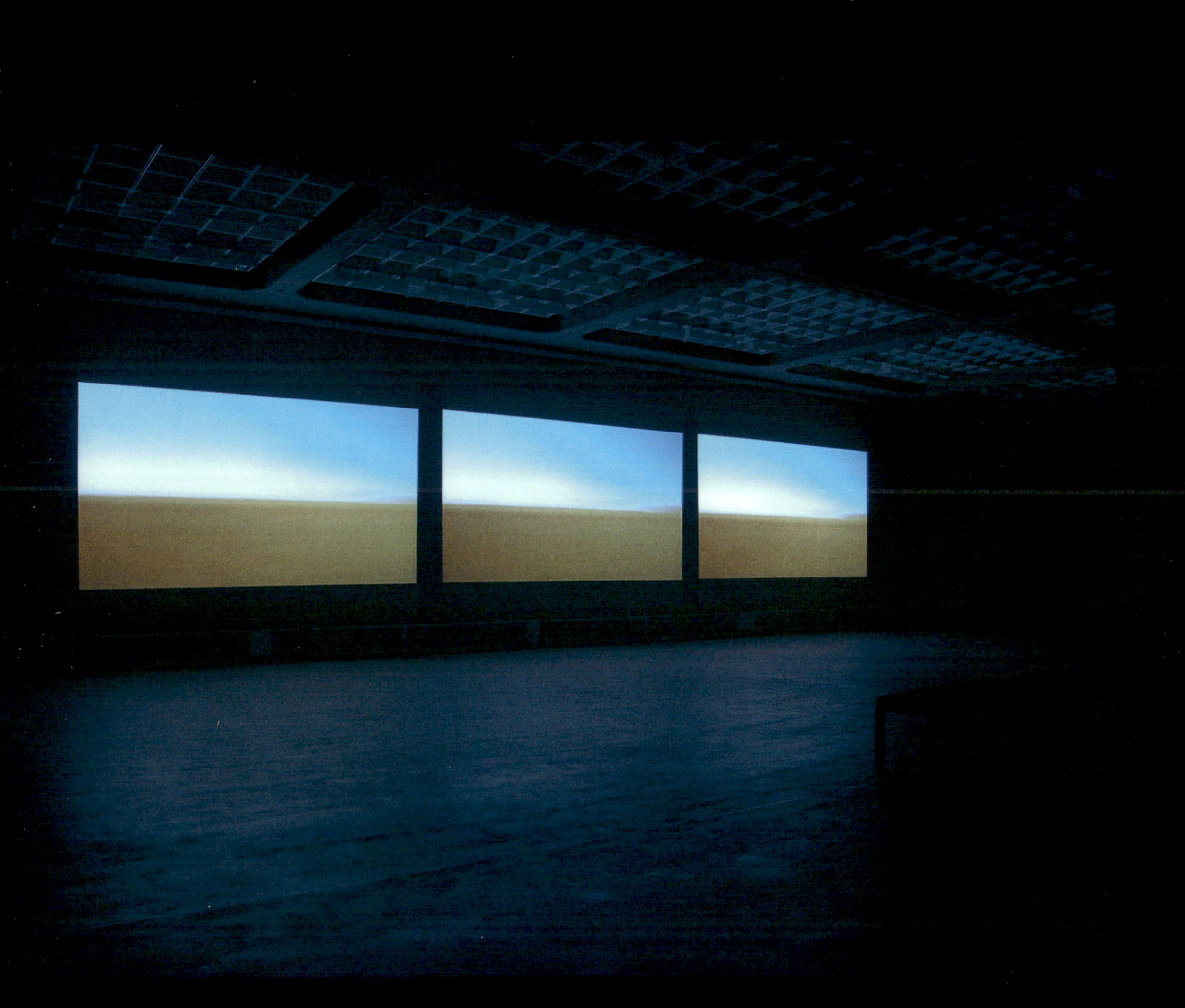

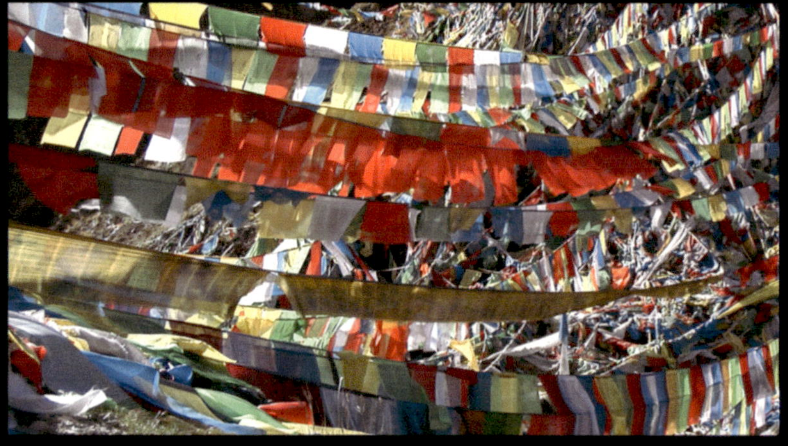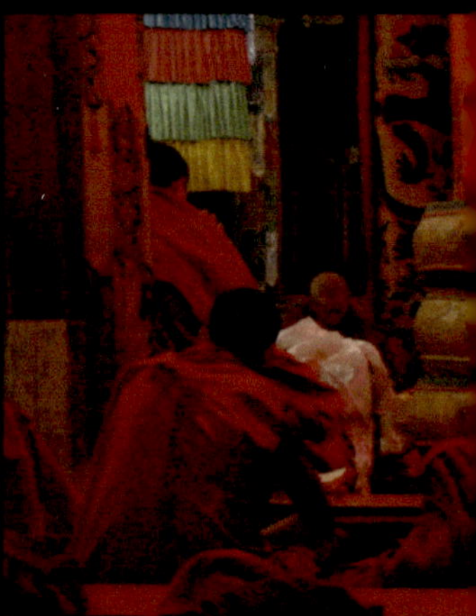

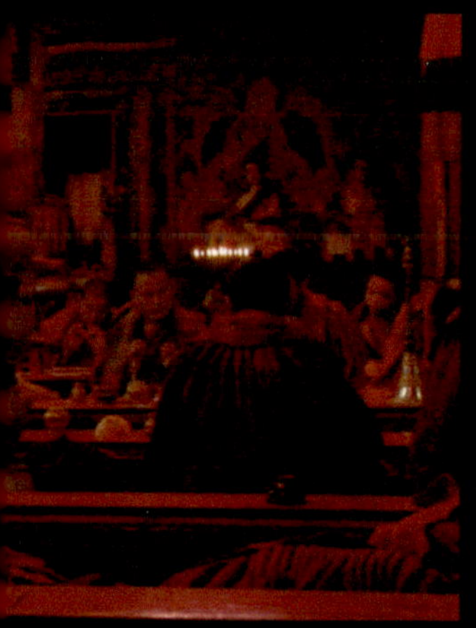

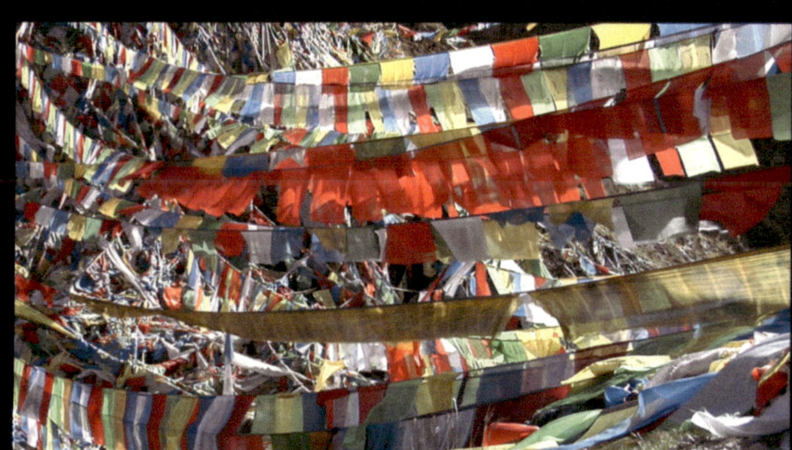

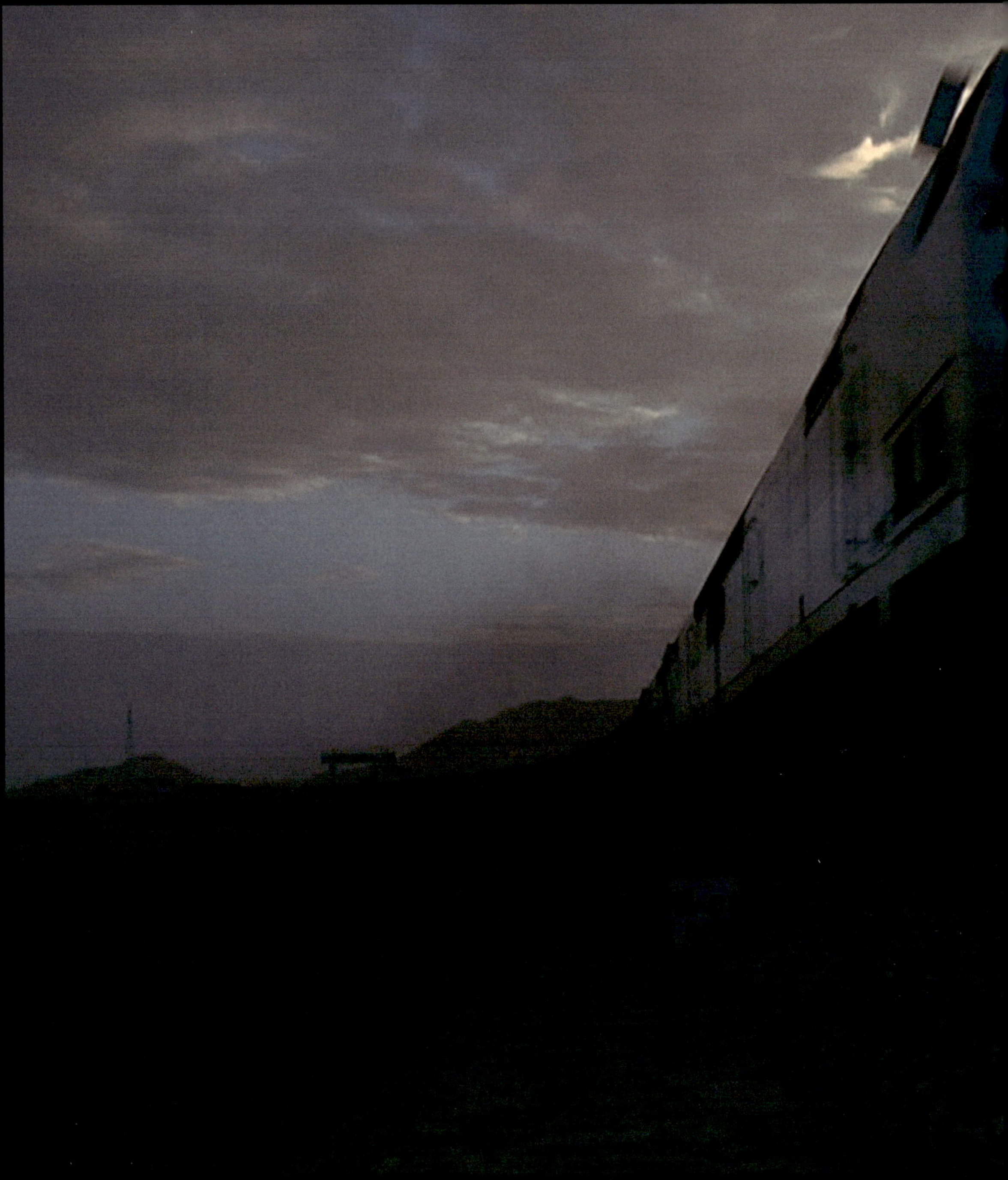

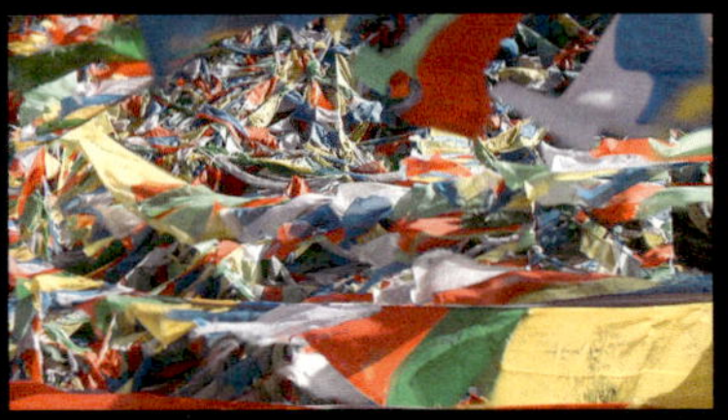

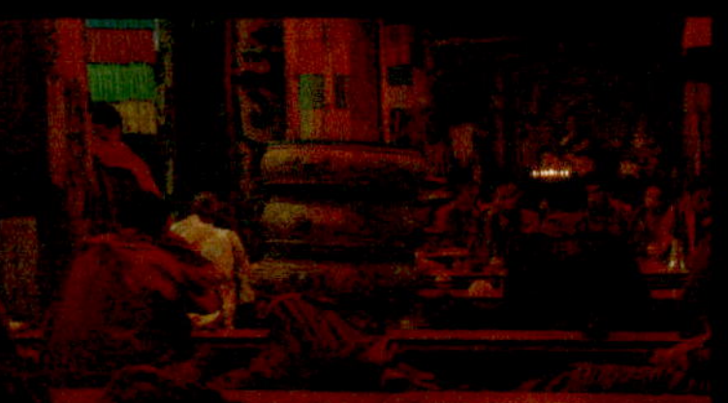

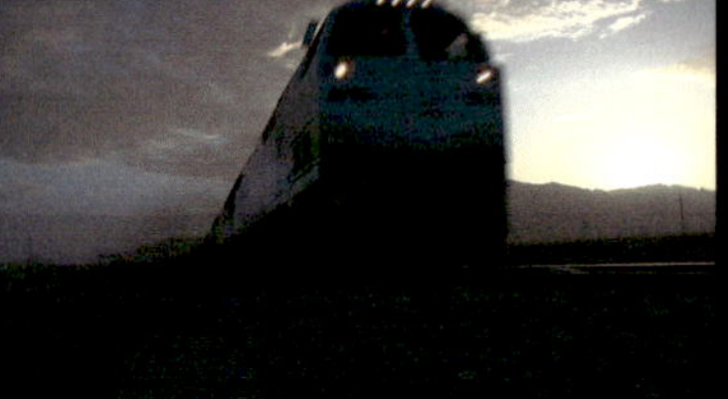

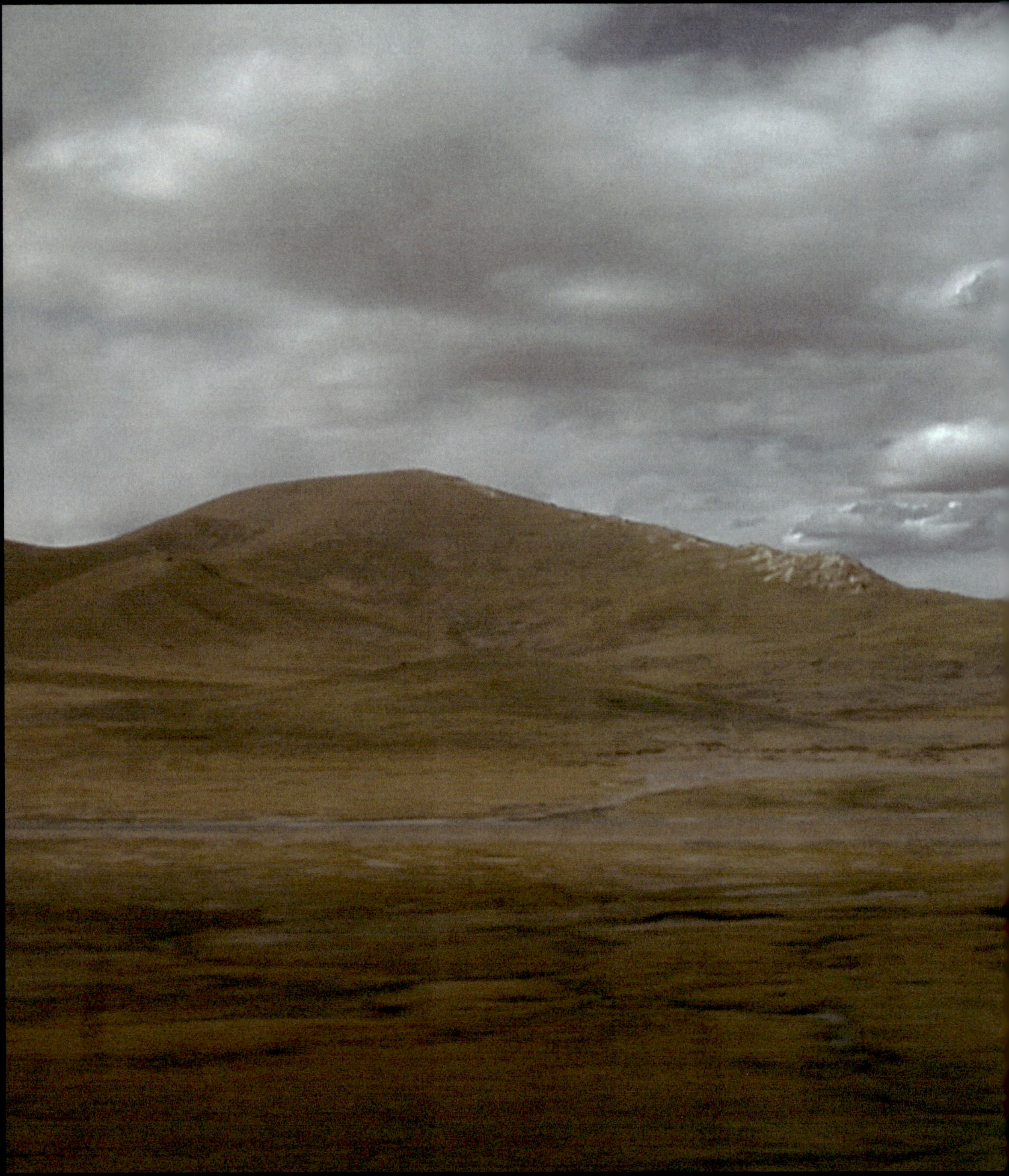

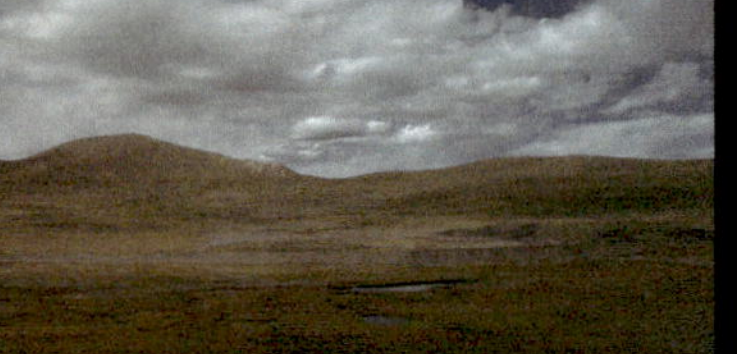

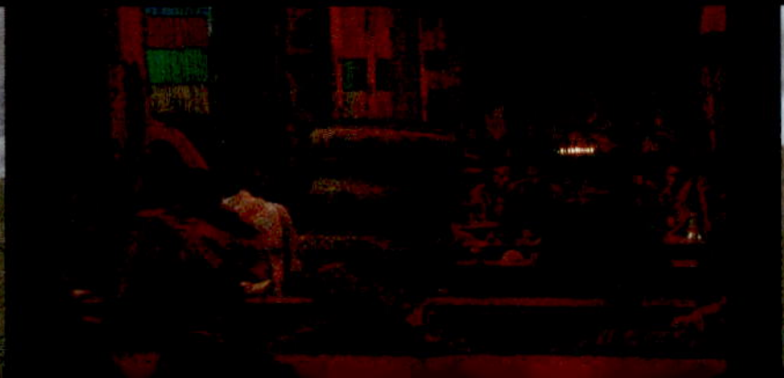

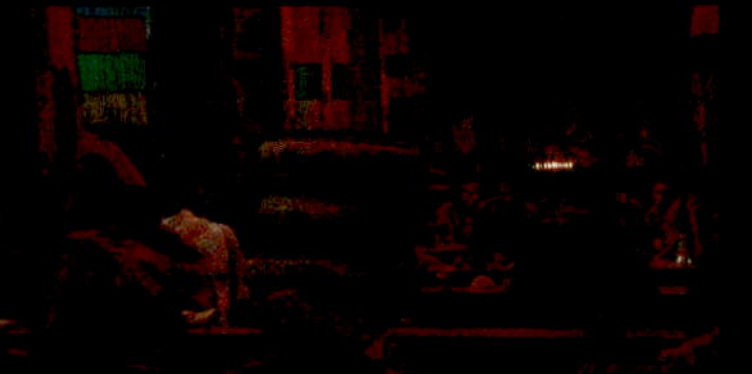

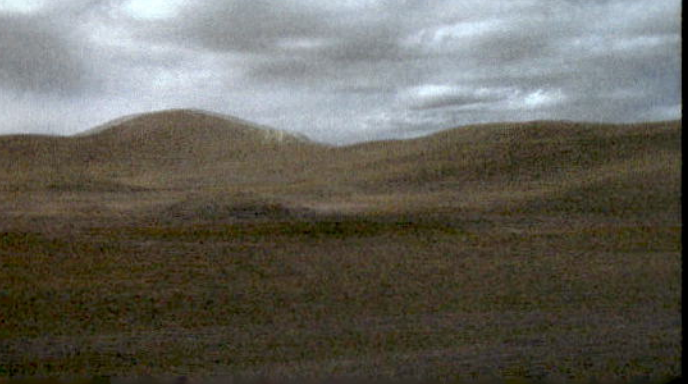

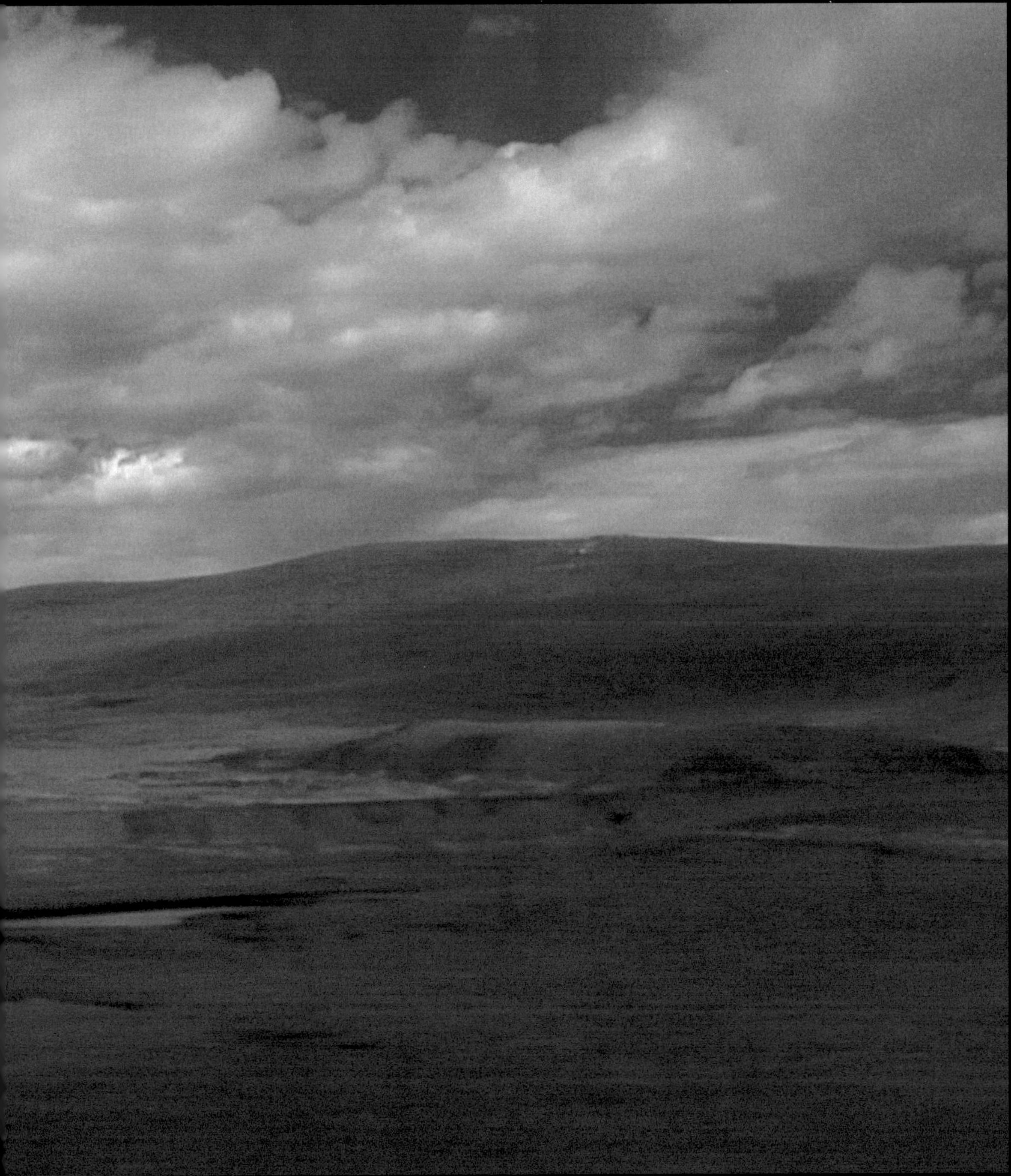

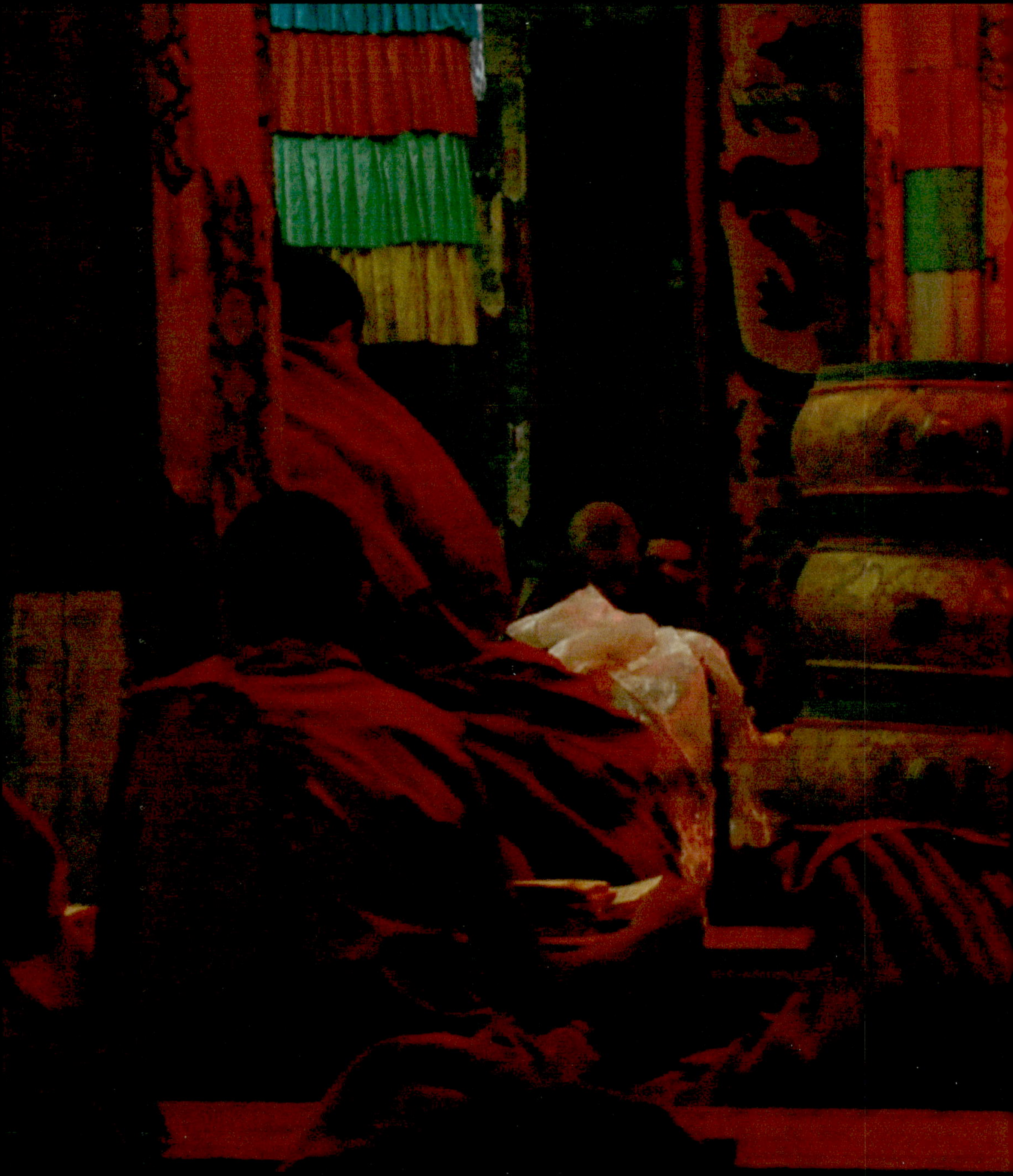

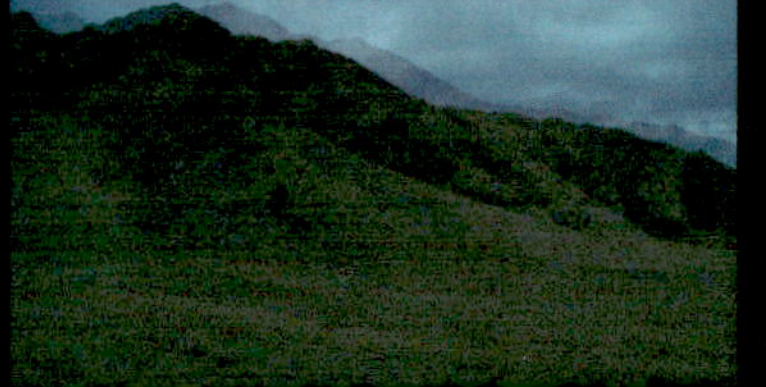
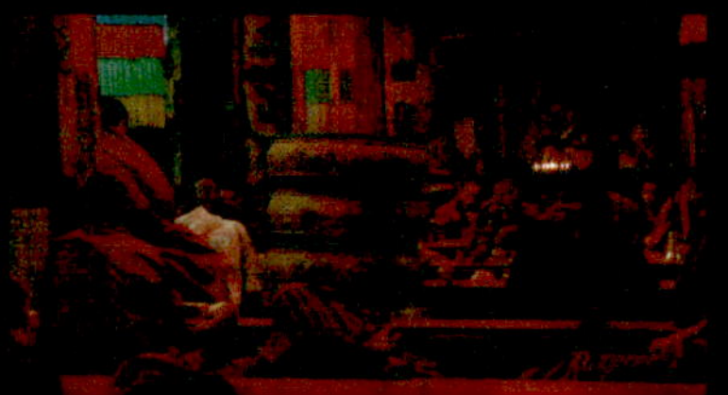
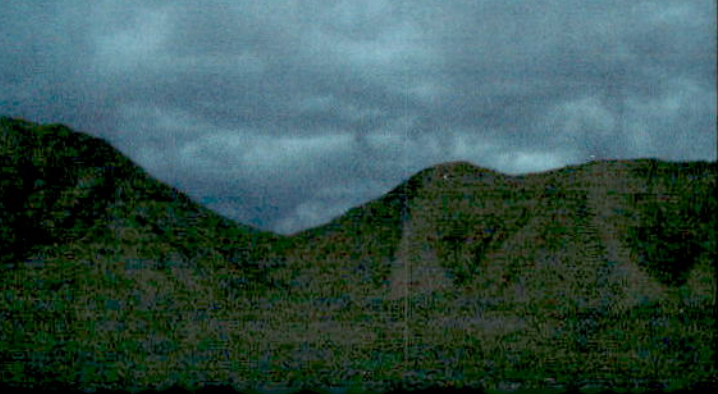

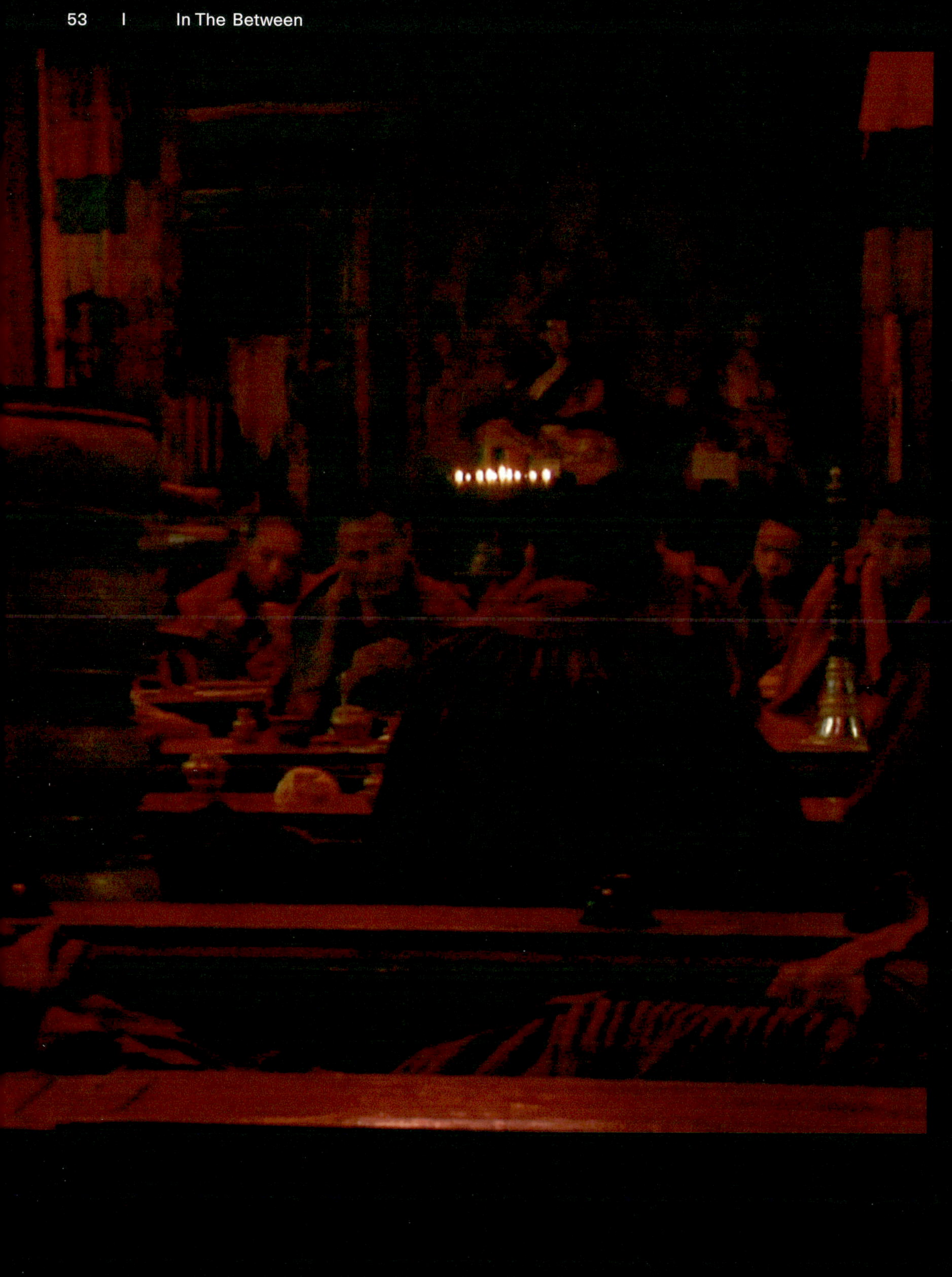

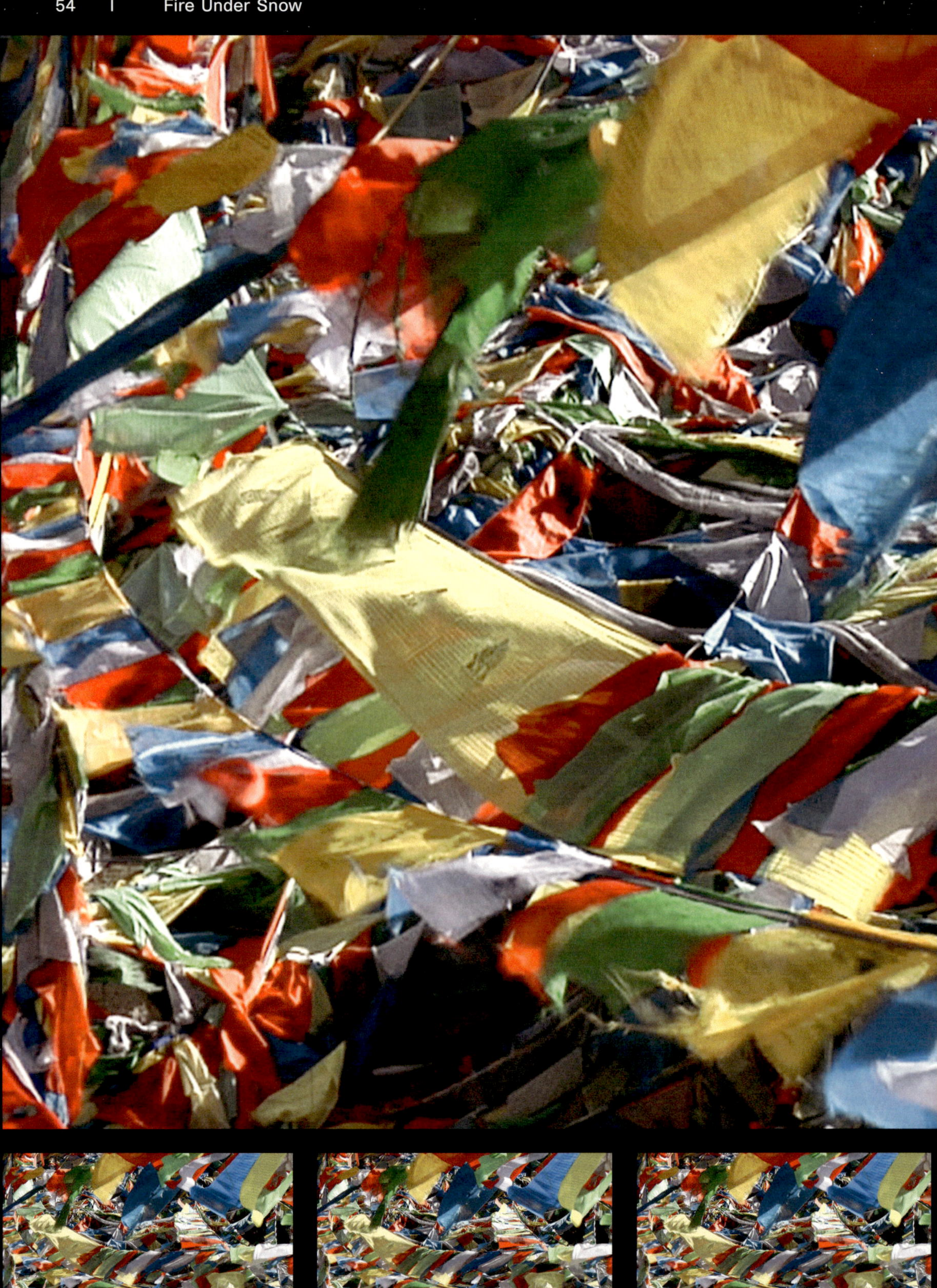

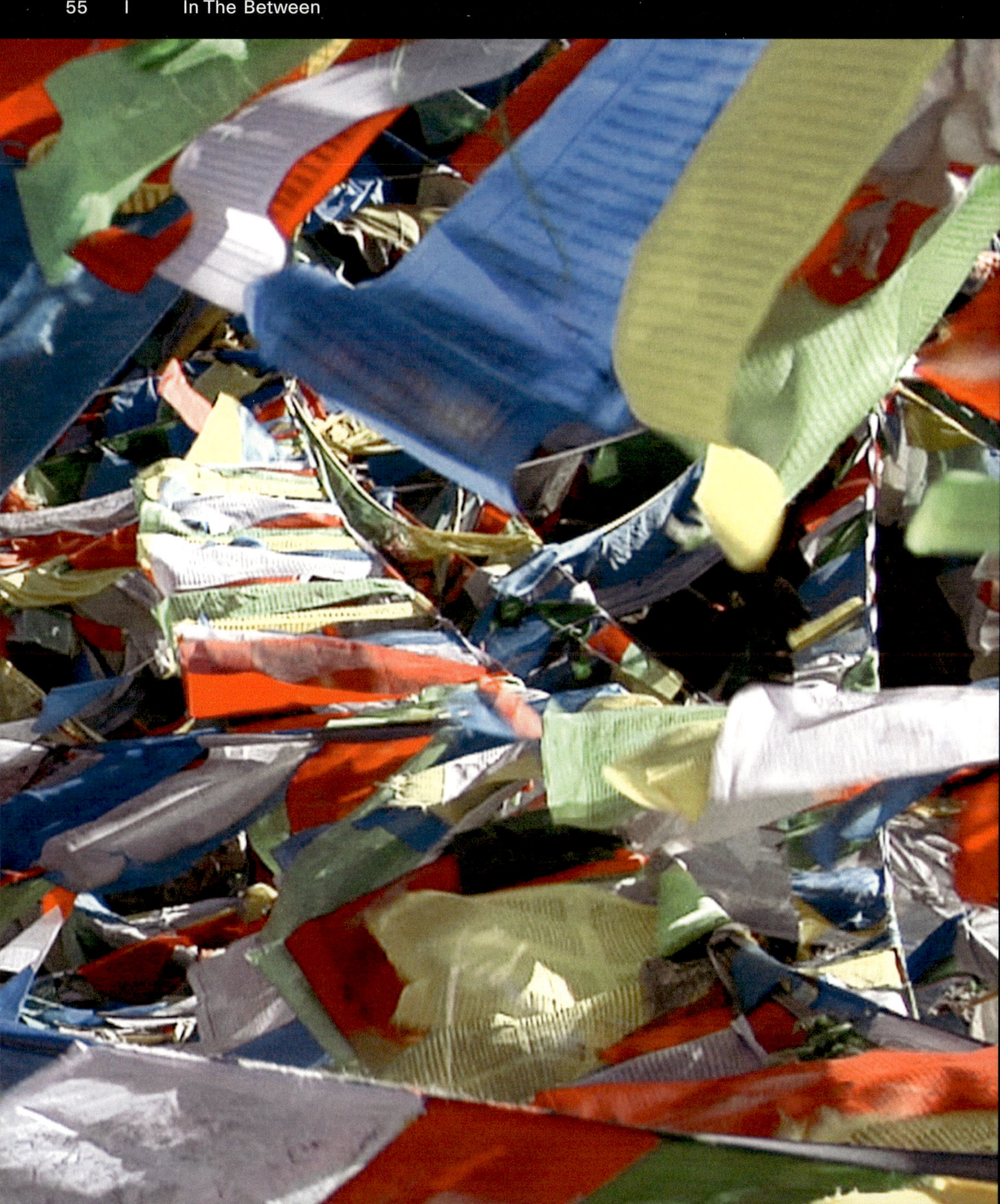

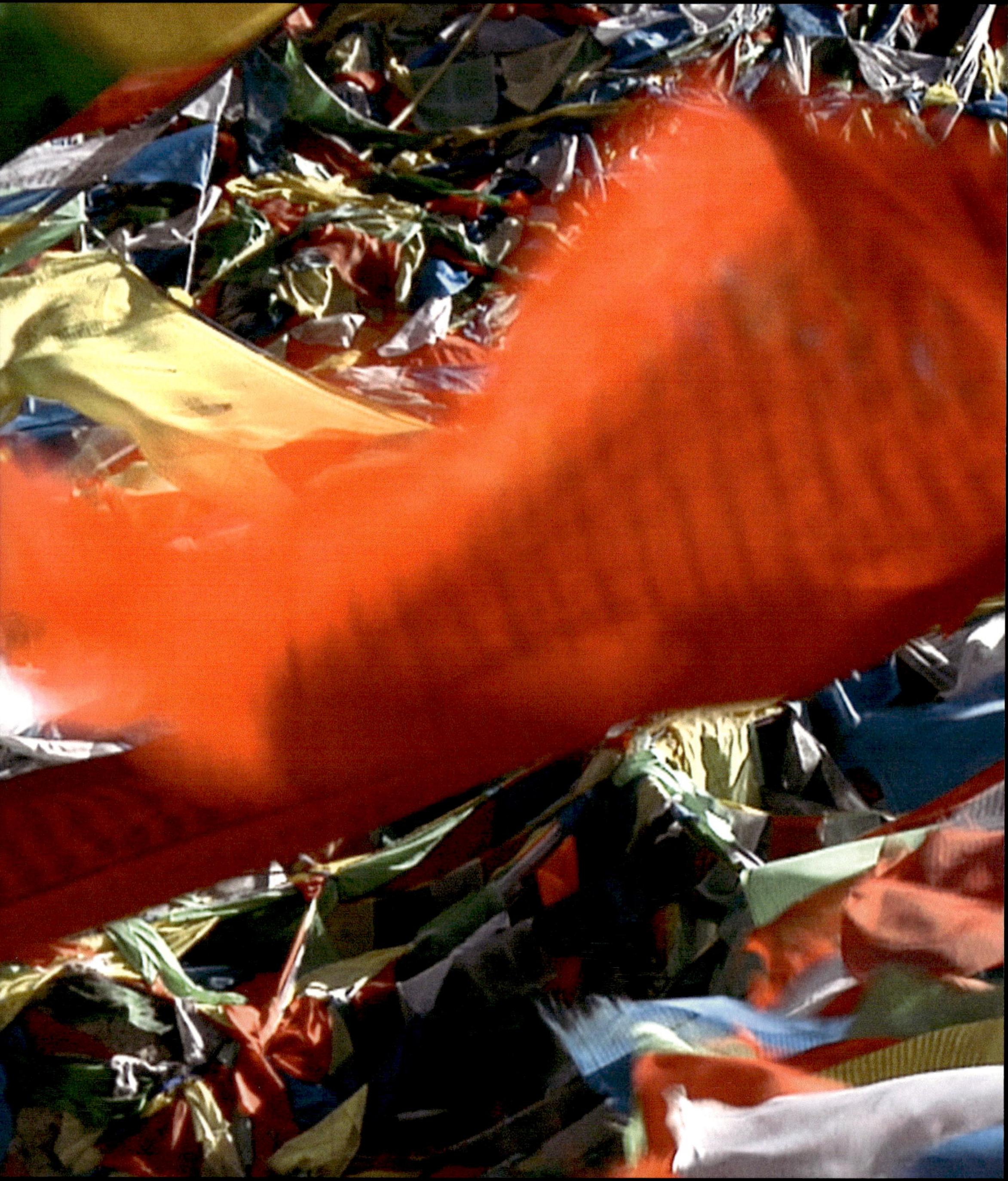

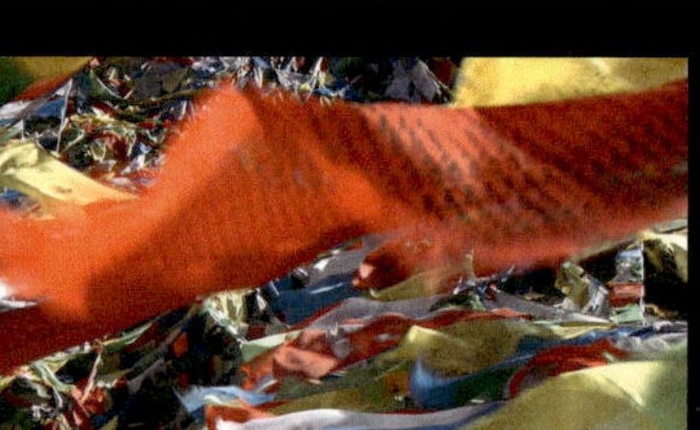
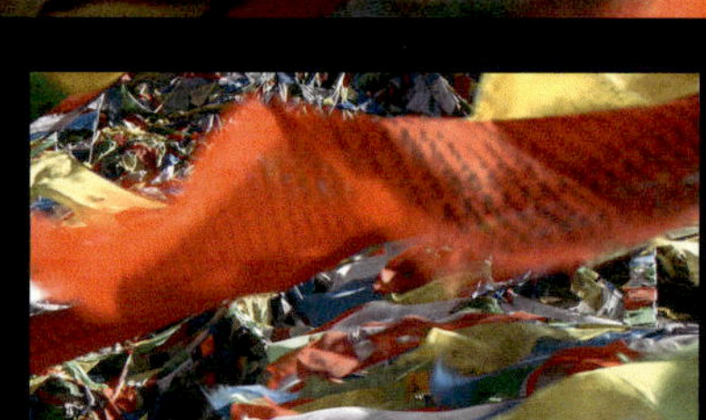
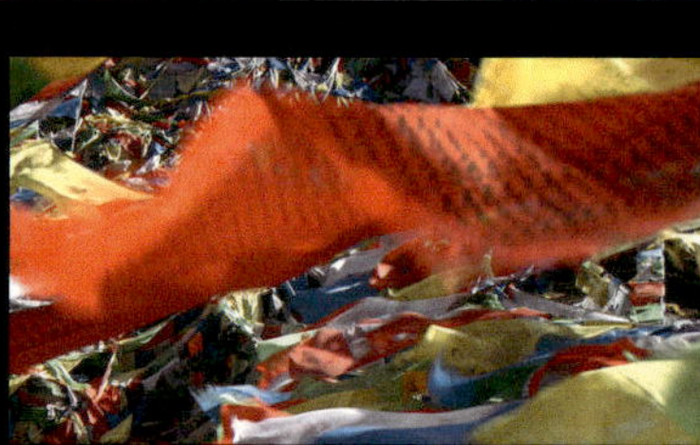

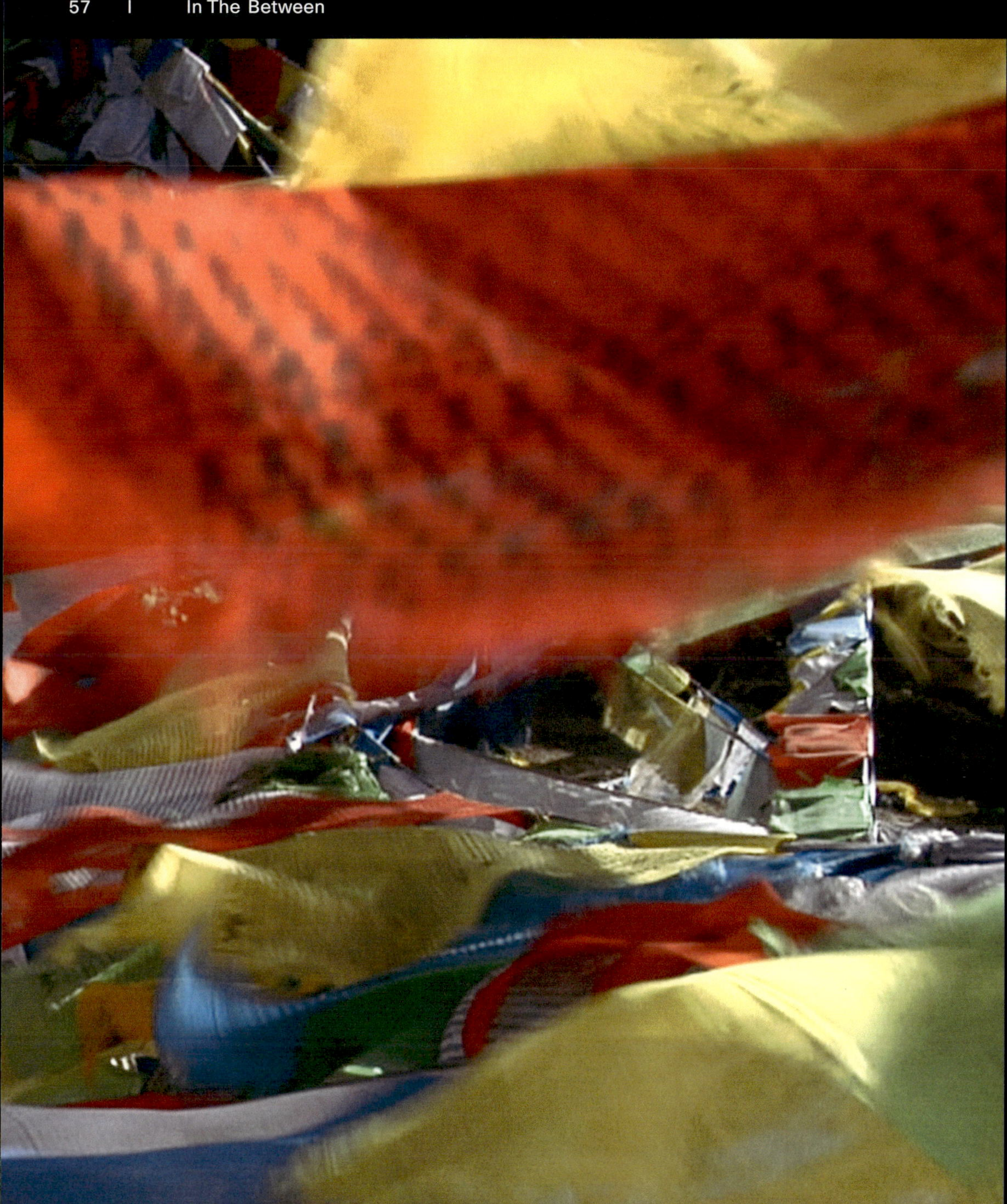

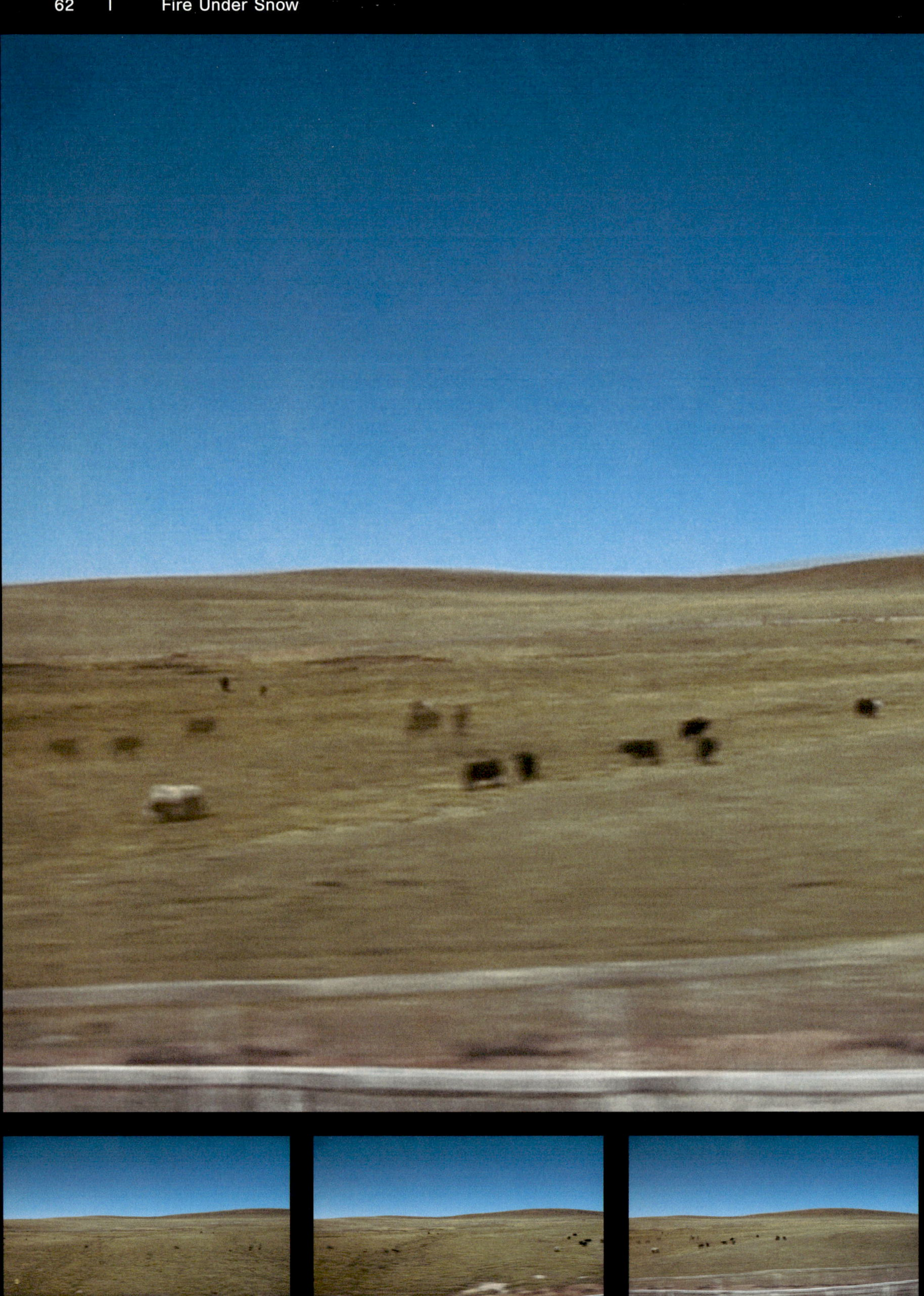

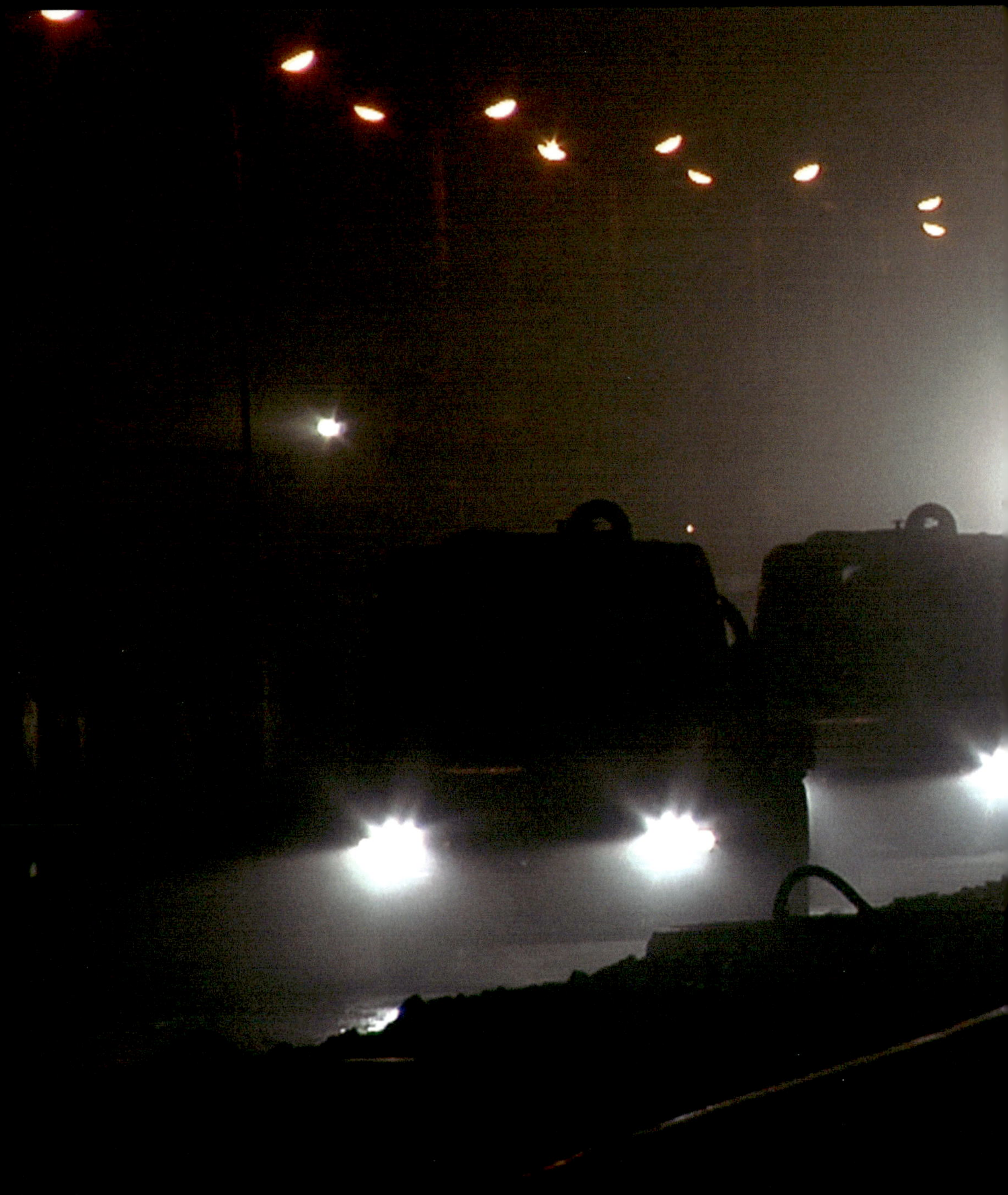

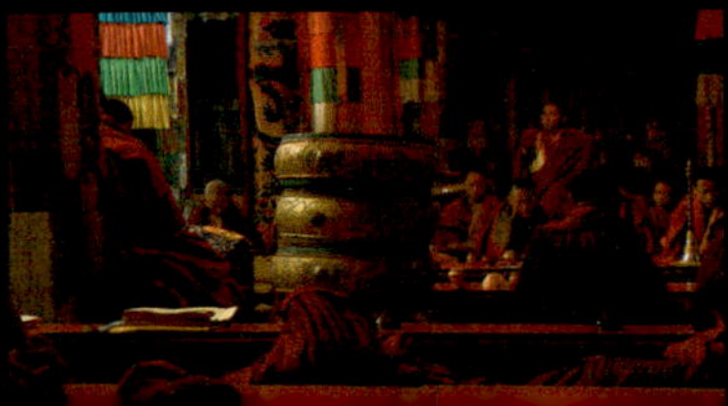

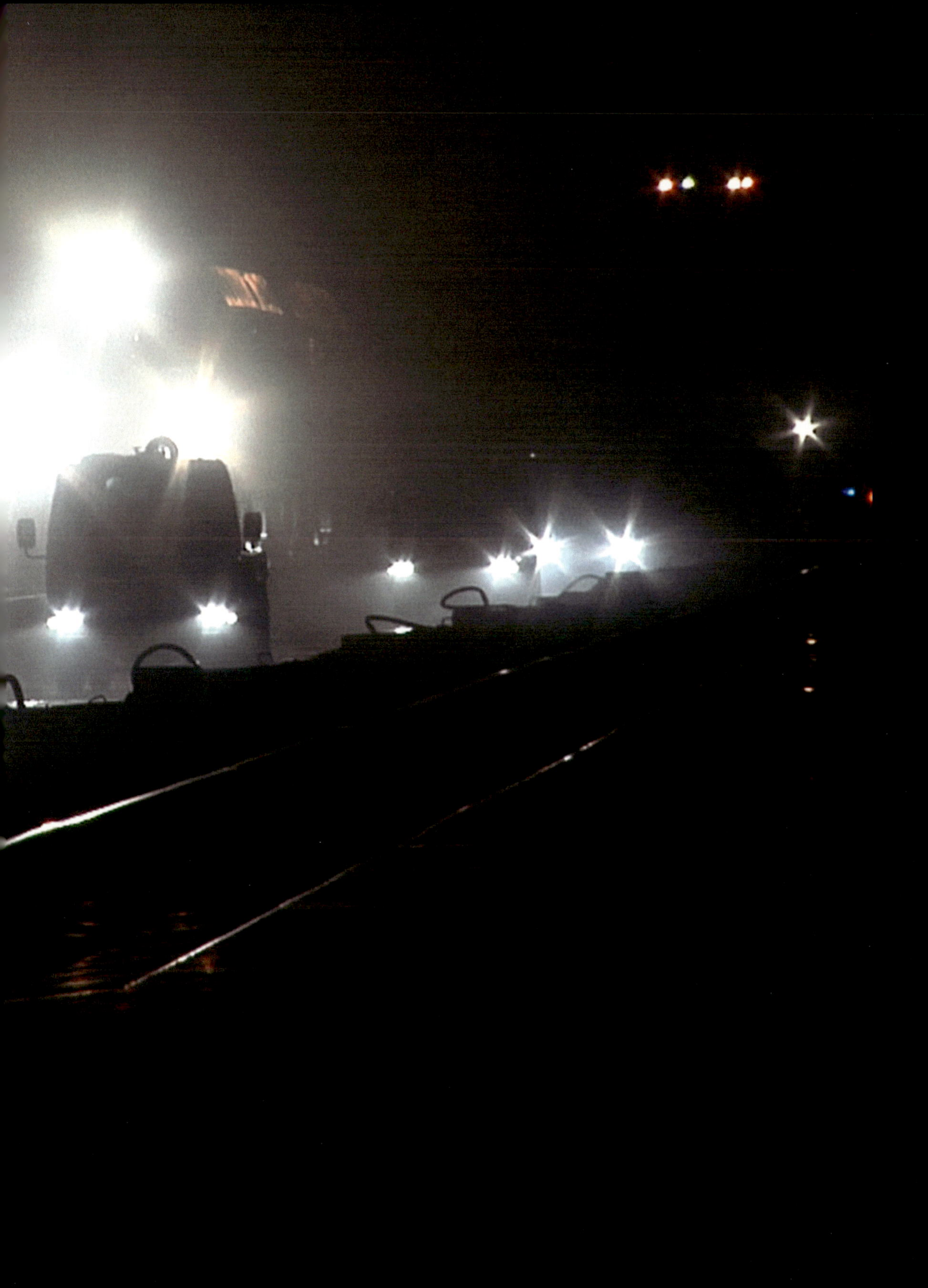

Meditation on *In The Between*

Robert Thurman

I am honoured to write a meditation on Darren Almond's courageous and powerful work of art. The Chinese rape of Tibet is evoked by the recording of a high-altitude bullet train penetrating a vast landscape rendered spectral by speed and steely machine disregard. The living heart of the three-mile-high landscape is represented by the temple of vibrant colours, the seventh-century Samyey, the very first Buddhist monastery ever built in Tibet. Therein, a group of leathery, weather-beaten, and funkily blissful monks gently chant prayers of taking refuge for themselves and others in the profound space of the foundational goodness of the universe.

For the sake of all my mother sensitive beings, I take refuge in the Buddha who is the discoverer for our times of the wondrous real nature of life and death, the universal mother of wisdom and freedom. I take refuge in the Dharma, choeu *in our Tibetan language, the reality of all beings and things, revealed as actually being bliss-void-freedom indivisible amid the delusory configurations of the mindless anguish and vast seething agony of egocentric creatures. I take refuge in the Sangha, the community of beings who lives according to the goodness of the Dharma, gently, intelligently, happily, compassionately. I take refuge in the Lama, whose mind and speech and body keep alive for us the Three Jewels of wish-fulfilling refuge. I vow to become perfectly enlightened myself as swiftly as possible, so that I may effectively free all my old mother beings – beings who in the infinite past have birthed me and mothered me in inconceivably many life forms unaccountably many times – from their needless sufferings. In order to accomplish that I give up any aims I may have just for this single human life, and I give up any hankering after any sort of great self-centred life in heaven or paradise, and I adopt only the eternal aim of indestructible blissful beauty of buddhahood.*

The monks are chanting in this vein, then building up on the refuge foundation of positive universes, mandala mansions, filled with invocations of the myriad forms of enlightened beings already engaged in terminating suffering, who work tirelessly in all realms in all ways to help beings.

And on the two sides of the screen, the train rolls on, determined to reach its 'goal of this life', as Tibetans call what is least important because it only lasts until death brings on the next 'between'. 'Get to Hlasa! Get to Hlasa! Get to Hlasa!' the clattering wheels seem to repeat as the train howls past peaceful yaks and bewildered nomads and endless plains and hills and mountains. (People write 'Lhasa' because the British did. The Tibetan letter 'L' sits above the 'H' in the Tibetan consonant cluster, and yet it is pronounced with the 'H' sounded first, and phonetically should be written 'Hlasa' – how much more fun!)

And what awaits in Hlasa, what awaits the passengers? Who are they? Mostly they are Chinese tourists, officials, businessmen, adventurers, workers, grifters, because non-Chinese don't like to visit Tibet anymore, since it is a country under occupation, home of a dispossessed people undergoing a fifty-plus-year process of genocide.

Genocide by invasion and battle, though Tibetans were ill-suited for the fight after more than half a century of freedom from serious war.

Genocide by class struggle, thought-reform, reform by labour in vast gulags, and by the destruction of religion and spirituality, although the Tibetans remain immensely resistant to that, as spirituality has become the central preoccupation of their culture.

Genocide by mismanagement, as huge famines, previously unknown in Tibetan history, were engineered by totally unsuitable agricultural collectivization and arbitrary crop imposition.

Nowadays, there is genocide by colonization, population transfer, and racial assimilation, by the systematic effort to settle three, five or even ten times the number of Chinese on top of the six million Tibetans. (In 1950, Mao vowed to settle one hundred million Chinese in Tibet by 1960. Luckily, he only ended up with around four million by then, and nowadays there may be some ten million.)

The key to this is psychological: genocide of the mind. Chinese propaganda requires the denial of the very existence of the Tibetan nation, the Tibetan people, by pretending they are only and have always been merely a sub-category of Chinese people. This pretence is automatically refuted by the very existence of Tibetan persons, with their different language, sense of identity, sense of history and culture, genetic adaptation of their lungs and bloodstream to the three-mile average altitude, and so on. *Ergo,* it becomes necessary for the Chinese to remove the Tibetan people from the picture, by all the above means.

And all these genocides end up in culturecide and ecocide, as the great Chinese nation is infected by the disease of money-obsessed industrialization, which has already ruined most of the land, water, climate, and air of the Chinese homeland and much of Manchuria, Mongolia, and East Turkestan/Sinkiang, and the Tibetan Western headwaters of the Yellow and Yangtze river systems, where clear-cutting of primeval forests has caused massive flooding in Western lowland China proper. Spreading this industrial cancer in Tibet would, if it ever succeeded, ruin the headwaters of the Mekong, Salween, Irawaddy, Ganga, Yamuna, and Indus river systems. Fortunately, it can never succeed. The great Tibetan plateau itself, anciently envisioned as a giant demon goddess lying on her side, will never allow it. If tens of millions of lowland people could live on the three-mile-high plateau, they would have been there already, millennia ago!

No one likes it when we talk frankly about what is going on. It is impolite. The Chinese are going to be the big 'superpower' of the twenty-first century. The Chinese have an ancient culture. We mustn't be racist or prejudiced about the Chinese, or we'll get into nineteenth-century 'Yellow Peril' paranoia. Global 'Business' thinks China is the promised land, the last great achievement of capitalism. General Motors, Daimler and Toyota want to fill it with cars. Yahoo and Google can't resist 'the China market'. They are all addicted to what we have for years called 'the billion shoe-lace syndrome'. But they are not going to buy our billion shoelaces made in Massachusetts. They are going to make a billion shoelaces and bankrupt Massachusetts, unless we think of a cure for the money-obsessed industrialization cancer we carry and spread and which has infected this one-quarter of all human beings.

So, Almond's work of art is a profound challenge to this misperception by the elite of our culture of the reality of China today, as revealed in its ongoing rape of Tibet.

But it's not that simple either. It is not only the Chinese; not really their fault. It's nothing personal. It is modernity, it is the machinery of industrialization itself. It is the separation from nature, ecological as well as human, represented by the powerful machine, its phallic sleekness, its speed and power, its hard metallic deadliness, a disease the Chinese got from us. After all, it was we in the West who taught them to make such trains. Their own ancient culture invented many things – gunpowder, the compass, advanced metallurgy, many medicines, etc. – before us, but their wise people realized that such inventions would be misused, and would imbalance human and natural life and death. And they were able to restrain their greed and aggression somewhat better than we were. They enjoyed their lives. They had Chan/Zen centuries before us, they encountered the brilliant beauty and peaceful calm of the Buddha two thousand years ago. They had beautiful gardening – from a sense of continuity with nature that is integral to Buddhism and Taoism/Confucianism – and much better cooking! They used toilet paper millennia before the European pirates who came to their shores five centuries ago.

But the post-Mao Chinese are not the same as those who grew up with the ancient culture. It is mostly lost to them, or forgotten. They lost their spirituality to the Marxist and now capitalist version of the industrial dream of creating a mechanical paradise on Earth, a material paradise for purely material beings for purely material comfort until a meaningless death puts an end to a short but hopefully well-fed meaningless life. So the train is just their attempt to do our Euro-American train-thing better than us. They are hyping it like our East-West transcontinental railroad of the nineteenth century – built largely by Chinese and Irish immigrants – and trying to confirm our wrong thinking that what we did then was great. Actually, it was an instrument of the enormous genocide we perpetrated on the hundred million or so native peoples of the 'Americas'. The slaughter of billions of buffalo. The rape of 'Turtle Island', which turned it into a self-depleting pit of industrial agriculture and resource extraction.

And this is of course the deepest reason why the industrial world lets the Chinese destroy Tibet, because to challenge it with absolute clarity would require us to acknowledge our own genocides, culturecides, ecocides; an acknowledgement only a few of us have so far managed, though everyone dimly feels it in their bones.

Almond's work reaches right into our unconscious, wherein we actually 'like trains'. We love the sound of a train whistle in the night, and can become all sentimental when we hear it. We fall asleep peacefully in the overnight train we may occasionally take to some distant destination. We see train wrecks on the television news as if we are watching the end of the world. As children, especially boys, we are given toy trains. The train going through the tunnel is a profound sexual stereotype used in countless 'Orient Express' movies, with lovers in train cabins; James Bond making love to beautiful spy women before having to throw the bad guy, who has invariably stalked and interrupted them, out of the window after a fierce fight. A passing train can make anyone of a dreamy disposition long for cities, beauty, liberation, freedom from the humdrum and hard routines of life. Great industrial fortunes were built on trains; nations have held together the many disparate regional peoples of their landscapes with trains. Capitals have held sway over vast empires by trains. We think nostalgically of steam engines, loco-motives (motives of crazy persons?), and empires.

Fashionable historians point to the terrifying post-modern world and recount for us the glories of empires past. Politicians still lead us into obsolete, fruitless and atrocious wars based on such delusive dreams of imperial conquest. And there may be more to come.

Almond calls this work *In The Between* – which was a thrill for me. It is really why I took up the task of meditating on it. When I was commissioned years ago to re-translate the *Book of Natural Liberation Through Learning in the Between,* the so-called *Tibetan Book of the Dead,* one of the main reasons I took the job was that I can't stand the habit translators have of calling the *bardo* – the Tibetan word for 'gap', the space 'between' two things – 'the intermediate state'. They could only call it that because they cannot envision it as an experientially real condition, like a far more intense dream state, 'between' falling into deep sleep and waking up. So I felt it a dream come true to encounter a work entitled, *In The Between.*

The 'between' translates the Tibetan *bardo,* the amazing Buddhist concept that stems from the Sanskrit *antarabhava,* 'between state', which describes the transitional state of every living being's subtle bodymind after having died away from a particular coarse mind and embodiment and before either achieving nirvanic liberation and then consciously emanating incarnations, or involuntarily entering another coarse mind and embodiment driven by the blind delusion of grasping selfhood and the egoistic impulses of lust and hatred. Almond was familiar with that usage of 'between' from my translation of the mis-named *Tibetan Book of the Dead.*

By calling the work *In The Between,* Almond is hinting at the near-death condition of Tibet and Tibetans. The chanting monks are not being loved. They are not the beneficiaries of the romance of the speeding train. The train to Hlasa is a harbinger of their death. It brings people who have no use for them, who only wish to speed through them, to penetrate their land, their hearts, their temples, their prayers, their vitals.

But Almond is an artist, and artists are connoisseurs and articulators of the ambiguous, the ambivalent, the cognitively dissonant. The *Tibetan Book of Natural Liberation in the Between* is not a 'book of the dead', because its message, its ontology, is that *there are no dead people, there is no 'state' of death for people to be dead in.* After 'death', which is simply the instant of disentanglement of the subtle and extremely subtle bodymind-being from the preoccupations of the coarse mentality, from the coarse embodiment and its coarse environment. The soul-being is not at all dead, but very much alive. If it expects, due to ideology and conditioning, to simply enter oblivion, it is very much surprised when it arises in a dream-like state in a body of pure virtual imagery (like that of Neo in the *Matrix*), and perceives a highly volatile and unstable dream-like environment and hosts of dream-like subtle energy beings. Death is like a line crossed, a space that has no width, no dimension, and so is not a state – just as you are never really on a line, anything you can be on is a long rectangle, a line by definition is a concept of position and has no width. Death is merely the instant of severance of the connection between the subtle and extremely subtle bodyminds from the coarse bodymind consisting of five sense organs and six-fold mental consciousness – and no one can stay in an instant of severance. No one stays dead! So, the implication of this depiction of the train being 'a between' is that – if the speeding bullet train the Chinese send into the heart of Tibet is to disrupt the endless prayer of Tibet, to extract the wealth of Tibet, to intrude upon the solitude of Tibet, to kill the soul of Tibet – it fails. The subtly embodied soul of Tibet simply continues in the between, simply finds there the bliss of compassion to embrace even the speeding train.

In calling his film *In The Between,* Almond touches these themes, as he is dealing with death and continuing existence and even life on a multiplicity of levels.

There is the between of the distance between Beijing and Hlasa, China and Tibet. The train is bridging this, carrying people from one place to the other, and the passengers are this *in the between.*

There is the between of the pre-occupation of industrial workers who are exploiting time and materials for a productive purpose and the dis-pre-occupation of the renunciation, the monastic, who considers mundane enterprise paltry, impermanent, inconsequential, and seeks liberation in the depths of reality with a supreme purpose, to share the supreme happiness of enlightenment with all beings.

There is the between on the screen of the monks chanting calmly and evenly in the peaceful but colourful temple between the reflecting images on two sides of the train rushing through the landscape, through stations, along nomadic encampments with staring yaks.

There is the between of machine and human, hooting clattering train and chanting monk, though occasionally the monks when they make music in offering sequences in their rituals blow a deep horn quite like a train, and clatter cymbals, and play a haunting clarinet like big-bone trumpet, and it all sounds quite jolly and clattery in its own right. They consider that the deities of fierce wisdom use the forms of ultimate ferocity to turn back evil and transmute it into good.

There is the between of time, the linear time of the train and the machine that is going somewhere, getting something done, and the seeming timelessness, the free time, of the monks' ritual and prayer, calling on eternal forces of wisdom and compassion to deal with the pain and suffering caused by ignorance and delusion.

There is the between of sound and silence, felt when the landscape, through which the train tries to rush, emerges in its utter vastness, its far steppes and high mountains, wherein the thrusting roar of engines and sound of its whistle and clatter of iron wheels are lost in the silent vastness of the three-mile-high plateau.

There is also the political between, the state of relations between Tibet and China nowadays, when things are not settled. China claims it has always had Tibet; scholars know that this is not so. The Tibetans are quite clear that they are not Chinese. The Chinese, also, do not think the Tibetans are Chinese, except for the purposes of disguising their colonial occupation of Tibet, trying to keep an empire of subjugated nations at a time when empires are *passé,* when their vestige of Marxist liberational rhetoric wants them to keep repeating slogans and thinking of themselves as liberating people from *imperialism* (the very thing they are perpetrating in Tibet, Uighuria, Mongolia, and Manchuria).

The between is actually a place of beauty and vibrancy. When one catches the vision of the between, one realizes everything is a between. The essential Buddhist vision of the relativity of all beings and things – which was discovered by Buddha 2500 year BE (Before Einstein!) – leads us inexorably to the discovery that we are always in a between. The Indian and Tibetan Adepts had six of them: the death point between, the reality between, the becoming between, the life between, the dream between, and the trance between, but there are infinite betweens. After all, we are only here in relation to there, or there in relation to here, and always between here and there in other matrices.

All these betweens have a message of hope. They show something beyond death, for both sides. They bridge from one side to the other. They link up beings in their relationality. A between follows a death but also is followed by a rebirth. The Chinese and foreign passengers on the train can visit the Tibetan monks and enjoy their prayers, and learn how to do the prayers themselves. The monks can travel on the train to Beijing, and perform their rituals and share their peace and vision and calm with the frenetic, industrially toxicated and addicted Chinese. The Tibetans, the Chinese, we ourselves and the whole world are all living together in the between of the last days of millennia of violence and not attending to our great teachers, Buddha, Confucius, Lao Tzu, Moses, Zoroaster, Isaiah, Jesus, Muhammad, Deganawida, and so on. They have all told us that hate brings more hate, violence more violence, destruction more destruction and so on; and that we are all related and all connected, and now face the first days of realistically facing the music of the planet, and universally realizing that we now must live that way. If anything can get us through that between more quickly and cheerfully, it is the vision of our artists, calling us to realism and liberation. So I congratulate Darren Almond for this brave and highly significant creation.

Night + Fog

2007

Bromide prints, b/w, mounted on Kapamount
119.3 x 149.1 cm (47 x 58¾ in)

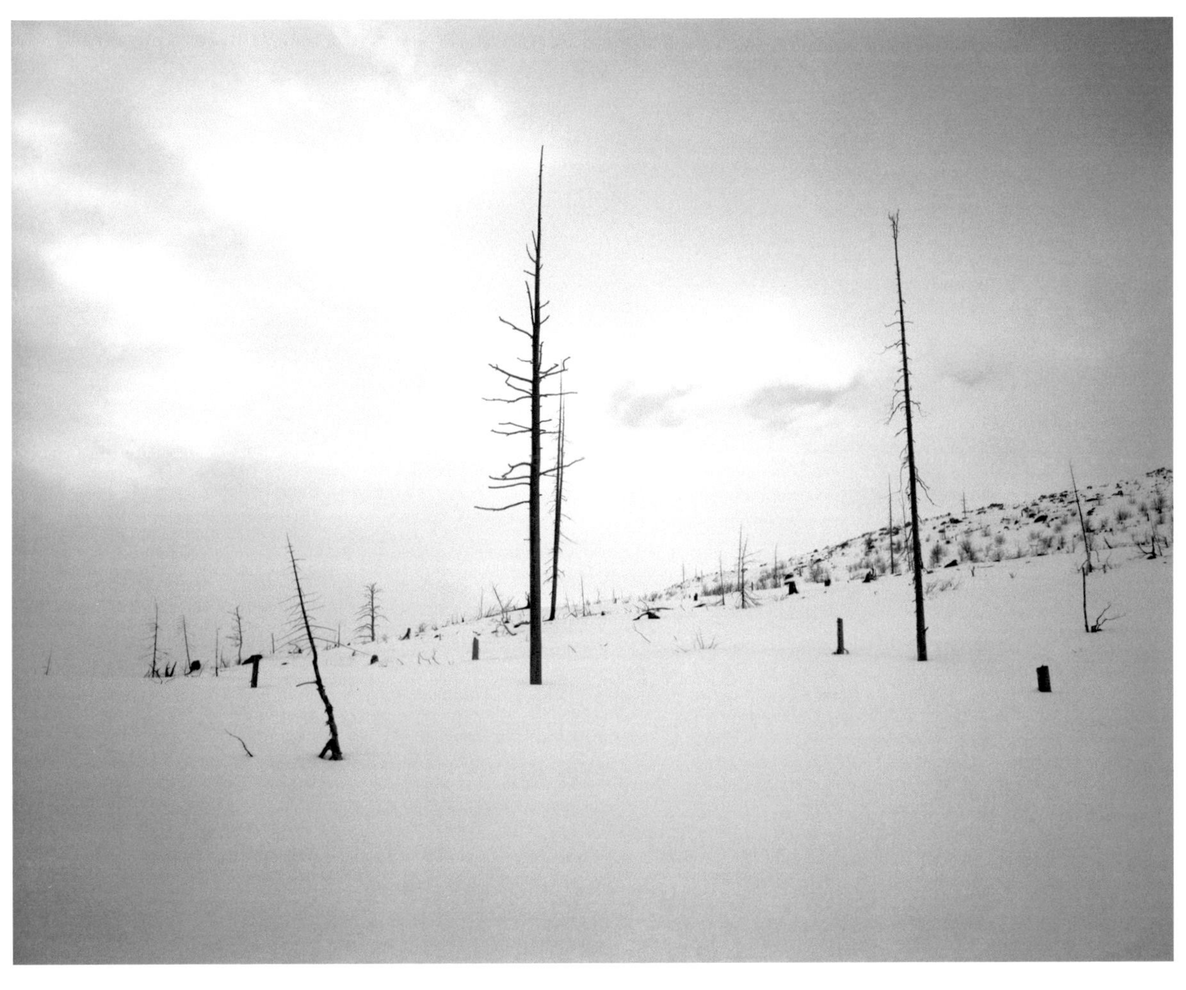

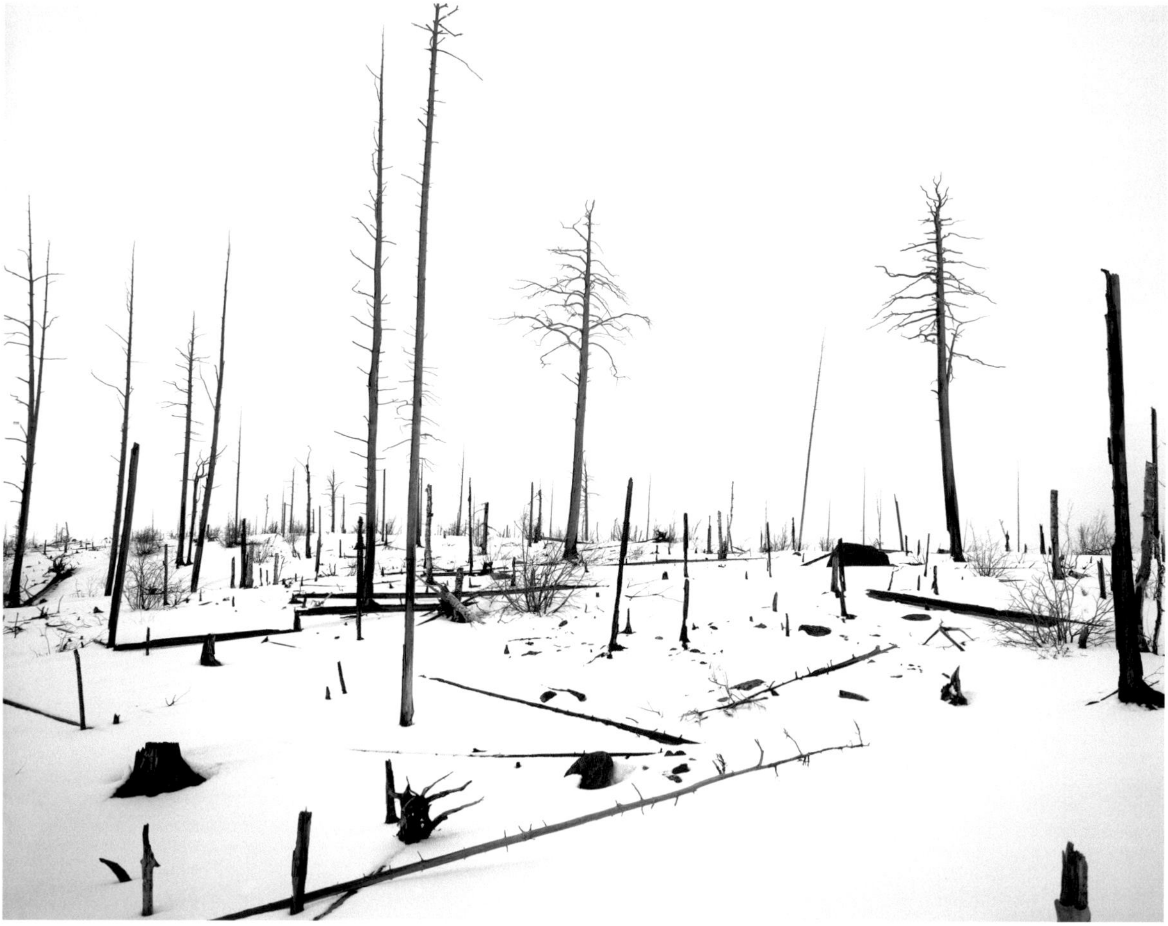

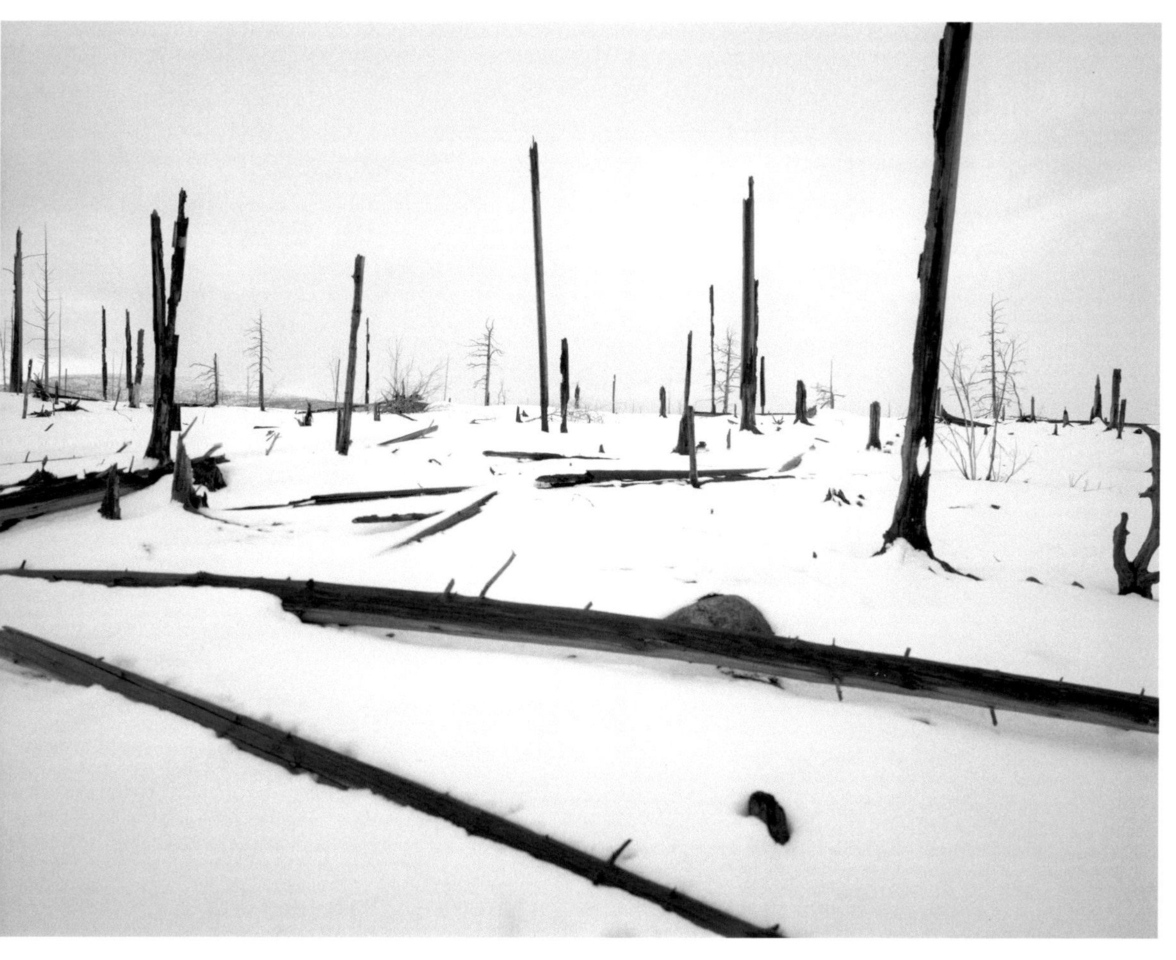

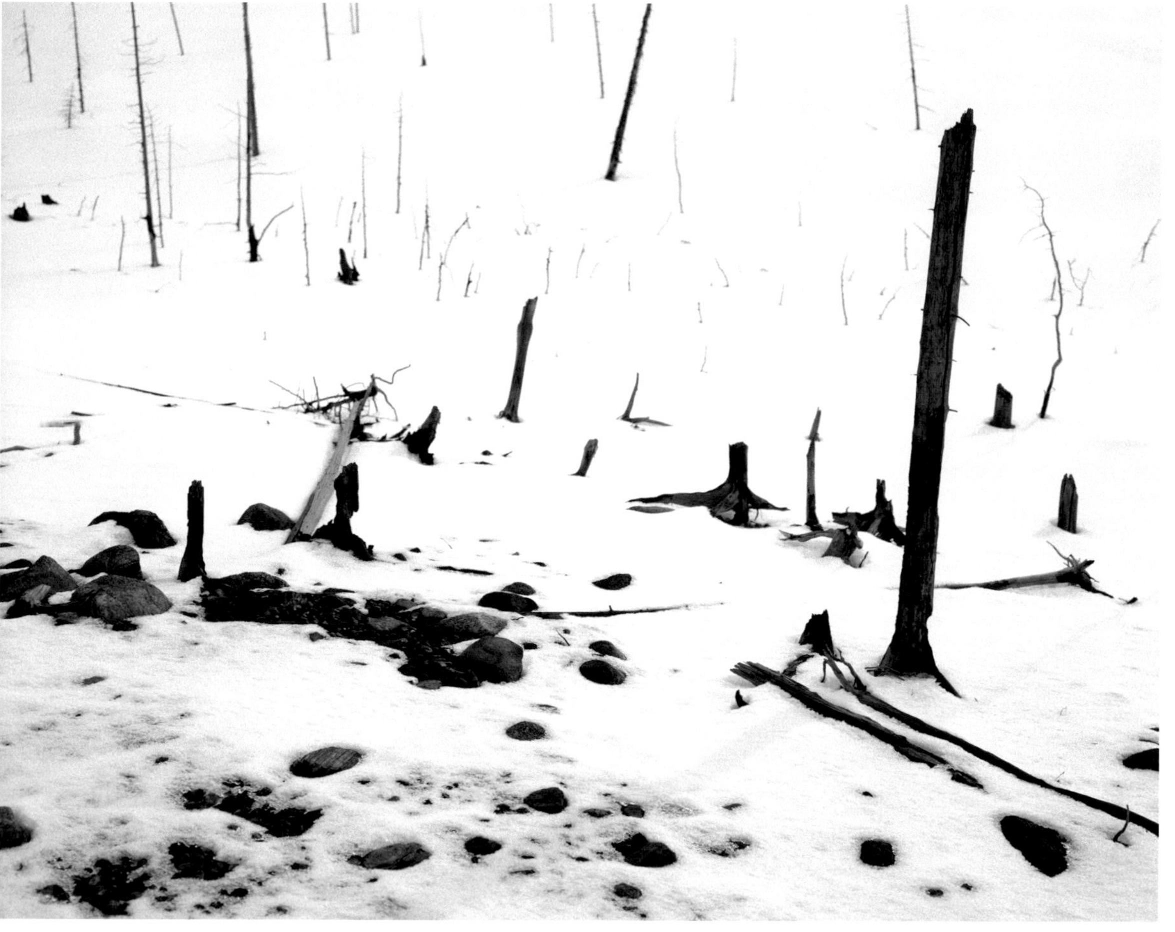

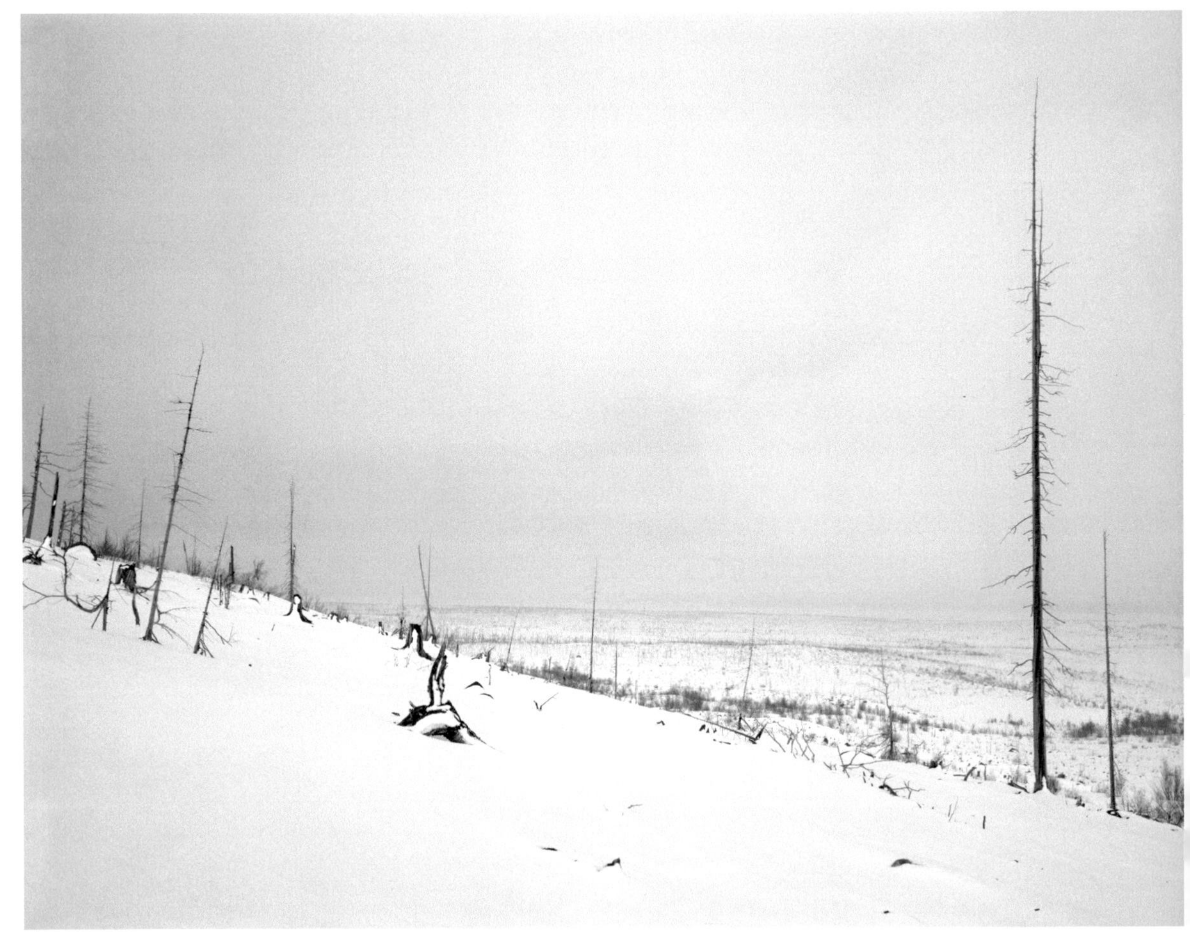

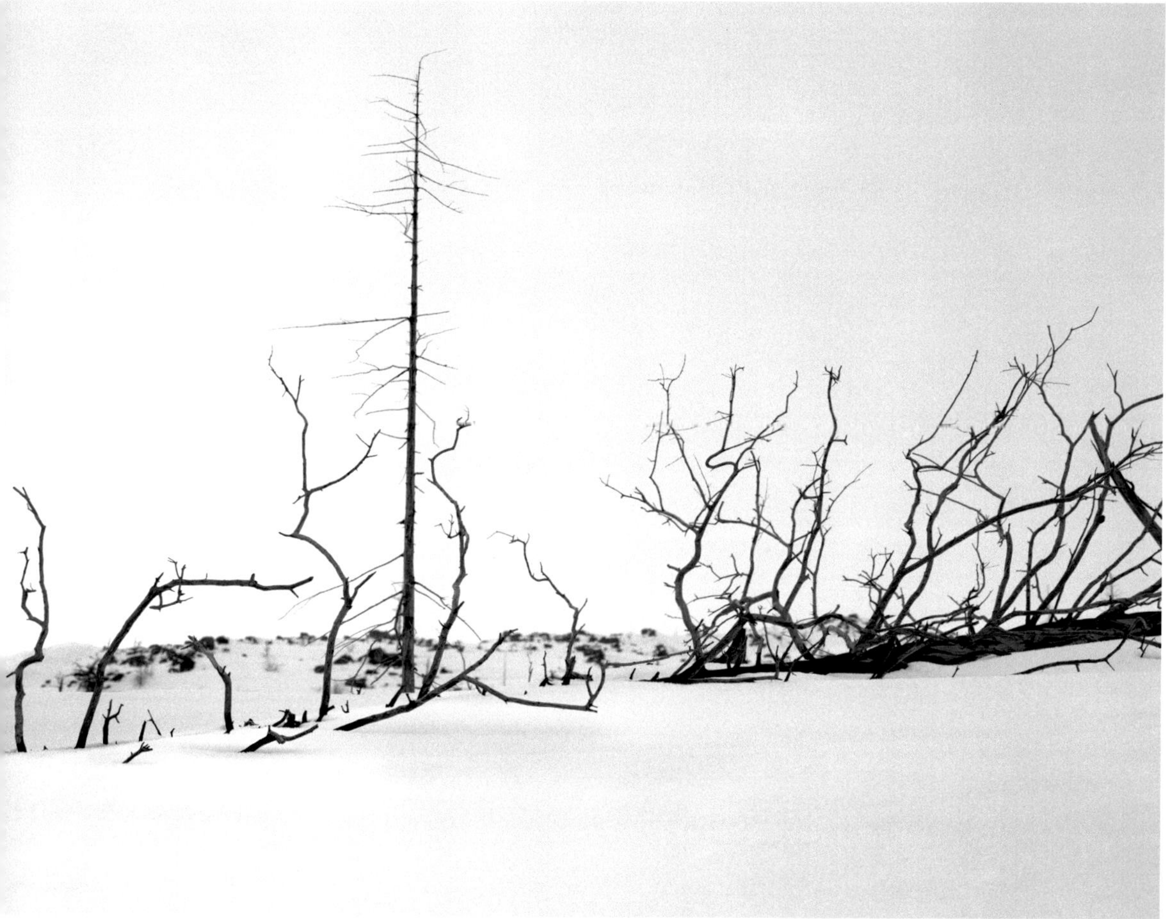

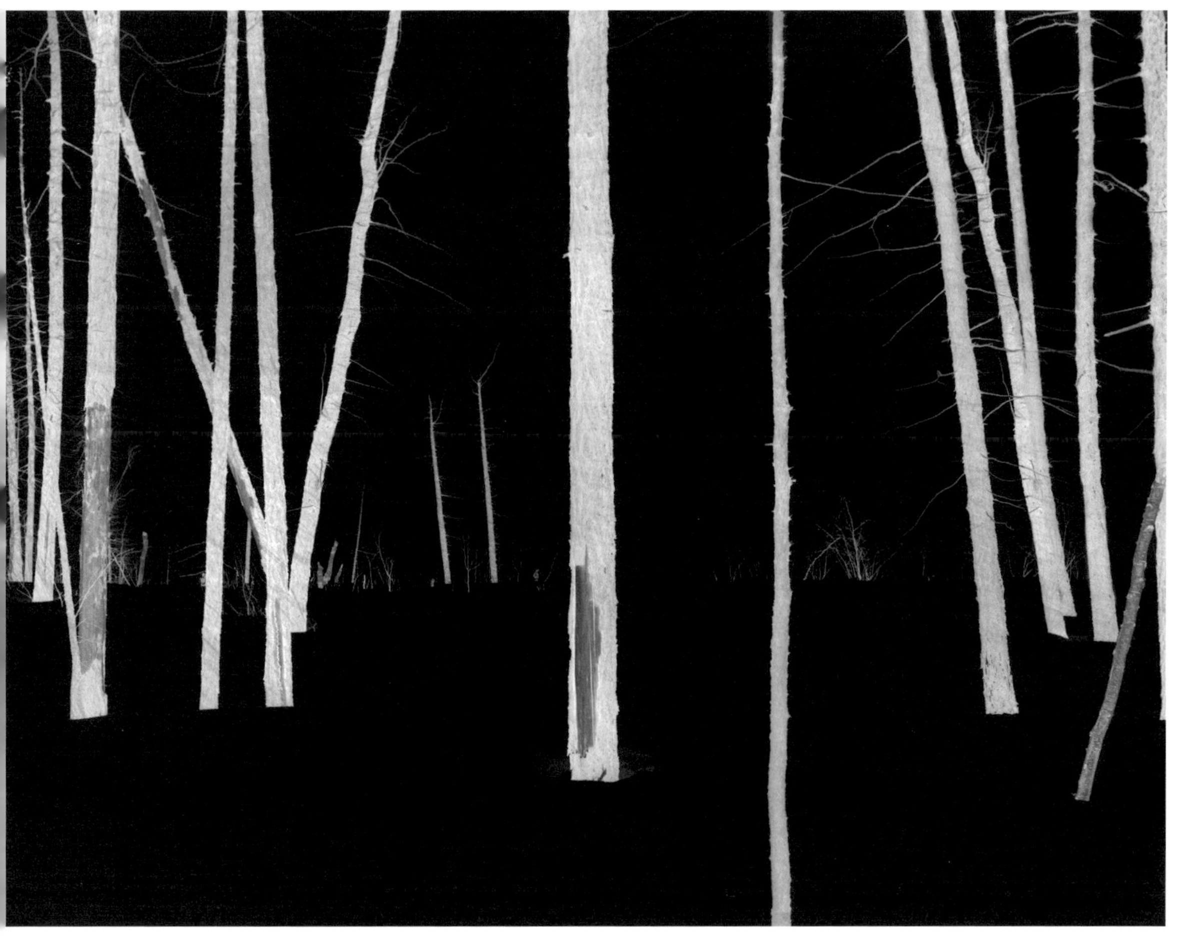

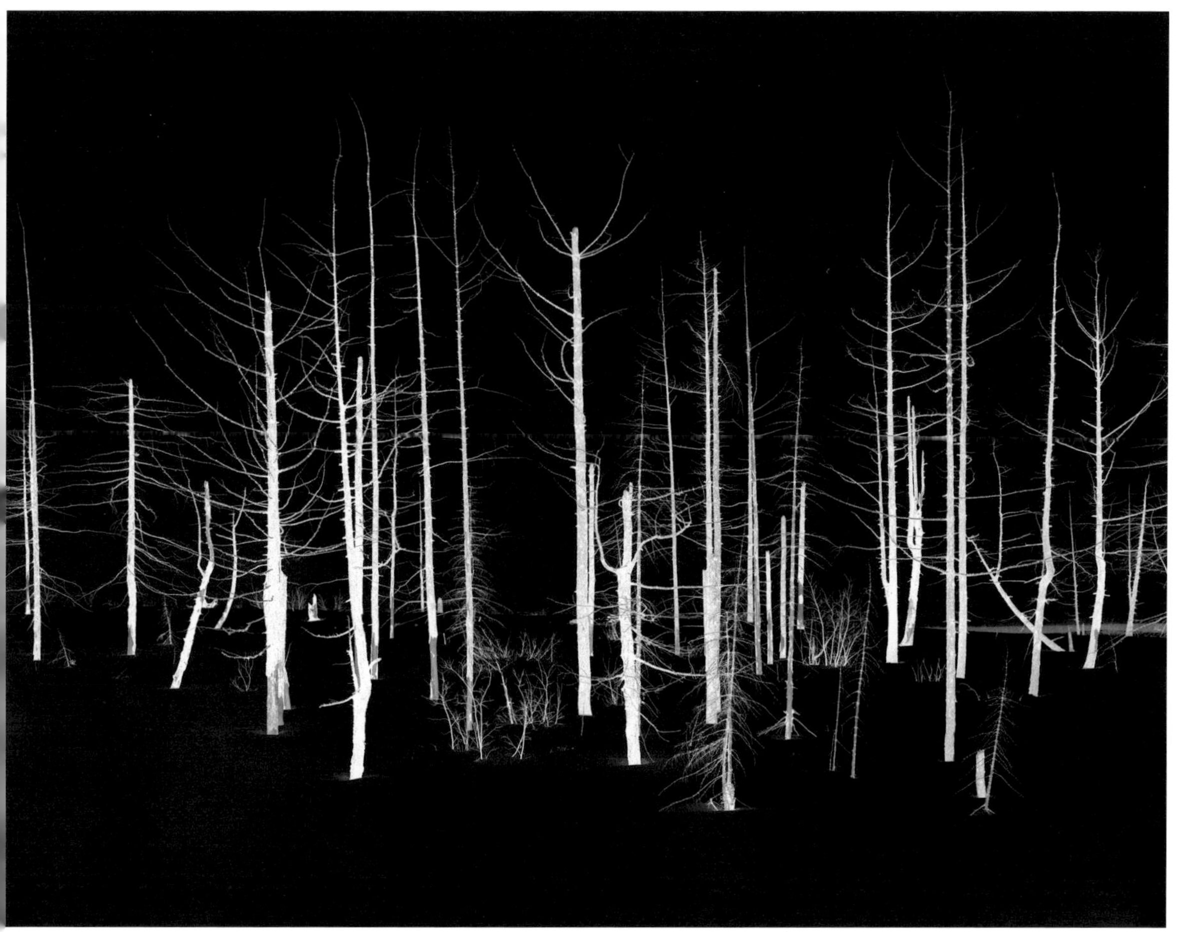

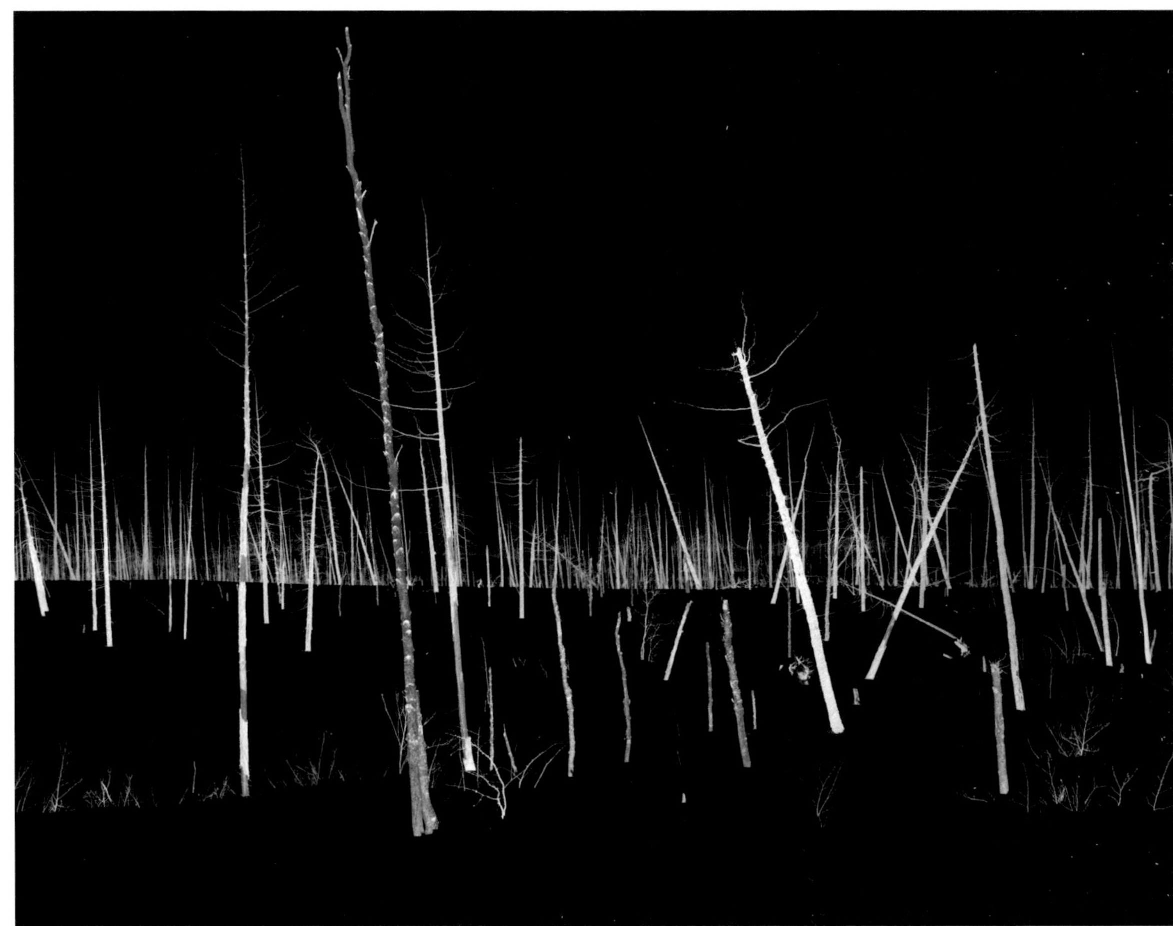

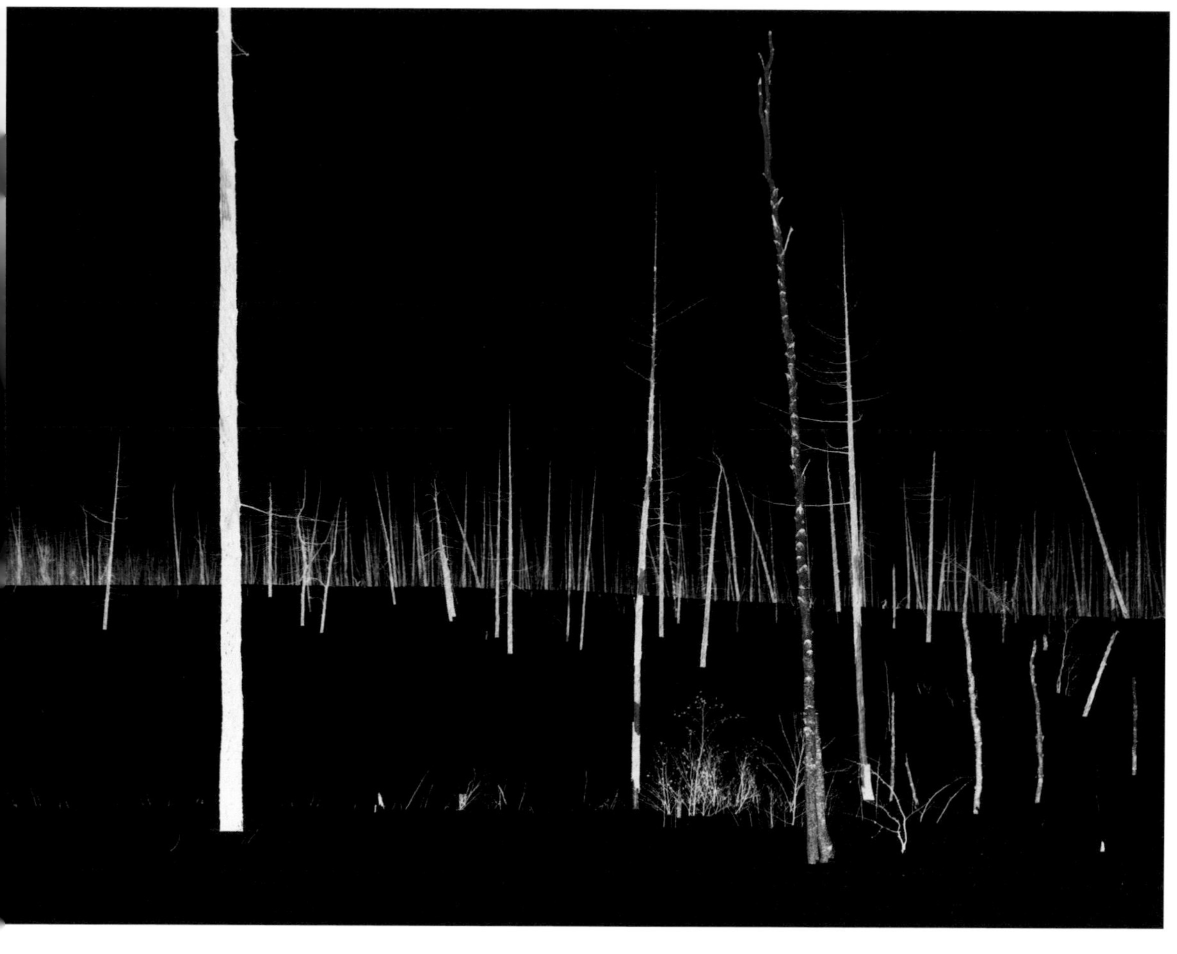

This text by Simon Ertz is Chapter 7 of the book *The Economics of Forced Labor: The Soviet Gulag,* a comprehensive academic study of the economic, social and political conditions of the Soviet Gulag, Norilsk, edited by Paul R. Gregory and Valery Lazarev. It is reproduced here with the permission of the publisher, Hoover Institution Press. Copyright 2003 by the Board of Trustees of the Leland Stanford Junior University.

Building Norilsk

Simon Ertz

Norilsk is today a city of some two hundred thousand residents located in the Krasnoiarsk Territory of Northern Siberia on the Taimyr Peninsula. It is the northernmost major city of Russia and the world's second largest city, after Murmansk, above the Arctic Circle. It is linked by rail to the Kara Sea, and its mineral products can be shipped by the Northern Sea Route. In winter the temperature drops to minus 45 degrees Fahrenheit, and Norilsk is without sun for months at a time. The Norilsk region contains more than a third of the world's nickel reserves, and 40 percent of the world's reserves of platinum as well as significant amounts of cobalt and copper.[1] Between 1935 and 1953, Norilsk housed one-third of a million prisoners of the Soviet Gulag, who constructed its facilities and then mined and processed its minerals. This chapter describes the building of this remote and gigantic industrial complex by Gulag prisoners.

The Gulag economy can be studied through its history, its administrative structure, or its economic functions.[2] Yet if we focus on the working arrangements of the Gulag, we may learn more about them by studying the parts of the Gulag than by studying the whole. This chapter provides a case study of a Gulag camp and its associated industrial complexes, located in Norilsk and its environs. Chapter 5 described the Norilsk labor force. The current chapter deals with the construction of the Norilsk metallurgical complex, its transportation infrastructure, and the Norilsk Correctional-Labor Camp, called Norillag (meaning Norilsk camp), which was created in 1935 and operated until 1956. This chapter examines the decision to build Norilsk, the subsequent decision to turn the project over to the NKVD [People's Commissariat

(Ministry) for Internal Affairs] and its Gulag administration for development, and finally, Norilsk's difficult construction starting in 1935. This account is based on original Norilsk archival documents from the Soviet state and party archives.

Exploration and design

The geological study of the Norilsk area began in earnest in the early 1920s,[3] but the first large expedition, consisting of 250 experts, was dispatched to Norilsk only in 1930. This expedition was under the auspices of the Main Administration for Nonferrous Metal and Gold of the Supreme Council of the National Economy, which took on the initial responsibility for developing Norilsk's reserves. The expedition concluded that the Norilsk deposits were rich enough to warrant the start-up of development. In 1933 about 500 workers, employees, engineers, and technicians were already working on this task at Norilsk, but their number was too small for significant progress.[4] The exploration and development of Norilsk remained largely under the heavy industry ministry until 1935, when it was transferred to the NKVD and its Gulag administration. This transfer was legalized by the top-secret Council of People's Commissars Decree No. 1275–198ss., dated June 23, 1935, "About Norilsk nickel industrial complex construction,"[5] which documented that the infrastructure surrendered to the NKVD was minimal.[6] Thus, the Gulag administration had to start the construction of Norilsk practically from zero.

The minerals of the Norilsk area were significant for Soviet industry. The most valuable mineral was nickel, contained in local ores, which also had significant traces of copper, cobalt, and precious metals, such as platinum. Although platinum, copper, and cobalt later acquired considerable significance, nickel was at the time considered the basic product to be produced in Norilsk. As today, nickel in the 1930s was mainly used in the production of high-quality stainless steel, which was sought after by the military. In 1935 when the decision was made to proceed with development, only a small part of the actual deposits was known. Two years later, estimates of recoverable reserves were raised by a factor of six. According to 1939 data, Norilsk's deposits of nickel made up "48 percent of all deposits in the USSR and 22 percent of world deposits, not including the USSR." Copper deposits equaled "10 percent of USSR deposits and 2 percent of world deposits."[7] According to an October 1938 report, platinum deposits "... appear to equal 549,780 tons, which puts them in first place in USSR and accords them status of world significance."[8] Natural conditions were favorable for the mining and processing of Norilsk ores because large deposits of rich coal were located in the region and served as a power supply both for smelting and for the transportation facilities operated by the Northern Sea Route Administration, the Merchant Marine Ministry, and the Yenisei Steam Navigation Company.[9]

Thus, the enormous economic and military significance of Norilsk was well established at the start of the second half of the 1930s when responsibility for exploiting these riches was placed squarely on the shoulders of the Gulag. The Council of People's Commissars decree of June 23, 1935, assigned the NKVD the responsibility of constructing the Norilsk nickel complex and obliged the NKVD "to organize a special camp for this purpose."[10] The June 1935 decree made Norilsk a top-priority construction project and provided the basic specifications and terms of its realization. The complex should be designed to produce "10,000 tons of nickel annually," and its launch was scheduled for 1938, after three years of construction. The NKVD was obliged to "begin an open field operation of Norilsk deposits starting January 1, 1936," … "to complete its exploratory and research work in 1935," and "to ensure the completion of the fifteen-kilometer narrow-gauge rail link between Norilsk and Piasino and the 120-kilometer rail link between Norilsk and Dudinka by the end of 1936." The project design was assigned to a special design group of the Ministry of Heavy Industry, which was to be formed from the best experts of Union-Nickel-Project-Design (Soiuznikel'proekt). The deadline for completing the design was set for August 1, 1936.[11] Norilsk's priority can be seen in the way in which the Ministry of Heavy Industry supplied Norilsk fully and ahead of schedule with experts, scientific and technical consultations, and studies of "correct management of construction operations."[12] The financing for the design and purchase of equipment and materials was to come directly from the Council of People's Commissars' own reserve funds. Ten million rubles were assigned to Norilsk in 1935 alone. The State Planning Commission was authorized to allocate additional funds for equipment and materials within ten days to take advantage of the short navigation period in summertime.

The decision to assign Norilsk to the Gulag administration of the NKVD was made gradually. The original intent was to assign construction and operation to civilian ministries while the Gulag supplied prison labor force. The Politburo issued its most important decisions as joint decrees with the Council of People's Commissars. According to this practice, the July 1932 joint decree of the Central Committee and the Council of People's Commissars, "About Norilsk deposits of platinum and other rare metals," was introduced and accepted at the July 10, 1932, meeting of the Politburo. Paragraph 8 called on the OGPU (the predecessor of the NKVD) to "ensure exploratory work with the required labor force." Since the OGPU managed only penal labor, it is clear that the Politburo had already decided in 1932, just as the White Sea–Baltic Canal was being completed, that Norilsk would be built by Gulag inmates. The first group of prisoners arrived in Norilsk three years later. The 1932 joint decree assigned Norilsk projects to different authorities. The surveying for railway construction between Norilsk and the Yenisei River was assigned to the Ministry of Transport; equipment and expert geologists were assigned to the Ministry of Heavy Industry and the Committee for Labor and Defense; radio communications were assigned to the communications ministry; and geological exploration was assigned to "Eastern Gold" (Vostokzoloto). Geological exploration was supervised by the Main Administration for Nonferrous Metals and Gold (Glavtsvetmetzoloto). The OGPU was responsible only for the delivery of labor force.[13]

The leadership's conception of Norilsk changed in 1935, when Norilsk was assigned exclusively to the Gulag administration of the NKVD. The 1935 about-face is explained by the Gulag's growing reputation for managing large projects in remote regions and difficult conditions and by the civilian ministries' aversion to working under such hazardous conditions. The development of Norilsk deposits was extremely difficult because of its remote location beyond the Artic Circle. The Ministry of Heavy Industry, which was responsible for metallurgy, for all practical purposes refused to take on the Norilsk project. In fact, the heavy industry ministry lobbied to be relieved of responsibility for such a difficult project. The People's Commissar of Heavy Industry, G. K. Ordzhonikidze, wrote to Stalin the following: "Taking into account serious difficulties in the realization of exploratory and research operations, completion of construction and the development of production in polar conditions, and also the enormous experience of the OGPU in carrying out complex construction projects in extremely difficult conditions, we conclude it is expedient to entrust the OGPU with the organization of operations on the basis of a special camp."[14]

Geologist A. E. Vorontsov supervised the exploration of Norilsk deposits from the beginning of the 1930s, and in 1935 he was appointed the first chief engineer of "Norilsk-construction" (Norilstroi). In the spring of that year, he was present at a Politburo meeting in which the draft of the 1935 decree was discussed. Vorontsov gave the following brief account of the discussion: "Stalin recommended that the project be transferred not to Otto Ul'evich Shmidt [then chief of the Administration for the Northern Sea Route]; he has enough to worry about. It should go to the construction organizations of the NKVD."[15] Although it was unusual for the Politburo to discuss basic decisions in the presence of outsiders, the reason for the decision to transfer responsibility for Norilsk to the NKVD was obvious. The Gulag administration had evolved in the minds of top Soviet leaders from an organization that supplied prison labor to an administration that could, on its own, carry out complex construction projects of the highest priority. As noted in Chapters 3, 8, and 9, the Gulag's potential had become apparent with the construction of the White

Sea–Baltic Canal, the beginning of construction on the Baikal-Amur Railroad (BAM) in 1932, and the organization of camps formed to carry out other significant economic projects.[16] Hence, the assignment of the Norilsk complex to the Gulag administration in 1935 was yet another step in this logical progression.

Organizing the Norilsk project

Only two days after the approval of the Council of People's Commissars decree, the NKVD Commissar, G. G. Yagoda, signed top-secret order No. 00239 of June 25, 1935, "About the organization of Norilsk Nickel Complex construction."[17] The camp was named "Norilsk Correctional Labor Camp" (acronym Norilsk ITL) and was generally referred to as "Norillag." Yagoda's order assigned to the NKVD's Gulag administration more complex and detailed tasks than the Council of People's Commissars decree upon which it was based: Yagoda called for the permanent exploitation of mineral deposits and for the development of the whole area in accord with the now-customary practice of assigning large-scale projects in remote northern and eastern regions to the Gulag. The Gulag's labor camps were to provide labor and other services to the associated industrial projects, such as the Norilsk Construction (Norilstroi) and then to the mineral and metallurgical plants to be built.[18] A precursor of the Norilsk complex, the Northeastern Labor Camp, was organized in April 1932 to provide labor for the "Dalstroi" trust (see Chapter 6).[19] The amount of detail in Yagoda's order underscores the significance of Norilsk in comparison with other large Gulag projects. Norilsk had strategic importance, and its difficult geographical conditions made the project a technologically difficult and complex undertaking. Norilsk had long winters and violent snowstorms and was remote from all means of transport. Construction, which was carried out under conditions of permafrost, required new construction technologies. The difficult climate is mentioned directly in the ninth article of Yagoda's order: "Considering the importance of Norilsk and its location in extremely difficult conditions, I impose as a duty on all bodies of the NKVD to respond immediately to all inquiries of Gulag or Norilsk camp concerning this construction."[20] Another indication of Norilsk's importance is that Yagoda directly assigned Norilsk to the Gulag administration. In May of 1935–one month before the order to organize the Norilsk camp–most camp administrations were subordinate to territorial NKVD administrations. Only five camps "occupied with construction of major economic projects," were directly subordinate to the Gulag administration.[21] Norilsk was added as the sixth by order of Yagoda.

During the first three years of the project, Norilsk development was based on two entities–the Norilskcamp (Norillag) and Norilsk construction (Norilstroi). The second was the agency in charge of building Norilsk's infrastructure using penal labor from Norillag. The director of Norilstroi was initially in charge of the overall project. The draft plan of 1935 called for a production capacity of ten thousand tons of nickel a year starting in 1938, a figure that was first achieved (approximately) only in 1945. As it became clear that start-up schedules could not be met, amendments to the original plan were made. A Council of People's Commissars decree of April 26, 1938, proposed to start exploitation of the first production line (with a productive capacity of five thousand tons a year) in 1940 and to complete construction in 1941.[22] Documents from 1939 and 1940 did not project dates for when the complex would reach its proposed productive capacity and targeted only insignificant quantities of nickel production for the near future.[23] Soviet accounts of the Norilsk project remained silent on the significant delays; instead, Norilsk was described as entering production after a period of speedy construction.[24]

Norilsk construction suffered from significant cost overruns. The draft plan of 1938 called for a capital expenditure of 515 million rubles. This cost estimate was raised to 1.1 billion rubles in 1939 and 1940 and was later set at 1.3 billion rubles. These cost overruns were partly related to the difficult climate and to transport difficulties, but they also reflected fundamental changes in the nature of the project. As geologists discovered ever-richer mineral deposits in the region, the design focus changed from a complex that would produce semi-fabricated metals to one that would finish metals. As geologists found unusually rich lodes with high nickel content, the decision was made in 1939 to expand the Norilsk plant from an experimental plant to a significant industrial complex.[25] According to the original plans of 1935, Norilsk's major product was to be semi-processed nickel, rather than anodic or electrolytic (cathode) nickel, which was supposed to be processed in Krasnoyarsk.[26] Yet the 1939 decision meant that facilities for the final part of the production process were to be installed at Norilsk. Correspondingly, by 1940 the capability of the complex was defined not in terms of semi-finished material but by "10 tons of nickel and 17 tons of copper annually." The increase in the construction budget (noted above, from 515 million to 1.1 billion rubles) was due in part to the change to final processing.[27] It is difficult to disentangle the cost overruns due to such fundamental design changes from those associated with normal construction difficulties. Nevertheless, we will examine endogenous reasons for cost overruns in the next section.

Failures, excuses and progresses

Norilstroi, the Gulag organization in charge of building Norilsk's infrastructure, had to fulfill plans imposed on it by the Council of People's Commissars and by the commissar of the NKVD. Like any other Soviet organization responsible for fulfilling plans, Norilstroi wished to present its work to its superiors in the most favorable light. Its failures had to be explained as caused by the failures of others or by forces outside of management's control. Until 1941, Norilsk's reports were sent to the Gulag administration for review by the NKVD; thereafter they were sent to a new central administrative board within the Gulag, the Central Administration of Mining Enterprise Camps.[28] Norilsk's reports included not only statistical results but also narratives describing the course of construction and special problems and difficulties encountered. The Norilsk administration used these reports to justify their claims on resources and to ensure that their superiors understood the difficult conditions under which they were operating. Norilsk was so remote that it was difficult for Moscow to check the reports, giving Norilsk a certain leeway to fudge them.

Reports from the first three years, beginning in 1935, when the first group of more than one thousand prisoners arrived in midyear, show the extreme difficulty and hardship associated with creating new infrastructure in such a hostile environment. During this period, the mining of coal and ores began, but construction activities concentrated "almost exclusively on construction of subsidiary facilities,"[29] such as transportation systems. For this reason, reports from the scene are less detailed than in later periods.[30] The first three years coincide with Norilsk's first management team, led by Vladimir Matveev. It fell to Matveev to explain to Gulag authorities a series of plan "failures"; the 1936 report had to explain why the plan of capital construction had not been executed. Although 33 million rubles of investment had been planned (in constant plan prices), actual investment was only 78 percent of that planned. The physical construction plan was fulfilled by only 51 percent, and construction costs were 9 percent higher than scheduled. Despite shortfalls in construction results, expenditures on construction materials exceeded the planned amount by 21 percent.[31] The 1936 report also explained why some important projects were not started (such as an experimental concentrating mill and a second temporary power station).

The management explained some plan "deviations" by citing decisions to redirect resources because of unusual circumstances, such as "the necessity to promptly launch temporary railroad traffic." Other narratives explained deviations that were outside of management's control.[32] The delay of a forty-ship expedition loaded with materials and equipment was particularly catastrophic:[33] "... From the 22,700 tons of consignments expected, only 6,000 tons reached the settlement nearest to Norilsk; 1,700 tons were sent back; and 15,000 tons were kept on Lake Piasino for the winter."[34] Not only was the delivery of building materials and equipment incomplete, but because of the congestion at the port of Dudinka, the over-expenditures on labor for loading and unloading cargo were significant. The 1936 report complained that the slow delivery of prisoners due to "supply and transport difficulties"[35] caused the loss of four hundred thousand man-days "during the best construction season."[36] The 1936 report also complained about the bad physical and "moral" state of arriving prisoners, about cost limits that were unrealistic for Arctic conditions, and about "conducting work without preliminary drafts and without effective management."[37]

The minutes of the industrial managers' meeting of Norilstroi and Norillag were added to the 1936 report as an extraordinary communication to superiors to summarize the immense difficulties under which Norilsk was operating:

> *It should be noted that materials of the annual report and its narrative reflect insufficiently the circumstances of construction work under absolutely abnormal conditions: ... In 1935 an advance group of workers was sent to undeveloped tundra without necessary materials to prepare for expanding construction in 1936. This contingent had to do difficult and time-consuming preparatory work under permafrost conditions, under the most severe snowstorms, which dissipated their energy and mental state. Only a person who had experienced it himself knows what it means to preserve the necessary vitality and working energy after months of constant winds with a force from 18 up to 37 meters per second that blow continuous clouds of snow, so that visibility is about 2 meters. Stray workers were lost due to loss of orientation. They had to work in temperatures reaching 53 degrees below zero. Workers were dispersed in the tundra to prepare new areas for habitation and to prepare the area to receive new labor force, create stocks of materials, and to equip work places. In these conditions, Norilstroi workers conducted the first operations in making tractor and cart roads from Dudinka to Norilsk....*[38]

The winter of 1936 was the first Arctic experience of Norilsk's first general manager, Matveev, who had grown up in Central Asia.[39] It was Matveev who included these graphic pictures of Norilsk working conditions for his superiors in the Gulag administration. The descriptions were designed to drive home the point that norms and plans drawn up in Moscow were unrealistic when applied to Arctic construction. Norilsk's superiors, however, did not accept Matveev's "excuses" at face value. "The commentary to the report of Norilstroi," signed jointly by the Gulag's chief of the mining sector and by the deputy head of the finance-planning sector, complains of "inept maneuvering of the labor force" [underlined in red pencil] and of significant over-expenditure of funds, where the "available data do not clarify reasons for the large gap between the supply plan and its fulfillment."[40] Despite Matveev's attempt to explain to the Gulag administration why the work was over budget and behind schedule, these comments show that the Gulag administration considered Norilsk as a construction project that, although complex, should be finished on time and with the allocated resources. Although they recognized that emergency situations influenced the 1936 results, they supposed that subsequent work could be completed according to schedule. The Gulag administration brushed off Matveev's doubts—that Norilsk could be finished according to plan—by offering increased mechanization, improvements in the qualifications of prisoners and workers, and the establishment of more strict control over Norilstroi by the Gulag administration.[41]

We have even richer documentation for the economic activities of 1937 because this year produced two reports, one by the soon to-be-fired management team of Matveev, and the second by the incoming administration led by A. P. Zaveniagin.[42] Matveev's report contains a litany of plan failures: "1937 was supposed to be the year of completion of preparatory work. In 1937 it was necessary, first of all, to solve the issue of the main supply base located on the coast of the Yenisei River in Dudinka village" by completing a narrow-gauge railway line connecting Dudinka and Norilsk. Matveev reports that "this basic task of 1937 was not completed; the railway was opened only at the end of October in a condition unsuitable for exploitation in the severe climatic conditions of the Arctic Circle."[43] As a result, "the whole construction plan was foiled." The secondary power station and the experimental-enrichment factory "were not only incomplete; they were still in a rudimentary state at the end of the year."[44] These important failures are reflected in the lag of construction behind schedule: only 40 percent of scheduled investment was carried out,[45] although 212 percent of the scheduled costs were expended. The totals for 1937 were disastrous from the point of view of central economic administrators. Yet nothing suggests that the 1937 annual plan was changed when it became clear that its execution was impossible. As in 1936, Matveev continued to blame the plan failure on insufficient construction materials: "In the first half-year and in the third quarter there was no extensive construction in Norilsk, a fact explained by the lack of construction materials."[46] The missing construction materials were then explained by the failure of the 1936 supply mission and by problems in railway construction. Matveev had the temerity to place some of the blame for supply problems on Moscow: "All major supply questions are resolved in Moscow, but Norilsk is remote from Moscow and the frequently severe conditions of Norilstroi are not taken into account," such as the difficulty of navigating the Yenisei River and the "carelessness and mismatch of the scheduled and estimated norms that regulate the operations of

Norilstroi."[47] Matveev also complained about the application of "single all-union norms to Arctic Circle conditions," which had to be applied because there were no others. "Such high norms mean the underestimation of budget rates of work."[48]

The Gulag administration's reaction to Matveev's tales of failure is found in the protocol of a 1937 meeting of the Gulag balance commission chaired by the Gulag chief, I. I. Pliner. The Gulag administration's assessment of Norilsk management was merciless:

> *The improper use of labor has caused a failure to fulfill the plan of construction of the narrow-gauge railroad from Dudinka to Norilsk.... Not only was the directive on cost reduction not executed, but a large over-expenditure over the cost estimate was allowed... In view of the massive failure to fulfill the construction plan and the vast over-expenditures, we declare the industrial and economic activity of Norilsk construction to be completely unsatisfactory and uneconomical.*[49]

In light of its disastrous assessment of Matveev's performance, it comes as no surprise that the Gulag protocol mentions the appointment of a new general manager for Norilsk, A. P. Zaveniagin, who took over Norilsk operations in early April 1938.[50] The reasons for Matveev's firing are related in the classified NKVD Order No. 044, "About operation of NKVD Norillag," which was approved literally on the eve of these events, March 9, 1938. It cites the massive failure of the 1937 construction plan due to "poor organization of work," the "absence of work discipline," and "cronyism" and "drunkenness" among the camp management. The management of the Gulag was ordered to develop a plan to complete the railroad construction before the end of 1938, to introduce a system of monthly operation schedules and strictly monitor their fulfillment, to finance Norilsk on the basis of work accomplished to prevent cost overruns, and to strengthen its management and engineering staff. Ominously (since this report was issued during the Great Purges), the Gulag administration issued a "stern reprimand" to Matveev and warned him "that in case of non-fulfillment of the plan for the first six months of 1938 he will be prosecuted." These warnings appeared too late. Matveev, the first general director of Norilsk, was arrested one month later.[51] On April 9, 1939, the military tribunal of the Moscow NKVD sentenced him to death, a sentence later commuted to a fifteen-year prison term.[52] In 1955 he was rehabilitated post mortem.

The new general manager, Zaveniagin, in his first report concerning the 1937 Norilsk performance, places the blame on his predecessor. After an exposition of the huge cost overruns, Zaveniagin concludes that "the 1937 over-expenditure was not justified by any external factors." The report criticizes the extremely low labor productivity of separate construction projects, including railway construction, "the absence of means of mechanization in the construction place, the performance of labor-intensive operations in wintertime, and insufficiently qualified workforce...." As for the problem of the delivery of materials to Norilsk, the report concludes that despite the "poor organization of the shipments from Krasnoyarsk to Dudinka," ... "the quantity of deliveries to Dudinka during the navigation period of 1937 was sufficient for fulfillment of the capital construction plan. The solution of the supply question required only the prompt delivery of materials by railroad to Norilsk."[53]

The new management began its work with a significant reorganization of both the camp and the construction organization. The camp, Norillag, which "included the camp divisions and the department of general supplies and its commercial network," was separated from Norilstroi, the construction company, and was placed on an independent accounting system. Several new departments were formed, including a budget department with a staff of up to two hundred people, a department of work organization, an operations department, a department of design, a maintenance subdivision, a subdivision of subcontracting enterprises, and a chief mechanic's department. This reorganization was supposed to "define precisely the obligations and responsibilities of each division." The functioning of the management of construction before this reorganization was criticized as follows: "Before the second quarter there were so-called 'areas,' which merged production and camp functions."[54]

The 1938 report of the new management team spelled out its assessment of the situation and its accomplishments since the new management team took over: "January to May was a period of complete stagnation of construction due to the lack of materials that remained in Dudinka and could not be dispatched owing to unavailability of railway transportation. From June to the second half of August, forces were concentrated on the completion of the railway to make it operative. September through December saw a period of normal turnover of goods from Dudinka and full-scale operations in Norilsk."[55] Zaveniagin's statistical results also showed marked improvement. Capital investments composed 52 million rubles or 104 percent of the authorized investment plan without, remarkably, cost overruns. Originally a higher 60-million-ruble investment plan had been authorized, but it was cut back to 50 million in October.[56] However, the level of 1938 investment was approximately twice as high as in the previous year. Norilsk's ability to carry out construction work blossomed after the start-up of normal railway transportation.

Figure 7.1 [p.108] shows planned and realized investments in Norilsk for the period 1935–39. These data show that the crisis period for Norilsk construction was 1937, when Norilsk's managers and prison workers had to contend

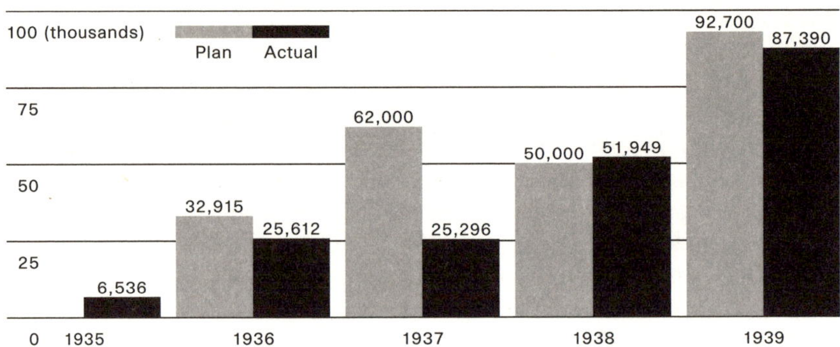

Figure 7.1: The Dynamics of Capital Investments at Norilsk Construction (in Thousand Rubles)
Sources: GARF 9414.1.854: 73; 969: 4; 1118: 16; 1.2977: 230ob.; 8361.1.102: 4.

with the rigors of work in Arctic conditions and with the plan failures that were bound to occur, such as the failure of the forty-ship convoy in 1936. Once Norilsk's transportation infrastructure and reasonably reliable lines of supply were established, construction could proceed on a more normal basis. Matveev had the bad luck to be manager during this difficult period. Later management teams could build off the "failures" of his tenure. Significant construction problems remained. Although the 1938 construction plan had been fulfilled in investment expenditures, results with respect to putting finished projects into operation were less satisfactory. The completion of several major projects, such as the temporary Power Plant Number 2 and a few construction-materials plants scheduled for operation in 1938, were postponed until 1939, though many of them were almost finished. The delays in putting these plants into operation were caused by defects of planning, analyzed in detail in the explanatory notes to the 1938 report. For example, many of Union-Nickel-Design's plans were not suitable to Arctic conditions and had to be redesigned at the site. Supply problems continued to be severe, particularly the shortage of lumber.[57] The start-up delays, however, were also explained by frequent design changes brought about by changing circumstances. The mining of rich ores that could be smelted without enrichment required the redesign of several factories under construction. Moreover, there was no construction-financial plan, which "deprived management of the possibilities of monitoring and controlling budget discipline."[58] Even if there had been a better financial plan, it may have been beyond the capabilities of the camp's accounting departments, which "[had] only a tiny share of qualified workers; the majority of the accounting departments [were] staffed by barely literate people."[59] The optimal use of labor was another problem. The timing of the beginning of large projects was determined by the availability of large numbers of prisoners in the middle of the year. There were too few prisoner laborers in the third and fourth quarters.[60] What's more, Norilsk prisoners were ill suited for construction; they were primarily unskilled workers whose training was conducted on the work site, thereby reducing efficiency and quality of work.

Memoirs of former Norilsk prisoners shed light on the use of prison labor.[61] Although accounts differ, former penal workers all agree on the hard and cruel working conditions in Norilsk. Some, however, recall their work with pride, citing honorary postings on the "red bulletin board" for outstanding brigade work. Those who engaged in physical labor emphasize the labor intensity of their work. Prisoners who had to level construction sites or to dig excavations in permafrost worked only with pickaxes. Workers transporting construction materials or moving earth worked with primitive wooden wheelbarrows. They had to develop their own primitive technology for working in permafrost, such as a heating machine cobbled together by a political prisoner. Prisoners were assigned to work without consideration for their physical state or qualifications. Some of the weakest and oldest prisoners were assigned to the hardest form of manual labor, while the accounting department employed able-bodied but scarcely literate personnel. Women assigned to conveyer belts that sorted ores in winter had to jump up and down on the belts until they started up again. Prisoners characterized their work as "hard, unproductive, and at times senseless." Some of them report being assigned street-cleaning duties on national holidays, after being told by their guards: "National holidays are not for enemies of the people." Thus the prisoners themselves echo the complaints of their captors, who pleaded with the Gulag administration for better equipment and technology. The NKVD and its Gulag administration continued to assign the same output norms to Norilsk prisoners, working under coercion and with primitive hand tools, as to the civilian work force. For the leadership, this prison labor was "free" and available in abundant quantities. There would be no great loss if it were wasted or not used to its full potential. Camp administrators viewed labor differently because plan fulfillment depended mainly on how effectively labor was used and how motivated prison laborers were. If they did not fulfill their plans, their managers would be demoted or, worse, imprisoned, as the first general director of Norilsk had been.

Surpluses and expectations

The first period of Norilsk construction and economic activity came to an end in 1938 as Norilsk's second management team took control. The chief transportation links had been established. Norilsk mining operations were substantial. Norilsk produced 5,050 tons of ore in 1939; 30,130 tons in 1940; and 81,099 tons in 1941, of which 2,270 tons were high-grade ore. Norilsk was producing 4,000 tons of refined nickel by 1943. The Council of People's Commissars' original production goal of producing 10,000 tons of nickel by 1938 was met in 1945 as Soviet troops were placing the Red Flag atop the Reichstag in Berlin. The war years were a difficult period for Norilsk because of the increased demand for nickel and the diversion of resources and workforce to the front. Throughout the period, the Gulag administration continued to receive complaints from Norilsk about the lack of labor and of scarcities in supplies. However, these complaints were not as vocal as in early years.

Conclusions

The story told here, based on the Gulag's own archives, is of how the Gulag administration took on a large priority infrastructure project that civilian ministries would not touch because of its risks. Civilian ministries, such as the heavy industry ministry, pleaded for the transfer of Norilsk to the Gulag administration with its masses of prison laborers that could be dispatched without complaint to the remotest and most arduous locations in the Soviet Union. After a difficult start, beginning at zero, prisoners were placed in a remote Arctic climate to build the housing and transportation infrastructure for what would become the Norilsk metallurgical complex. In this chapter the story has been told largely from a bureaucratic perspective. We have related how the NKVD willingly accepted the 1935 order to build Norilsk on its own and how the minister of interior imposed tough deadlines and tasks on the Gulag administration to complete the work on time. The NKVD refused to accept excuses for plan failure, even though plan failure seemed inevitable given the circumstances under which Norilstroi was operating. The first general manager was sacrificed, and the second management team arrived in time to take advantage of the enormous sacrifices that had taken place during the first three years of construction.

The ministry of heavy industry's near refusal to build Norilsk could be taken as a sign that it could have been built only by the Gulag—but this supposition would not be true. The heavy industry ministry simply recognized the difficulty and cost of the project and understood that the chance of failure was high. They followed the best course in opting out, particularly when the Gulag administration appeared ready to take over the project. The Gulag's own willingness is probably explained by their unrealistic expectation that prison labor could solve all problems.

The Norilsk reports show the clash between the reality of construction in the Arctic Circle (as viewed firsthand by Norilsk managers) and the expectations of the NKVD and its Gulag administration. The NKVD assumed that prison workers could be forced to be as productive as free labor working with better equipment and in better climates. Some of these coercive measures, such as more workdays and longer work hours, are summarized in Chapter 5. Norilsk administrators pleaded with Moscow for lower work norms to reflect the lack of equipment, the poor provisions, and the Arctic cold. Moscow insisted that Norilsk fulfill the plan and not resort to excuses. This clash between reality and expectation is visible in the enormous cost overruns of the early years. Costs were calculated based on unrealistic work norms; as worker performance fell well below norms, costs soared above those planned. In effect, the NKVD's plan was to extract a surplus from Norilsk workers by forcing them to work as effectively as civilian workers in more favorable locations. The massive failure of 1937 showed the lack of realism of this plan.

1   Michael R. Gordon, 'Siberia Tests Russia's ability to Profit from Privatization', *The New York Times,* December 9, 1997. http://econ.1a.psu.edu/~bickes/norilsk.htm

2   M. Dzhekobson and M. B. Smirnov, "Sistema Mest Zakluchenia v RSFSR i SSSR. 1917-1930," Sistema Ispravitel'no-Trudovyh Lagerey v SSSR. Spravochnik (Moscow, 1998), p.10-24; M. B. Smirnov, S. P. Sigachaev, and D. V. Shkapov, *Sistema Mest Zakluchenia v SSSR. 1929-1960* (Ukaz. soch.) pp.25-74; O. V. Khlevnyuk, "Prinuditel'niy Trud v Ekonomike SSSR, 1929-1941," *Svobodnaia Mysl',* 1992. No.13. pp.73-84.

3   N. N. Urvantsev, *Otkrytie Norilska* (Moscow, 1981).

4   *Sovetskiy Taymyr.* May 30, 1933. Quotation from: A. L. L'vov, Noril'sk. Krasnoyarsk, 1985, p.28.

5   State Archive of Russian Federation (hereafter–GARF).5446.1.481: 194-199.

6   Ibid. See also GARF 9414.1.854: 4-28. Ibid. 968: 1-46.

7   GARF 9414.1.29: 54.

8   Russian State Archive of the Economy (hereafter–GAE) 9022.3.1694: 16.

9   GARF 9414.1.29: 53.

10   SNK Decree No.1275-198ss. of June 23, 1935, GARF 5446.1.481: 195.

11   Ibid. For a history of this design group, see A. A. Mironov, "25 Let Nikelevoy i Kobal'tovoy Promyshlennosti Sovetskogo Souza i Perspektiva ee Razvitiia," *Nauchno-Tekhnicheskoe Obschestvo Tsvetnoy Metallurgii: Dvadtsat' Piat' Let Nikelevoy Promyshlennosti SSSR* (Moscow, 1959), pp. 5-14.

12   SNK Decree No.1275-198ss. of June 23, 1935, GARF 5446.1.481: 195.

13   Russian State Archive of Social and Political History (hereafter–RGASPI) 17.3.891: 41-42.

14   L. P. Rasskazov, I. V. Uporov, *Ispol'zovanie i Pravovoe Regulirovanie Truda Osuzhdennyh v Rossiyskoy Istorii* (Krasnodar, 1998), pp. 61-62–quotation from Ordzhonikidze's letter is taken from S. I. Kuz'min, "Ot GUMZA do GUINa," *Prestuplenie i Nakazanie,* 1997, No.5, p.11.

15   V. N. Lebedinskiy, P. I. Mel'nikov, Ukaz. soch., pp.13-14. See also A. L. L'vov, Ukaz. soch., pp.28-29.

16   M. B. Smirnov, S. P. Sigachaev, D. V. Shkapov, Ukaz. soch., pp.30-33.

17   A. I. Kokurin, N. V. Petrov, *GULAG: Struktura i Kadry* (Svobodnaia Mysl', 2000, No.2), p.113.

18   M. Dzhekobson, M. B. Smirnov, Ukaz. soch., pp.18-19; M. B. Smirnov, S. P. Sigachaev, D. V. Shkapov, Ukaz. soch., pp.25-26.

19   *Sistema Ispravitel'no-Trudovykh Lagerey v SSSR. Spravochnik,* pp.382-385.

20   NKVD top-secret order No.00239 of June 25, 1935: A. I. Kokurin, N. V. Petrov, Ukaz. soch., p.114.

21   These camps were the Baikal-Amur, White Sea-Baltic Canal, Dmitrovsky, Uhta-Pechora and Temnikovsky camps. M. B. Smirnov, S. P. Sigachaev, D. V. Shkapov, Ukaz. soch., p.39.

22   This decree was published in *Ekonomika Gulaga i ee Rol' v Razvitii Strany, 30-e gody* (Sbornik dokumentov, RAN. Institut Rossiyskoy Istorii, sost. M.I. Khlusov, Moscow, 1998), pp.88-89.

23   GARF 9414.1.2977: 231b. Ibid. 29: 57.
Ibid. 30: 43.

24   E. Riabchikov, *Plamia nad Arktikoy* (Moscow, 1959); V. A. Dar'ial'skiy, *Noril'sku–25 let* (Noril'sk, 1960); V. N. Lebedinskiy, P. I. Mel'nikov, Ukaz. Soch.; V. N. Lebedinskiy, *V Serdtse Rudnogo Pritaymyr'ia*; V. N. Lebedinskiy, "Nikel' dlia Fronta," *Voprosy Istorii*, 1981 No. 5, pp. 181–185; B. I. Kolesnikov, *Forpost Industrii v Sibirskom Zapoliar'ie. 50 let Noril'skomu Gornomo-Metallurgicheskomu Kombinatu im. A. P. Zaveriagina* (Krasnoyarsk, 1985); A. L. L'vov, Ukaz. soch. For a short account of the plant's history see also M. Ya. Vazhnov, *Bol'shoy Noril'sk: Istoria Sotsial'no-Ekonomicheskogo Razvitia. 1960–1985* (Otechestvennaia Istoria, 1994, No. 6), pp. 74–75.

25   Yu. L. Edel'khanov, "Sovershenstvovanie Tekhnologii Proizvodstva Noril'skogo Gorno-Metallurgicheskogo Kombinata," Dvadtsat' Piat' Let Nikelevoy Promyshlennosti SSSR. Materialy nauchno-tekhnicheskogo soveschania, posviaschennogo 25-letiu nikelevoy promyshlennosti SSSR, August 4-5, 1958, Verkhniy Ufaley (Moscow, 1959), p. 74.

26   SNK Decree No. 1275-198ss. of June 23, 1935.

27   GARF 9414.1.30: 41.

28   *Sistema Ispravitel'no-Trudovykh Lagerey v SSSR*, pp. 108–109.

29   GARF 9414.1.29: 55.

30   T. Vensenostseva, *Sozdanie Opornoy Bazy dlia Stroitel'stva NGMK. Noril'lag pri V. Z. Matveeve* (Noril'skiy Memorial, vypusk October 4, 1998), pp. 23–25.

31   GARF 9414.1.854: 73–76, 93.

32   Ibid., 74.

33   RGASPI17.3.975: 16; G. Kublitskiy, "Khodilimyna Piasinu …," *Sibirskie Ogni*. 1968, No. 12, pp. 127–139.

34   GARF 9414.1.854: 9.

35   GARF 9414.1.854: 2b.

36   GARF 9414.1.854: 74.

37   GARF 9414.1.854: 2b.

38   GARF 9414.1.854: 2-3.

39   V. N. Lebedinskiy, P. I. Melnikov, Ukaz. soch., p. 22.

40   GARF 9414.1.854: 74, 76.

41   GARF 9414.1.854: 83.

42   GARF 9414.1.968: 1–46; GARF 9414.1.969: 2–17.

43   V. A. Dar'ial'skiy, Ukaz. soch., p. 16; RGAE 8704.1.948: 14.

44   GARF 9414.1.968: 2, 4–5.

45   GARF 9414.1.968: 14; GARF 9414.1.969: 4–6; GARF 8361.1.10: 19.

46   GARF 9414.1.968: 19.

47   GARF 9414.1.968: 2–3.

48   GARF 9414.1.968: 45.

49   GARF 9414.1.969: 108

50   Zaveniagin was appointed chief of Norilstroi by order No. 840ls NKVD SSSR of April 8, 1938 (A. I. Kokurin, N. V. Petrov, "Gulag: Struktura i Kadry." Statia Sed'maia. *Svobodnaia Mysl'*. 2000, No. 3, p. 106). His assignment was approved during the Politburo meeting of April 25, 1938 (RGASPI 17.3.998: 15).

51   *Sistema Ispravitel'no-Trudovykh Lagerey v SSSR*, p. 339.

52   A. I. Kokurin, N. V. Petrov, Uraz. Soch., *Svobodnaia Mysl'*, 2000, No. 3, pp. 107–117; Pritcha o Noril'ske. B.m., b.g. p. 7. (Post-Soviet publication of the Museum of Development and Evolution of Norilsk Industrial Complex).

53   GARF 9414.1.969: 6, 8, 10.

54   GARF 9414.1.1118: 6, 9.

55   Ibid.

56   GARF 9414.1.1118: 5, 9.

57   GARF 9414.1.1118: 6, 10, 12.

58   GARF 9414.1.1118: 7.

59   GARF 9414.1.1118: 20.

60   GARF 9414.1.1118: 10.

61   Memoirs of former prisoners can be found in the Archive of the Moscow Society of "Memorial" as well as on the website of the Krasnoyarsk Society of "Memorial" (http://memorial.krsk.ru/memuar).

Part II
Selected Works 1995–2007

A Journey Through Time
But No Arrival

Julian Heynen

When he was asked a few years ago why he was more interested in digital than in analogue representations of time, Darren Almond answered with a memory.[1] He described an incident when he was riding his bicycle and was hit head-on by a car travelling at high speed. That brief but extremely dramatic moment was indelibly etched into his memory. But what he remembers most vividly is not the car suddenly speeding towards him and the moment of the inevitable impact – all the things that a movie director would try to capture – instead he finds himself reliving his own responses: 'At the moment of impact I remember very distinctly and clearly to this day all the processes and mechanical functions and signals that I asked myself to perform in order to contort and avoid serious impact.' What stayed with him was the way that his unconscious had acted at one remove from the actual situation, allowing it to instigate conscious and useful actions. The fascination of this multidimensional memory lies in the short 'pause' and the 'moment of reflection' that intervenes in the unstoppable passage of time. For Almond it is as though the sight of the jerkily changing numerals in digital clocks – particularly older models with mechanical workings – embodies this intervention, this moment when time seems to stand still. And it is as though memory is located 'somewhere between the analogue and the digital'. It is situated, one might extrapolate from this, between the feeling of being connected with everything that captures fleeting time and those moments where this indivisible

1   'A glance is accustomed to no glance back. A conversation between Darren Almond and Julian Heynen', in *Darren Almond – 50 moons at a time,* K21 Kunstsammlung Nordrhein-Westfalen, Düsseldorf, Verlag der Buchhandlung Walther König, Cologne 2005, supplement, unpaginated.

continuum is as it were suspended, because something else from outside prevails upon it and a crevice for reflection opens up. Or to put it another way: the two poles between which Almond's work increasingly seems to operate are the continuity of the world we live in, on one hand, and the isolated occurrence, on the other.

Time + Space

This work with time has not only taken shape in a variety of media (from meticulously executed drawings to films to large-scale sculptures), it has also developed in a number of different directions exploring diverse manifestations of possible responses to and reflections on time. In a sense the sundry digital clocks that Almond has made amount to an exposé of his work, for they thematize time in a fundamental, even relatively abstract form. The 'flip' mechanism controlling the leaves of the numerals beats out the continuum in a manner that is as relentless as it is actually arbitrary. We watch it just waiting for the next change, looking to the future only to be thrown back on the immediate past. It seems that since the invention of measurable time, it is only in these shifts forwards and backwards that the modern mind can negotiate its passage. But even if the clocks prompt such fundamental deliberations, they are also very striking physical objects, with each in its own place. There is no mistaking the sound of their workings, particularly since they are amplified in certain cases; one even 'talks' (a 'shit' every minute). Others make no secret of their inner lives as mechanical devices and reveal the time as we look through them to the space beyond. And the very biggest clock (*Meantime* [p.158], 2000), a converted freight container, is currently making its way around the world. It is set to Greenwich Mean Time, giving striking visual form to the relativity of time and space. This link between time and space, as categories, already featured in Almond's early work *Fan* [p.136], 1997, and in the numerous drawings connected with it, where the rotating blades of the fan, extending and retreating, also pace out the corners of the room, continually exploring its geometry. This 'squaring of the circle' turns the relationship between the rotation of the blades and the stasis of the space into an image of the inseparability of time and space. Bathed in white light, this almost hypnotic constellation calls to mind the famous words from Richard Wagner's *Parsifal*: 'time here becomes space' – and, vice versa, in this case space becomes time.

Besides these rather general connections, in other works there are very specific couplings and extensions of the two phenomena. All his life Almond has been fascinated by railways of every kind – be it the *Schwebebahn* [p.132], 1995, in Wuppertal, the *Geisterbahn* [p.148], 1999, at the Prater in Vienna, the name and number plates on British locomotives that have given rise to numerous metal plaques, pit railway systems (*K-Hole,* 2000; *Schacta* [p.160], 2001), the route of the Qinghai–Tibet railway (*In The Between* [p.44], 2006) or the track running through a former Gulag area in Siberia – in all these instances the railway is a space-time system that is wholly bound up with real places, cultures and epochs. Perhaps it is in the railway films that we see most clearly that Almond's work with time always has a very material basis. A railway system can never be separated from the physical, economic, social and political conditions of its existence. Moreover it has a definable history which coincides with the industrial age, an era that can now be seen, more or less clearly, to be coming to an end. The trains in these works not only travel between specific places, and they not only require a defined measure of time for their journeys, they also always carry with them the past as a historical dimension. Their locus and their theme is, broadly speaking, the route they travel.

Individual Time

Amongst Almond's earliest pieces is a live video link that transmits a nearly life-size image of the artist's studio into the gallery space (*A Real Time Piece* [p.134], 1996). Nothing seems to be happening, except for the fact that we can observe the passing of time in two different ways. Every minute the display on the digital clock on the wall changes with a BOOM, and anyone who looks long enough will see the light entering through the window changing as day becomes night. In so far as the video link connects two separate places, it makes a fairly general statement about the interconnectedness of space and time. But in addition to this the work also has a personal dimension in the shape of the chosen motif. Traditionally the general public in the bourgeois epoch has elevated the studio into a place dedicated to artistic creativity, a home for the myth of the artist. And when artists depict this space, it is usually deliberately arranged so that this particular 'home story' will chime with their own work. One of the most complex representations of an artist's studio from the past is Gustave Courbet's *The Painter's Studio*

(1854–55), which he described as a 'real allegory' for a reason. By contrast Almond's studio looks like the work station of an engineer, someone designing and experimenting with products in close contact with the manufacturing process. The atmosphere is neutrally functional; the 'business' here seems to be about determinedly connecting ideas and tools. The electronic link between the studio and the exhibition space attests just as dispassionately to the reality of contemporary art production that no longer makes a strict distinction between 'actual' artistic activity and presentation.

What is seen in this work in purely factual terms – namely the artist's own private sphere – is laid bare very differently in two other video installations. Both of these works are connected very movingly with personal, even intimate aspects of Almond's life. The protagonists are members of the older generation of his own family, and their 'stories' are of existential experiences. *Traction* [p.154], 1999, is about the life story of a working man and how it is reflected in his injuries; the actual account progresses systematically along a route leading from his feet to his head. With the piece consisting of three simultaneous projections, one camera concentrates entirely on the face of the man telling the story (Almond's father); a second focuses on the silent reactions of a woman (his mother). The third projection, like a ground bass, shows roadworks with heavy equipment. The longer the man's account lasts, urged on by Almond's own voice off camera, the more emotional the expression on the woman's face. The use of a triptych reinforces the pathos of this story of suffering, albeit a pathos that is a true reflection of the emotions of those involved. Listening to the man's words, there is no mistaking the objective, matter-of-fact nature of his recital of his injuries. Despite the often distressed reactions of the woman, *Traction* is not a protracted lament. This foray into the intimacy of the artist's own family becomes an expedition into an age when, unlike today, it was far from unusual for work to take a real physical toll on the individual's body. In this piece it is not a technological system, such as the railways, that is the focus of the artist's exploration of individual lifetimes – which in turn casts light on the increasingly 'historical' epoch of the industrial age – but rather the marks left on the physical body of an identifiable human being. *If I Had You* [p.170], 2003, homes in even more closely on the intimate life story of a particular individual. However, in this multi-part video installation revolving around an old lady's memories of life with her deceased husband, there is no speech. In this case 'statements' are made and distance is created by a series of gently moving pictures that seem to rise up within the slow-motion gaze of the woman. To the sound of elegiac piano music this work – never shy of any kind of emotion – seeks to make contact with the reality of one person's inner life. In so doing it touches on the sentimental side of memory, that deep-seated intermingling of desire and real facts. In this work the artist endeavours to take seriously the individual transfiguration of one part of life. Not everyone may wish to follow this lead, for the work crosses a threshold of intimacy beyond which the search for images to express the innately hidden is, by definition, a risky undertaking. It is a terrain filled with (justified) suppositions, but it is also a balancing act where a fall can only be prevented by observing the fragile borderline of aesthetic discretion.

Natural Time

A similar borderline is also in evidence in the landscape photographs. Taken at night, the only source of light in these pictures is the full moon. The long minutes needed in such poor light for even a recognisable image to be recorded are almost on a par with the extremely long exposure times that were used for early photographs. The old-fashioned slowness of this technical process already makes a connection between Almond's efforts to capture nature and the nineteenth century, *the* century for landscape art. Some of the motifs of these photographs are places that were painted in the past by artists such as John Constable (1776–1837) and Caspar David Friedrich (1774–1840), and even when there are no obvious precursors, the scenarios are reminiscent of those shaped by Romantic art in the widest sense. The idea of forming an image of nature via these historical models, so to speak, rather than showing the landscape from a present-day perspective after two hundred years of industrialisation and destruction was an entirely conscious decision. In the 'full-moon pictures', however, there is a subtle element of the Here and Now, by virtue of the medium itself. In conjunction with advanced photo technology and chemicals, the extended exposure time creates a mood that is irreal, in the truest sense of the word. Accustomed as we are to reflecting on all aspects of any medium, the sight of these photographs instils in us the sense that here we are being shown something that the human eye alone could never see. On the contrary, the colours and the materiality of the scenes is what sensitive photographic film 'sees' in conditions of almost-darkness. Thus the viewer's perception of these images wavers between their recognition of a Romantic schema and their awareness that the medium is being used to simulate that older model. Such views of nature, which range from philosophical to sentimental and which are part of a continuing, powerful tradition, come up against an almost common-or-garden scepticism with regard to the chosen medium. It is as though an alloy of different times were being fabricated. The idea of permanence, as embodied in nature, is taken up by Almond even as he casts doubt on the possibility of using pictorial means to understand it. In the indisputable beauty of these images there is a hint of poison, creating a tension that has something to do with the different time dimensions pertaining to the subject matter (the landscape, nature), on one hand, and to the artist or the viewer, on the other.

In the two series of photographs *Until MMXLI,* 2002, and Arctic Plates, 2003, and in the three-part video film *A–,* 2002, the relationship between nature and its observation is even more acute. The colour symphonies of the blue-white-green images of *Until MMXLI* are juxtaposed with the date, stated in the title, of the ending of the treaty limiting the commercial exploitation of the Antarctic. The monochrome nocturnal landscapes of the Antarctic ice cap are barely distinguishable from desert sands. Finally three filmic movements of an exploration of the Antarctic set to music contrast the apparently peaceable slowness of nature with its overwhelming power and, in an almost hallucinatory manner, upturn the viewer's standpoint which had pretty much been assumed to be secure. All these pictures of nature only function in this seductive form because they are in fact images of a distance or of a dislocation that really never could be synchronised. In the quest to seek out the time inherent to nature at its most stunning locations, the hardly commensurate time dimension of the observer is also always present. It is in exactly this gap between the two that Almond's images come into their own.

Collective Time

While the image of the studio with time passing was – despite his actual absence – concentrated on the single exemplar of the person of the artist and, as such, an indirect self-portrait so to speak, in the video projection *HMP Pentonville* [p.142], 1997, the focus is on a group of people. Once again the piece consists of a real-time video link to an empty room, although this time it is an unoccupied prison cell. The atmosphere of potential creativity in the studio is replaced here by maximum confinement, passivity and tedium. The absence of an inmate does not make this portrayal of the living conditions any the less vivid. The only thing that moves in this picture, besides the changing daylight, is a digital clock at the lower left edge of the image, with the tenths of a second racing by in a manner that is almost absurdly at odds with the complete absence of activity in the actual room. So much for the visible facts. At least as important to this scene is the presence of the world outside the cell; this is conveyed as a surround-sound relay that fills the space occupied by the viewer contemplating the image. Depending on the time of day the voices and noises can rise to the level of a nerve-wrenching cacophony or take the form of minor interruptions underlining the equally penetrating silence. The sound here is no mere backdrop, it is the main player. For a prison inmate living in isolation, sounds are a prime source of information on the social interaction outside the cell. However, the inmate's stake in that society is essentially passive. Anyone witnessing the live link in the museum is twice removed from the actual events of that situation and finds him or herself cast all the more resolutely in the role of voyeur. What seems to promise close contact and authenticity retreats to an almost un-bridgeable social distance. Once the cell light has been turned off, all that remains to be seen is the digital time racing by in complete blackness, and it is as though this locked place exists only in the free-floating imaginations of those observing it from afar.

Schacta [p.160], 2001, delves into a world of work unknown to most and already a thing of the past in vast tracts of one-time industrialised regions. In two projections the journey into the seemingly endless depths of coal mine is juxtaposed with a slow-motion view of the pithead bath where the miners change after their shifts. As in the video link from the jail, the actual activity of the place – the mining of natural resources – is not shown. The hard, dynamic work of men and machines remains out of sight. Instead the time Before and After stretches out, creating a strangely passive, almost dreamlike atmosphere. The kind of time that passes in this film, its calm, continuous, uneventful structure contrasts starkly with the social, techno-logical and economic implications of the time needed for this collective in-dustrial labour. In his duly cautious exploration of a social phenomenon such as work, different time modes offer Almond a way of escaping the tempta-tion to engage in pure illustration or documentation. But that is not all. The sound track consists of shamanic melodies sung by a single female voice. In the video images there are few if any indications that this mine is in fact in

Kazakhstan; however the style of singing does evoke a location somewhere in Central or Northern Asia. It suggests a site – certainly not a mine – with some traditional or religious use that does nevertheless have some strange connection with the almost archaic associations of mining. The sound track introduces another time dimension, bringing into play an epoch and a culture that were already lost in the depths of time long before our own industrial age and that no longer seem compatible with the Here and Now. These disjunctures of place and time are fundamental to the structure of the work. Although there are also ineffable affinities between them, they serve primarily to subvert any glib identification with sites (used for mining and religious ritual) overfilled with the extreme time dimensions. In both places and times there is a collective at the heart of things, albeit not clearly localisable. The position of the artist and of the viewer, that's to say, the outsider, the visitor or even the voyeur chafes at these disjunctures and, as such, is always implicitly present. However, here and in other works this built-in doubt in the powers of representation is not absolute; it is simply the other side of the artist's tireless efforts to arrive at an understanding of certain phenomena.

Historical Time

Almond pursues a similar contiguity and coupling of different times and places in a three-part projection with images from Tibet and the route of the new Qinghai–Tibet railway. Besides the metaphorical interpretation of the railway as a certain kind of life cycle, in the images and sounds of *In The Between* [p. 44], 2006, real history and politics are emphatically present – albeit only indirectly, once again. The artist's technical intervention in the sequence of images in the three projections turns the high-speed progress of the modern train through a monotonous, inhospitable landscape into the high-energy penetration of one culture by another. In the face of the stasis of monks at morning prayers in a Tibetan monastery or of a sea of coloured prayer flags fluttering in the wind, the onwards rush of the train seems like an act of sublime aggression. The historical and political background to this piece is the annexation of Tibet and its progressive colonisation by China. Further to that, we see here two fundamentally different attitudes to time: pre-modern and spiritual as opposed to technology-led and utilitarian. In this divergent configuration of historical, political, cultural, moral and philosophical issues, it would be hard to avoid at least a latent declaration of allegiance.

However, despite highlighting these various differences *In The Between* endeavours to present the interpenetration of supposedly irreconcilable conditions and the simultaneity of the non-simultaneous as the reality that the outsider will come up against in this region. Although in this piece equally real, symbolically charged images are found for both sides of the cultural conflict (the relentless train and the monk's incessant prayers), although meaningful elements of reality thus directly come into focus and together produce an antithetical composition, and although the film footage is visually extremely memorable – the specific disjuncture of places and times nevertheless introduces a need for a particular form of scrupulousness into any attempt at an assessment of this complex subject matter. The distance between the film and its subject is crucial to its success.

Terminus

For a decade Almond has been working on a group of works about a unique, monstrous kind of distance. Originally inspired by his preoccupation with prison life (as in *HMP Pentonville* [p.142]) to address the initially theoretical question as to the ultimate place of exclusion from the world, Almond found himself travelling repeatedly to the Polish town of Oświęcim. The works which ensued from these trips and which exist in a variety of media do not *de facto* deal with the real place associated with that town, namely the concentration camp known as Auschwitz. With a very few exceptions, the artist as it were imposes on himself a ban on any explicit images which are demanded of him by his own personal, intellectual and ethical sensitivities. As a tourist from a later generation, which is all he can be, he returns instead with objects and moments from an age after that period. It is as though he were searching for the dying, blurred echo that may still linger on in this place and in ourselves. More than the source of this echo, he is measuring out its present length and fragility. In purely spatial terms, these works take the viewer very close to the former camp, literally right to the fence around it. But with regard to time, they are locked in an impossible no-man's-land of no-longer and yet-still.

The earliest of these works, which also determines the main motif of most of the others, is a double-projection of two black-and-white films. Both show a bus stop seen from the other side of the street. The vicinity is unremarkable, cars pass by, people come and wait. All the movements are slowed down. The sky is overcast, it is late winter, heavy snowflakes begin to fall. Nothing else happens, the minutes stretch out – until everything starts all over again. The pictures would appear to have been shot in passing; the 8-mm format gives the scene a certain patina and it is obvious that the cameraman has been trying to keep a hand-held camera still. Sparing music, a litany of sorts, accompanies the otherwise silent images of *Oświęcim, March 1997* [p.140]. It is only the name of this Polish town that hints at what lies nearby. And knowing that this is a bus stop near the entrance to the present-day museum Auschwitz I, formerly the 'main camp', adds little useful information. Even the place name by the roadside (*Journey,* 1999) only vaguely invokes the past of this place that has become synonymous with the Holocaust. The concentration camp was a 'terminus' in the truest and most terrible sense; even one of the perpetrators called it the '*anus mundi*'.[2] In the ultimate dispatch of victims it was a place with an entrance but no exit. The people in the transports were deposited here for ever and for a single purpose. But when Almond films near this invisible place, he focuses on a bus stop on the open road, a place of transit with people passing through in both directions. The passengers that arrive or leave from here are as much visitors to the former camp as people going about their daily business in their town. But in the film they are indistinguishable; no one reveals their destination, they are all just waiting.

The next step for Almond was to give physical form to this moment: he removed and transported two of the shelters to an exhibition space in Berlin (*Bus Stop* [p.150], 1999). In the exhibition situation, they look out of place; now there is no traffic passing by any more. Everyday constructions have been turned into symbolic objects exposed to a new kind of scrutiny. There is no simple, logical route from their appearance in the exhibition space back into the daily life of Oświęcim and from there across the boundaries of time to that place of annihilation. The materiality of the objects and the visible traces of the 'lives' of previous users seem to suggest a continuity, as though the earlier events of that area had permeated the physics of the place and its structures by osmosis. We would like to read these objects as documents, as witnesses, and ultimately as monuments. We would like to counter that other connection to the past, to language and to its fragile relationship to the truth with something tangible. *Bus Stop* prevents that, precisely because the

2   The Holocaust survivor Wieslaw Kielar later used this phrase as the title of an account of the concentration camp at Auschwitz.

work takes us some way towards the imagined destination, into a town named Oświęcim and into the recent past. If – thanks to these uprooted bus stops – our senses and thoughts have at least progressed this far, they nevertheless come to a halt at the impenetrable barrier behind these otherwise readily comprehensible items. The work stages a form of seduction that ends in disillusion.

The most recent work in this series brings together fourteen versions of the original bus shelters (*Terminus* [p.174], 2007). They are all based on the same model as in *Bus Stop,* with only minor variations in certain details here and there. What does distinguish them from each other is their state of preservation. Time has variously left its mark on them: metal is bent, slats from the plastic seats have been broken, colours have faded, timetables have been scratched to the point of illegibility, Plexiglas panes are missing, graffiti and dirt of all kinds. Only the posts supporting the constructions are set into new, stable housings. That not only guarantees the stability of these small structures, it also precisely marks the spot where they were cut out of their original situation. In the ground in Oświęcim you can still see the sawn-off, square posts of the old shelters – like little wounds, witnesses to the earlier act of displacement. And the new housings for the supports in the exhibition point quietly to the fact that an arbitrary act of relocation has been carried out here. The technical adaptations to the new surroundings remain in view; the Here and Now is not to be confused with the There and Then. The fourteen bus shelters are all displayed facing each other; the best preserved are at the front, the less well preserved are further back. It is as though one were gazing into a decomposition of sorts. As in a classical landscape painting, distant objects have a less marked material presence, although here this is not achieved by optical suggestion, for there is a real disintegration of material and there are ever greater degrees of destruction. In this case the distance to the viewer, it seems fair to say, also reflects the distance in time.

The crowded group of bus shelters, all facing each other, signals a general level of traffic, or to be more precise, the notion of waiting in the midst of circulating traffic although there is no certainty as to its Whence and Whither. The multitude of bus stops multiplies individual stasis as a factor in the great movement through space and time. The halting of the individual at a particular place – their own place – determines their view of the general movement and measures out their expectations of or disappointment in it. A strange silence hangs over *Terminus,* as though an indefinite pause had set in. However, it is not the silence of complete absence, but a moment of in-wardness in which the senses remain alert to any possible continuation of what had gone before. The direction of the movement to be resumed is open as yet. But somewhere in this field of waiting there is an unsettling sign that seems to issue a challenge. On the edge of the roof of one of the shelters is the word MUZEUM, in upper case, with an arrow clearly pointing the way. This is the only instance of a sign of this kind. This bus shelter stood right by the entrance to the former concentration camp and present-day museum. In situ this sign was useful for strangers visiting the area, in the installation it points to another, different level of perception and reflection. What we see with our own eyes of the reality of Oświęcim/Auschwitz (the bus shelters), is only a temporary stop on a hypothetical journey to the 'real' place (the camp). But the word 'MUZEUM' creates another additional distance; it makes it clear that we will not find the actual thing itself, only a prepared version of it, spe-cially presented and interpreted for us. Metaphorically speaking: anyone who has made it to this place that we think we know the meaning of, has still not actually arrived. In this 'waiting room' the direction of the next step is shown, even as doubt is cast on the chances of us satisfying our desire for authentici-ty. 'MUZEUM' is itself only a substitute for the real thing, a 'closed container of history'.[3]

'Terminus' refers to the final destination, the last stop on a public transport route. But 'terminus' is also a frontier, the most distant reachable point. One only enters the territory beyond it under special conditions, in ex-ceptional cases; in the original sense it is a forbidden terrain that none may enter. 'Terminus', in the sense of 'term', also refers to a concept, a clear definition, the distinct division between one notion and another and hence, by implication, it also refers to the mental effort needed to grasp and order the phenomena one has experienced or sensed. Almond did not initially use this word for his work, choosing titles that referred to actual situations and objects (*Oświęcim, March 1997* [p.140]; *Journey; Bus Stop* [p.150]; *Shelter.* It first appeared some years later when he presented a second version of the bus stop (*Terminus* [p.174], 2005). He clearly felt a need, even at this level, to establish a distance between what we see before us and what is meant by the piece. Since then, and especially in the recent, large-scale installation,

3   Griselda Pollock, 'Holocaust Tourism: Being There, Looking Back and the Ethics of Spatial Memory', in David Crouch and Nina Lübbren (eds), *Visual Culture and Tourism,* Oxford and New York, 2003, pp.175–89.

the word 'Terminus' functions like a capsule or a black box that belongs to the work, with contents that are known, suspected or even feared, yet always out of reach.

With the individual works from this group Almond puts paid to the notion of a journey that has reached its destination. His stations are out in the open, they are only temporary halts, the journey takes the traveller through them. The focus is on the continuity of the world of life-since-then, although the event itself (the Holocaust) has never disappeared from it. None of the images or objects can be definitively located on a particular time level; they all deal with different modes of time – and place. What we are shown is subtly arranged so that the viewer remains ever aware of his or her own time – and place; there is no substitute experience to be had. The places that these works take us to remain closed to us. They leave us high and dry as unsuccessful but newly thoughtful voyeurs. The paradox of these works, the tension they create and sustain, has its roots in a radical, well-founded scepticism with regard to the possibility of ever really getting close to the unimaginable, combined with a scrupulous determination never to cease trying to understand. Neither seeing nor knowing will rescue us from this conflict. The forming of this dichotomy is the only thing that remains to us when there is no through-route to memory or empathy nor even to oblivion.

This essay is printed here in an abbreviated version of the German original, translated by Fiona Elliott, and commissioned for *Terminus* by Darren Almond, edited by Kathleen Madden, and published by Holzwarth Publications, 2007.

KN 120

1995

KN 120 was a ceiling fan illegally installed under the Westway, an elevated motorway in West London. The KN of the title refers to the KN-36 model number of a domestic fan with a diameter of 36 inches (91.5 cm). Almond replicated that fan on a larger scale with a diameter of 120 inches (305 cm) – a ten-foot span across the blades. A switch in Almond's studio, situated directly opposite the site of the installation, operated the kinetic sculpture, which Almond had made as a way of measuring cycles of movement as the fan blades circulated. *KN 120* is documented as a single-channel video.

Aluminium fan, motor, UV light, cable
Approximate diameter 305 cm (10 ft)

Schwebebahn

1995

An interest in movement as realized in *KN 120* led Almond to filmmaking. His preoccupation with trains and the indirect daily culture associated with them (timetables, stations, passenger traffic, etc.) emerges with *Schwebebahn,* the earliest film from Almond's trilogy of train films that also includes *Geisterbahn* and *In The Between. Schwebebahn,* shot on three rolls of 8-mm film, documents the world's first monorail train, the Sky Train. It was built in 1901 in Wuppertal, Germany, and is suspended over 13 kilometres (*c.* 9 miles) of the city. The film has two distinct sequences: the first shot in black-and-white, the second shot in colour. Both are inverted and played backwards so the train appears to be upside-down and the movement is in reverse.

Single-channel, 8-mm film transferred to video
12 minutes
Excerpt Black Secret Technology by A Guy Called Gerald

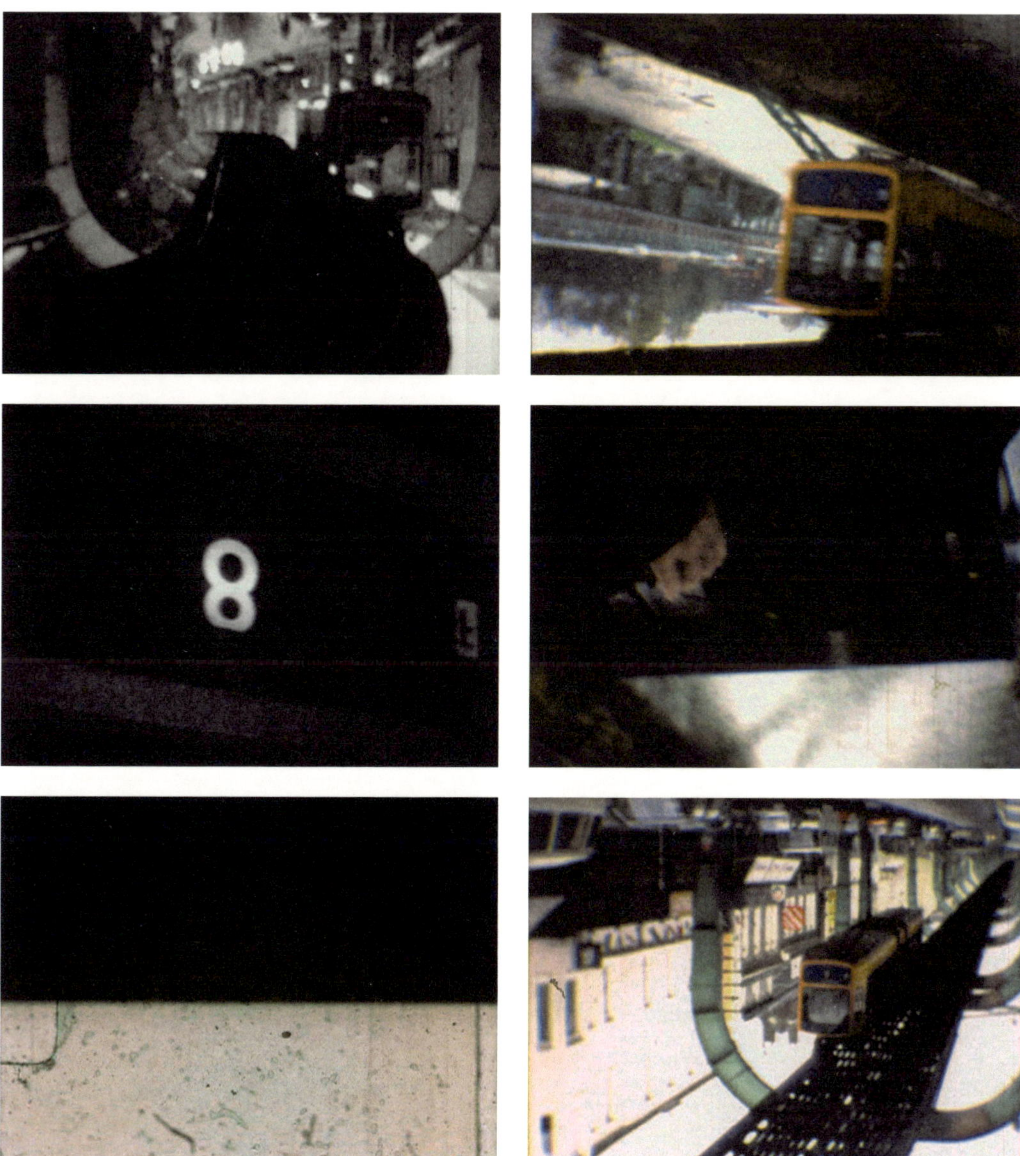

A Real Time Piece

1996

Almond's first exhibited work, *A Real Time Piece,* was transmitted from the artist's empty studio to an exhibition venue on the other side of London. It only showed a drawing board with a mechanical flip-clock nearby, with the changing digits of the clock amplified, and variations in the natural light coming through the window. Intrigued to see how compelling an almost still image could be, Almond orchestrated this intensified experience of time by which banality was transformed into a theatrical event. The BBC provided technical assistance to broadcast the signal from his West London studio to TV Central, thence underground to Crystal Palace and onward to the gallery. Initially, the duration of the work was the duration of the exhibition called *Something Else* installed in Exmouth Market. However, due to the nature of a live broadcast, the work is ostensibly endless. Emblems of waiting, temporality and transportation to another place emerge in *A Real Time Piece* to signal Almond's exploration of the physical and emotional effect of time on the individual. *A Real Time Piece* is documented as a single-channel video.

Originally a single-channel, live, satellite broadcast; archived as a single-channel video
A microphone placed within a flip-clock produces a loud sound effect, with an ambient hum heard from the sound of the studio building and the Westway in the distance. Projected life-size

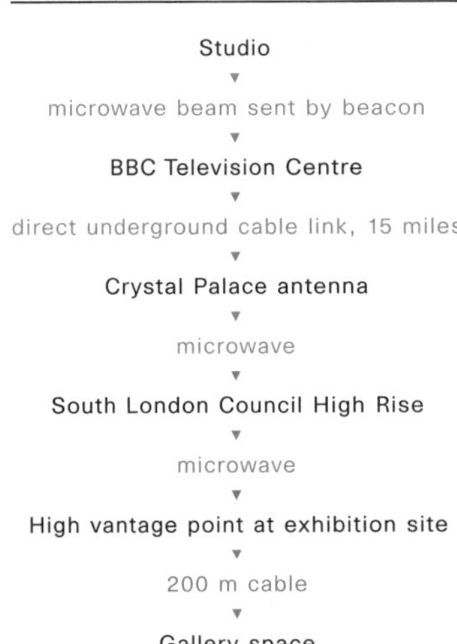

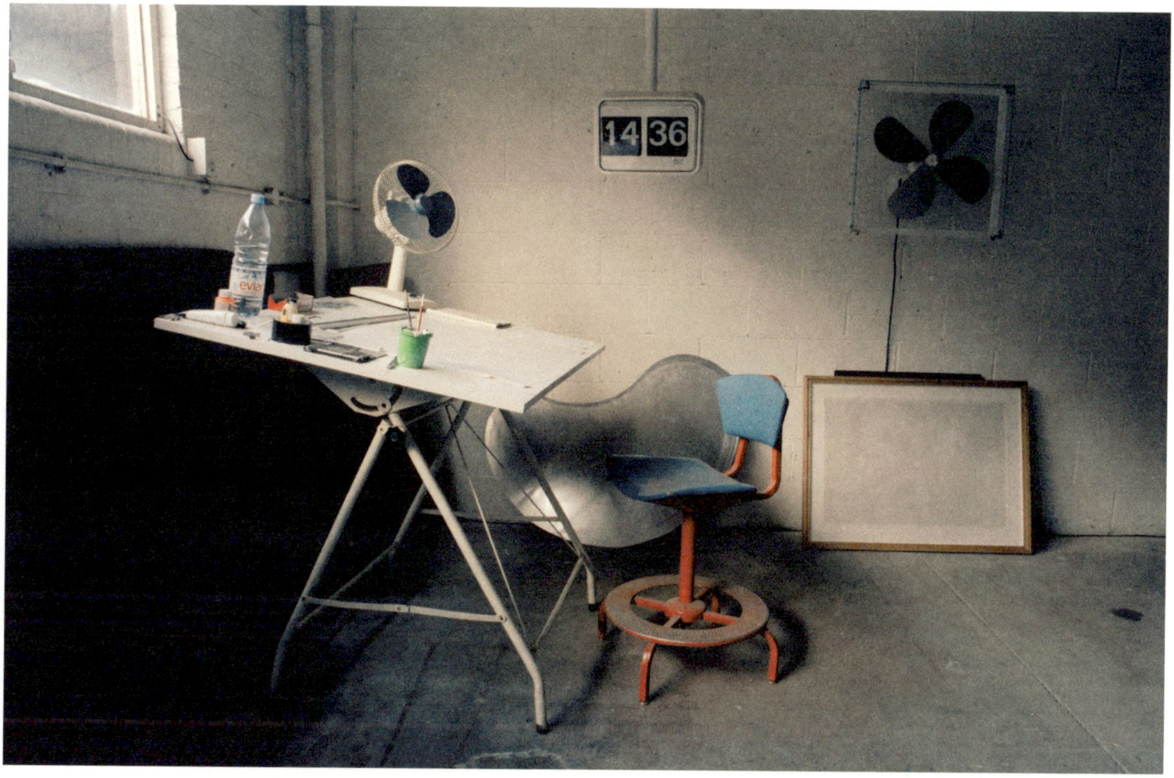

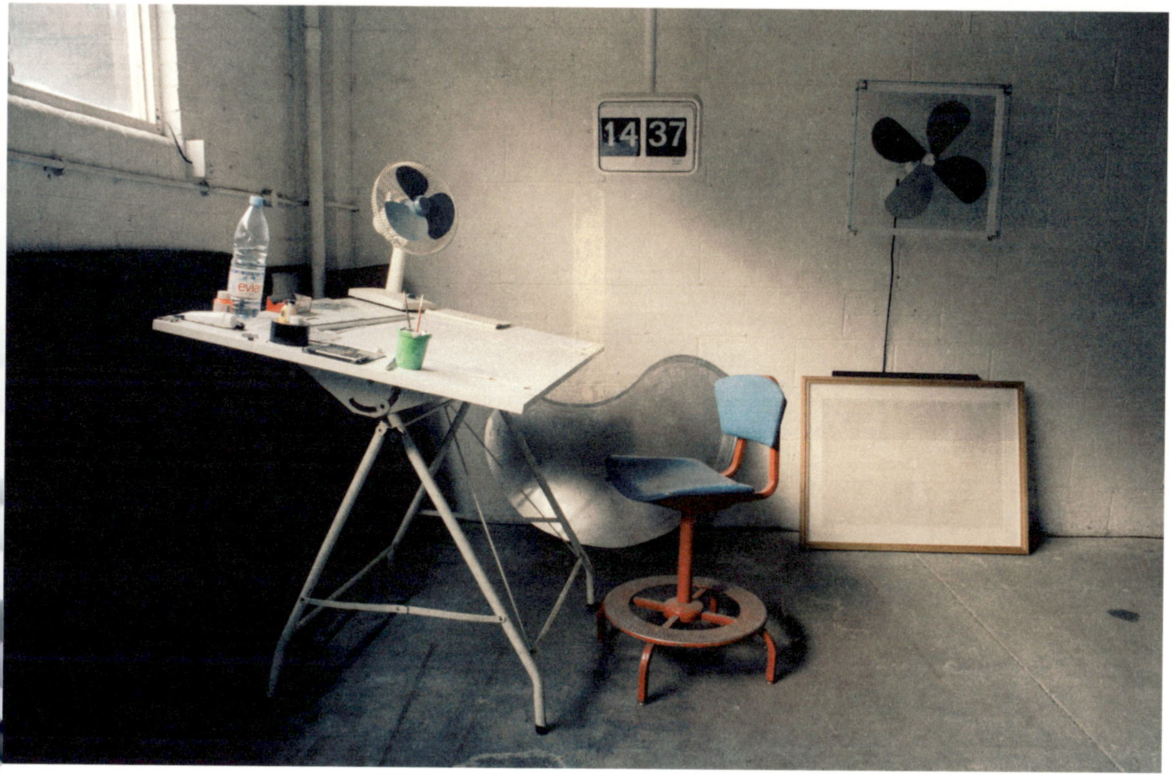

Fan

1997

Shown at Almond's first solo show at White Cube, London, in 1997, *Fan* was an oversized white ceiling fan with three extendable and retractable blades that slowly traced the space of the installation, demonstrating notions of circulation, flow, and extension, all of which have been considered metaphors for Almond's artistic activity.

Wood, plastic, microprocessors, paint, electro-mechanics
Approximate diameter 4.5 m (15 ft)

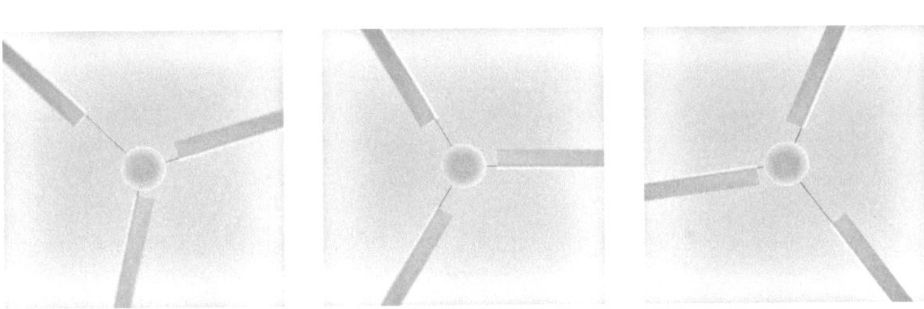

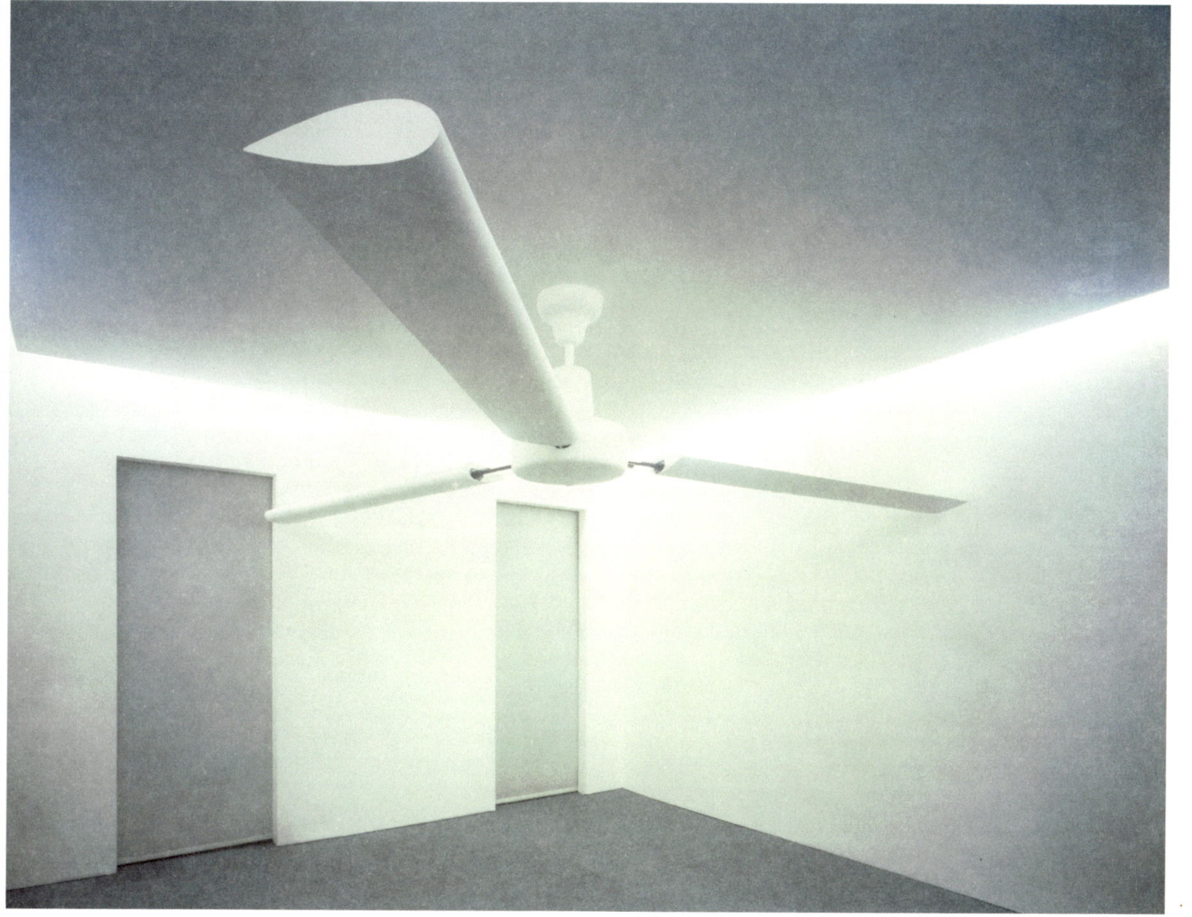

Trainplates

Ongoing series begun 1997

Coupled

2007

Almond initiated the *Trainplate* series in 1997 with *Intercity 125,* a sign made by British Rail, which read: 'Darren James Almond'. Concerned with transport, this series is emblematic of Almond's constant repositioning of his motifs of travel and exploration. Growing up in Wigan in the north of England, Almond became a keen train-spotter. This solitary and sedentary activity, with its prioritizing of periods of patient waiting, its concomitant and freely bestowed sense of being in the moment, and its precise attention to detail, is now deeply imbued in Almond's work. In these *Trainplates* Almond uses specific language, with a blunt and expository aesthetic, which is reinforced by particular fonts. The fonts reference the British Rail classification system used to distinguish different types of engine by a particular font. *Coupled,* which reads 'Drawn Together' has been composed using a Western Ranger font. Coupling is the technical term used to describe a mechanism for connecting railway cars. This train nameplate celebrates the union of two components.

Cast aluminium, paint
20 x 189 cm (8 x 74 ½ in)

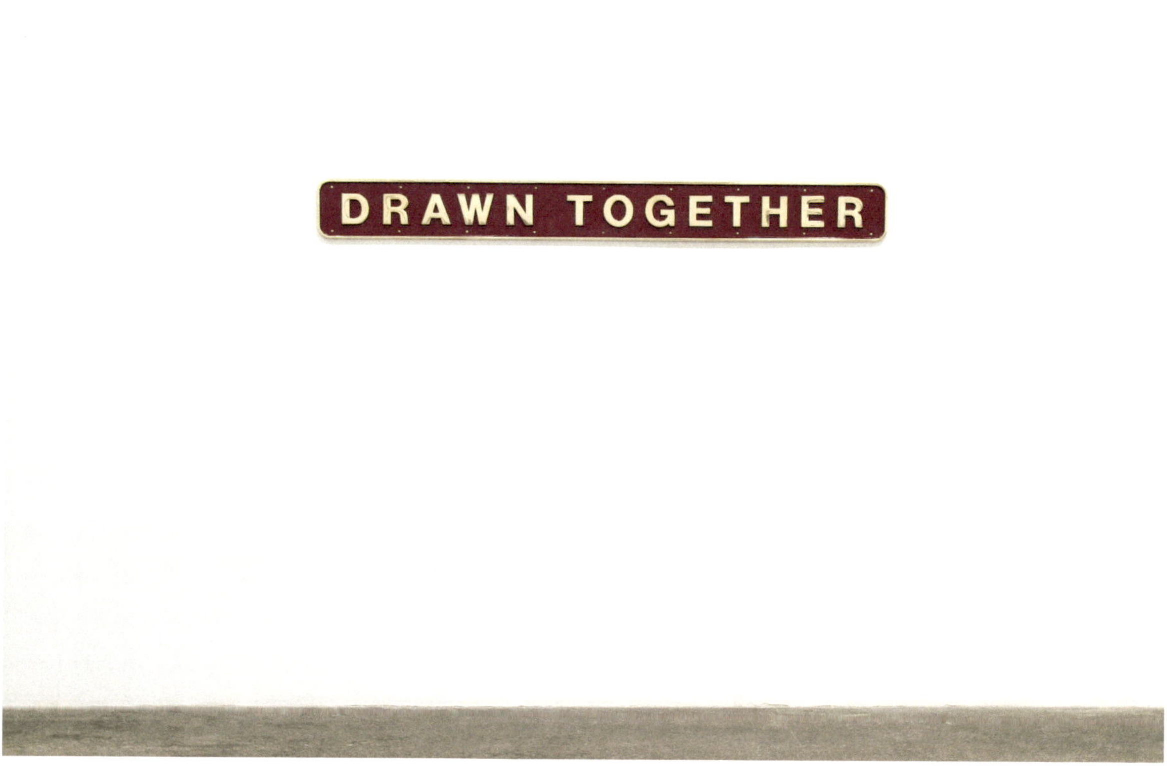

DRAWN TOGETHER

Oświęcim, March 1997

1997

Oświęcim, March 1997 was first shown in 1997, at the Institute of Contemporary Arts (ICA), London, together with *HMP Pentonville* and relates to Almond's preoccupation with incarceration and the time one serves when imprisoned. Recollection and remembrance permeate much of Almond's work, extending his exploration of highly charged subjects within the broader context of social and political history. *Oświęcim, March 1997* is a film of two commonplace bus stops where people stand and wait, come and go, but no bus ever arrives. The loop is a formal element that frustrates both the flow of time and the arrival of a bus, while emphasizing interminable waiting. Significantly, there is an audible human inhalation in *Trisagion,* one of the oldest Christian prayers and the standard hymn of the Divine Liturgy. The frames per minute speed has been slowed to 81%, referencing newsreel footage from the immediate post-war period. This work marks the inception of a ten-year engagement with the *Terminus* project and the bus shelters from Oświęcim, the Polish town formerly known under German occupation as Auschwitz. The place and time as noted in the title are intentionally specific.

2-channel, 8-mm, b/w, parallel films transferred to video
8-minute loop
Avro Pärt's Litany: *Trisagion*
Dimensions variable. Ideally 1.2 x 1.8 m (4 x 6 ft) each, shown in low light with walls and ceiling painted charcoal grey, each image projected on to a separate wall below eye level.

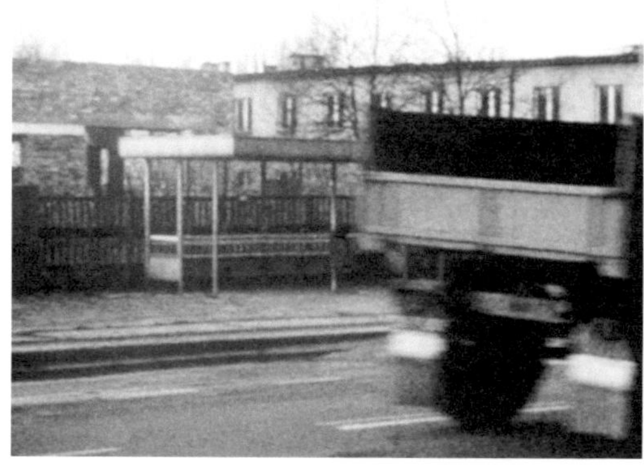
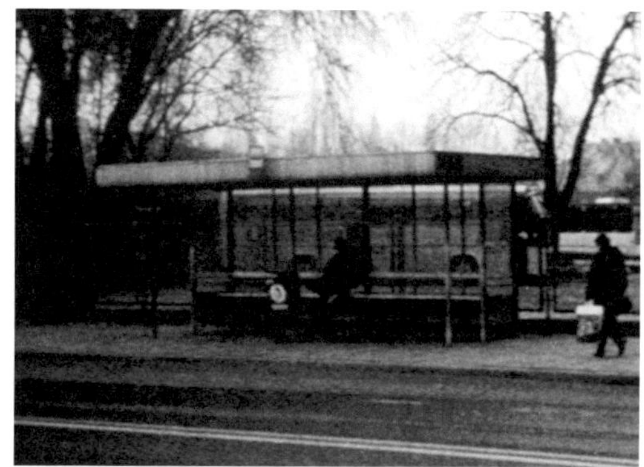
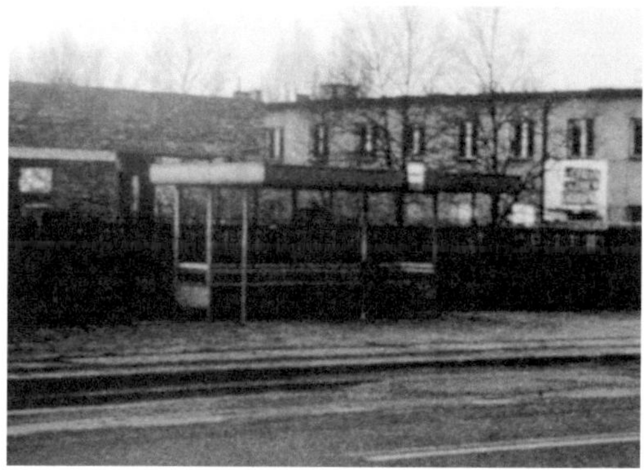
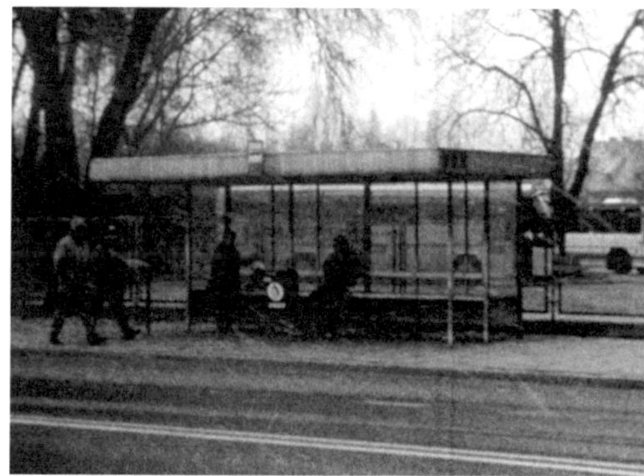
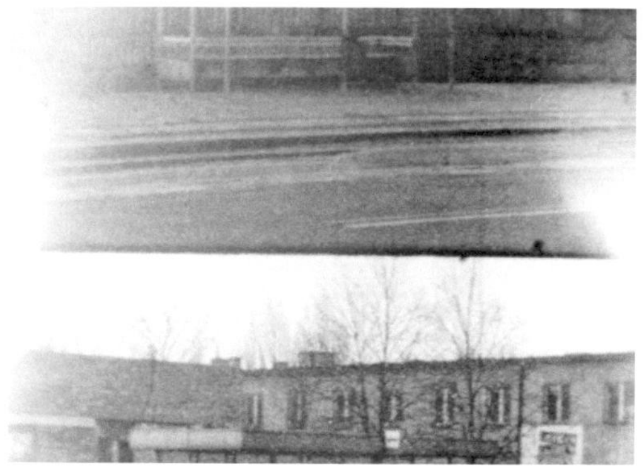
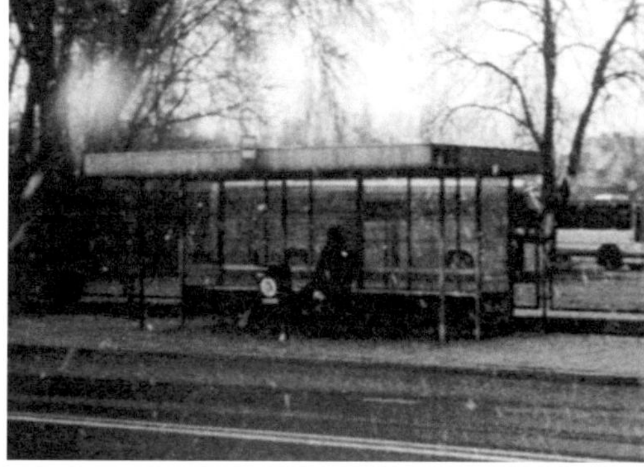

HMP Pentonville

1997

First shown in tandem with *Oświęcim, March 1997* at the ICA, London. The Governor
of the prison granted Almond permission to broadcast live from a cell, but after approximately 3.5 hours the transmission was terminated when a large number of new
inmates arrived and the Governor had to make use of the cell. The space of filming
in *HMP Pentonville* functions like a panopticon as described by Michel Foucault in
Discipline and Punish. The Victorian prison architecture has a very particular acoustic,
as the many accumulated layers of gloss paint add further reverberations to the
quality of sound that vibrates throughout the prison. On his way home one day, while
working on this piece, Almond sat at a bus stop outside the prison and began to
think about travelling to Auschwitz, thus anticipating his decade-long engagement with
Terminus. HMP Pentonville was reproduced as *Live Sentence* in 2004 at the Lentos
Museum of Modern Art, Linz, where Almond broadcast between the museum and a
local prison. Expanded to eight different points of view, this multi-channel work repeated a live broadcast from an empty cell, accentuated by recorded footage exploring the prison.

Originally a single-channel live satellite broadcast between Pentonville Prison and
the ICA, London, 7 May 1997; archived as a single-channel video
Broadcast intended for extent of exhibition; terminated after approximately 3.5 hours
of broadcasting; recorded documentation shown as 1-hour loop
Microphone transmission of hallway activity outside cell
Dimensions variable. Ideally larger than life-size

Cell
▼
BBC outside broadcast unit
(Pentonville)
▼
Satellite
▼
BBC outside broadcast unit (The Mall)
▼
ICA

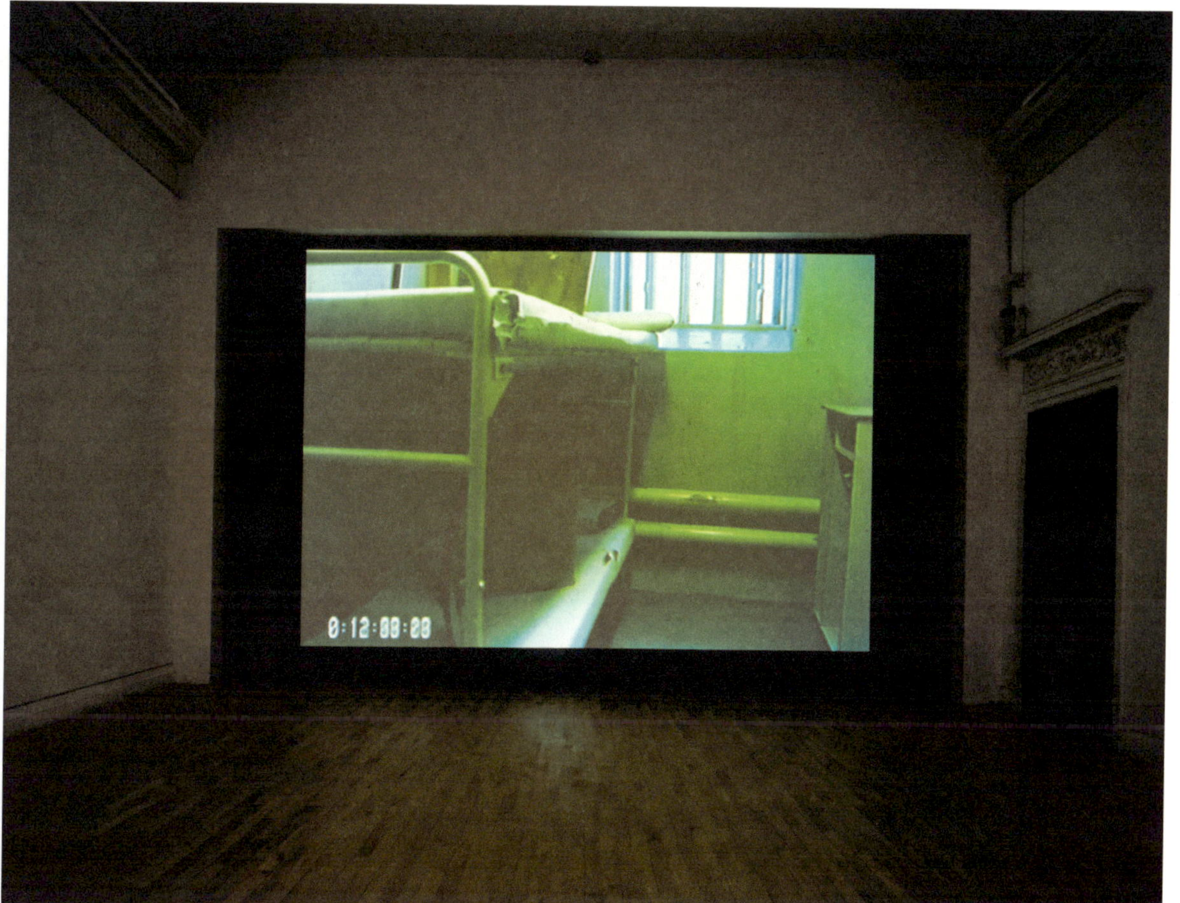

A Bigger Clock

1997

Almond was represented in the 1997 *Sensation* exhibition at the Royal Academy of Arts, London, by *A Bigger Clock,* a work inspired by the digital clocks at British railway stations. From the start, the ticking clock has been at the heart of Almond's art. *A Real Time Piece* provided a live satellite link from his studio, empty but for an industrial flip-clock on the wall amplifying the passing of each minute. *A Bigger Clock* is larger than the clocks commonly found in British railway stations and bears the artist's name like a signature. As the numbers rotate on the display, the clock makes a loud, amplified, and surprisingly piercing sound as it marks the passing of each minute. Ultimately, this kinetic object records changes in real time and space in relation to the physical presence of the viewer. *A Bigger Clock* puts a mirror up to technological hubris, and reflects on our poor attempt to domesticate, if not industrialize, one of the fundamental principals governing the universe: time.

Steel, Perspex, aluminium, paint, motor, electro-mechanics
154 x 206 x 98 cm (60½ x 81 x 38½ in)

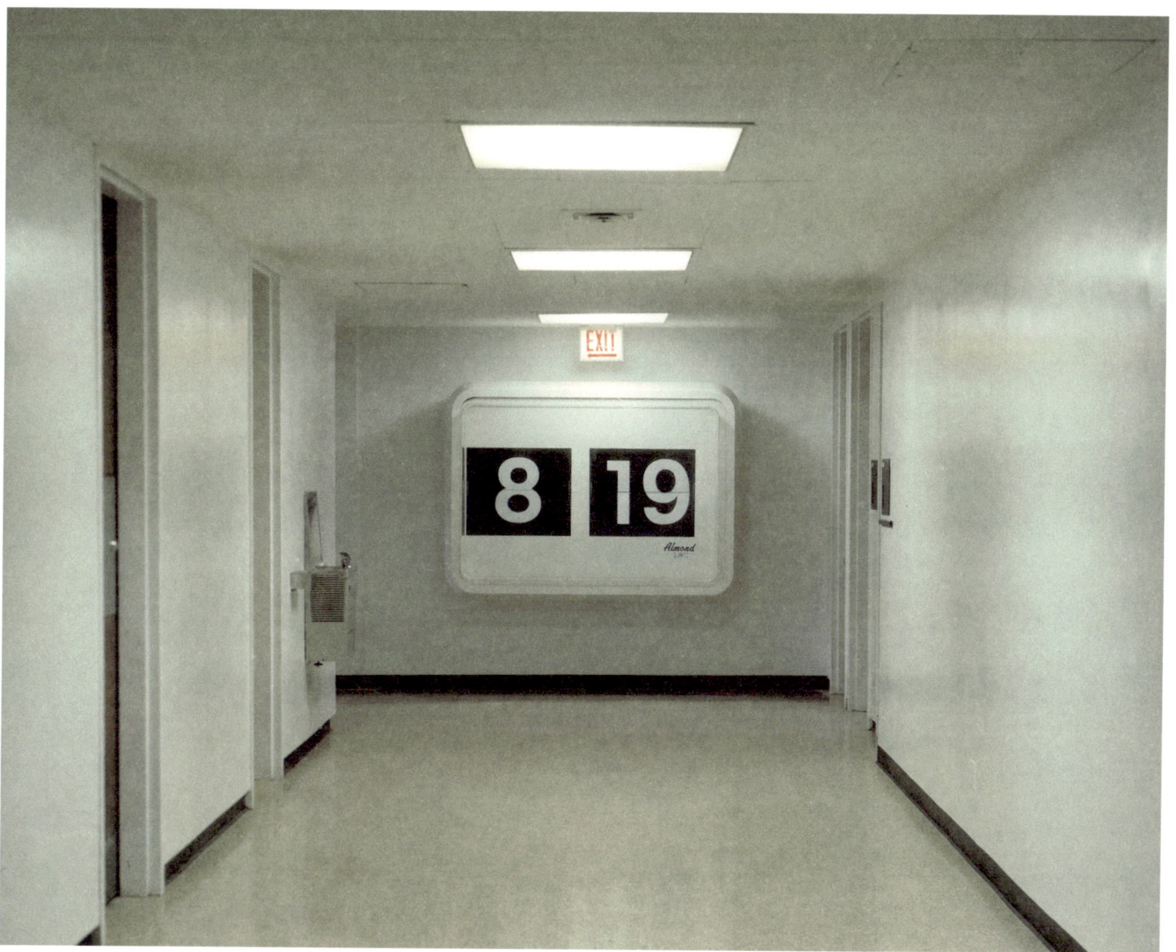
EXIT
8 19
Almond

Bad Timing

1998

Almond's continuing interest in keeping time is represented by foul exasperation in *Bad Timing* as, with the passing of each minute, the clock expresses an expletive. Almond was born in 1971, around the time of the first mass-produced digital clocks. The development of digital timekeeping was perhaps another instance of further ordering the routine day of industrial work. Almond has consistently formulated his experience in the form of clocks, some of them, like *A Bigger Clock* and *Meantime,* are larger than life. These clocks are artistic manifestations of the all-too-human attempt to control the analogue passing of time by means of a numerical (digital) system. With *Bad Timing* a sense of annoyance repeatedly erupts in the voice of the artist who, at the passing of each minute, furiously shouts out the expletive: 'Shit!'

Plexiglas, infrared sensor, electronic parts, sound recording
32 x 41 x 20 cm (12½ x 16 x 8 in)

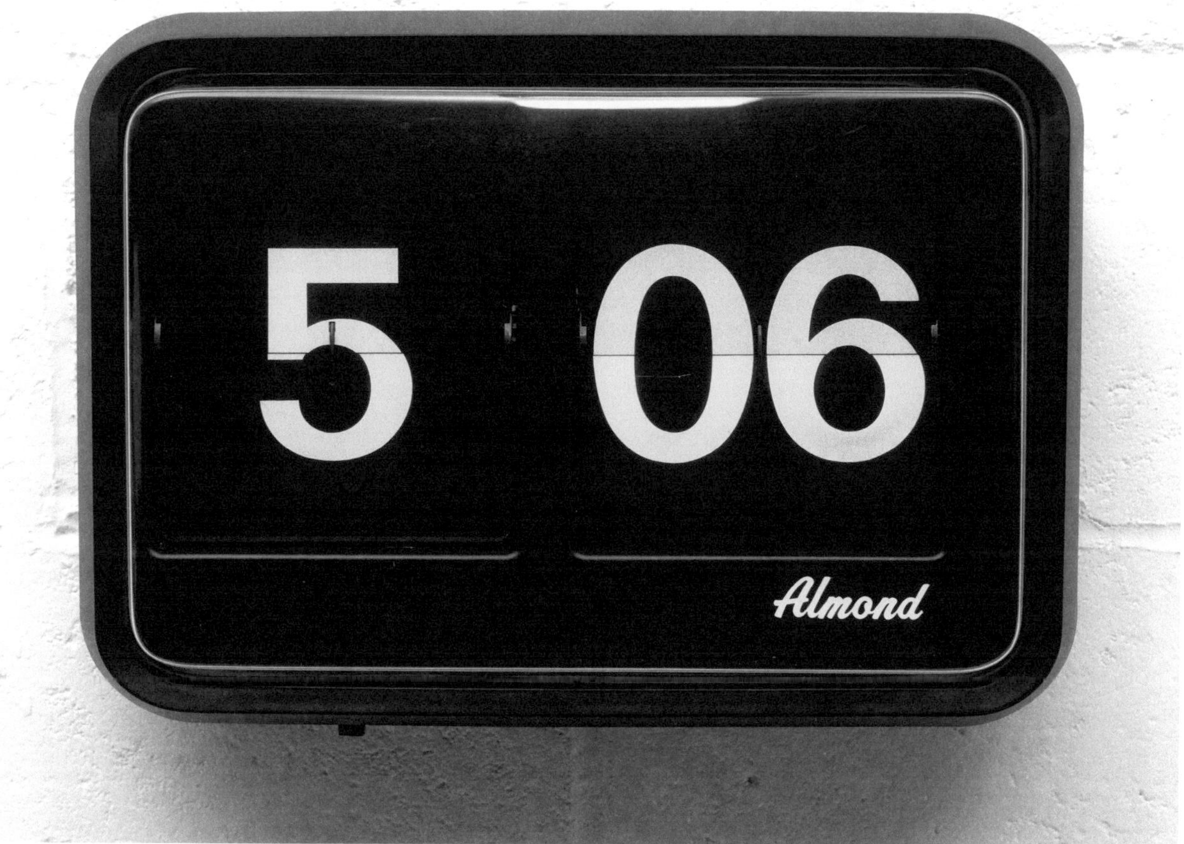
5 06
Almond

Geisterbahn

1999

Geisterbahn was shot at the Prater amusement park in Vienna, Austria, on a reproduction of the world's first ghost train, the original of which burned down during an air-raid in World War II. The camera was placed in the eye socket of Almond's skull-faced carriage at the front of the train and shows the macabre ghosts, ghouls and other miscellaneous startle-effects that the skull would have seen on its mechanical ride. *Geisterbahn* seems to be a self-portrait of a machine by a machine. Almost a documentary, the film is a straightforward record of what is there, put together with an insinuatingly seductive soundtrack of techno-dub by Stefan Betke, AKA Pole the DJ and producer associated with the Glitch Genre, on his broken Waldorf 4-Pole filter. *Geisterbahn* is the second of Almond's train film trilogy and represents the underworld in contradistinction to *Schwebebahn,* which is a train in the sky, and *In The Between,* poised on the horizon.

Single-channel, 8-mm, b/w film transferred to video
9 minutes
Fremd, a track from Stefan Betke, AKA Pole

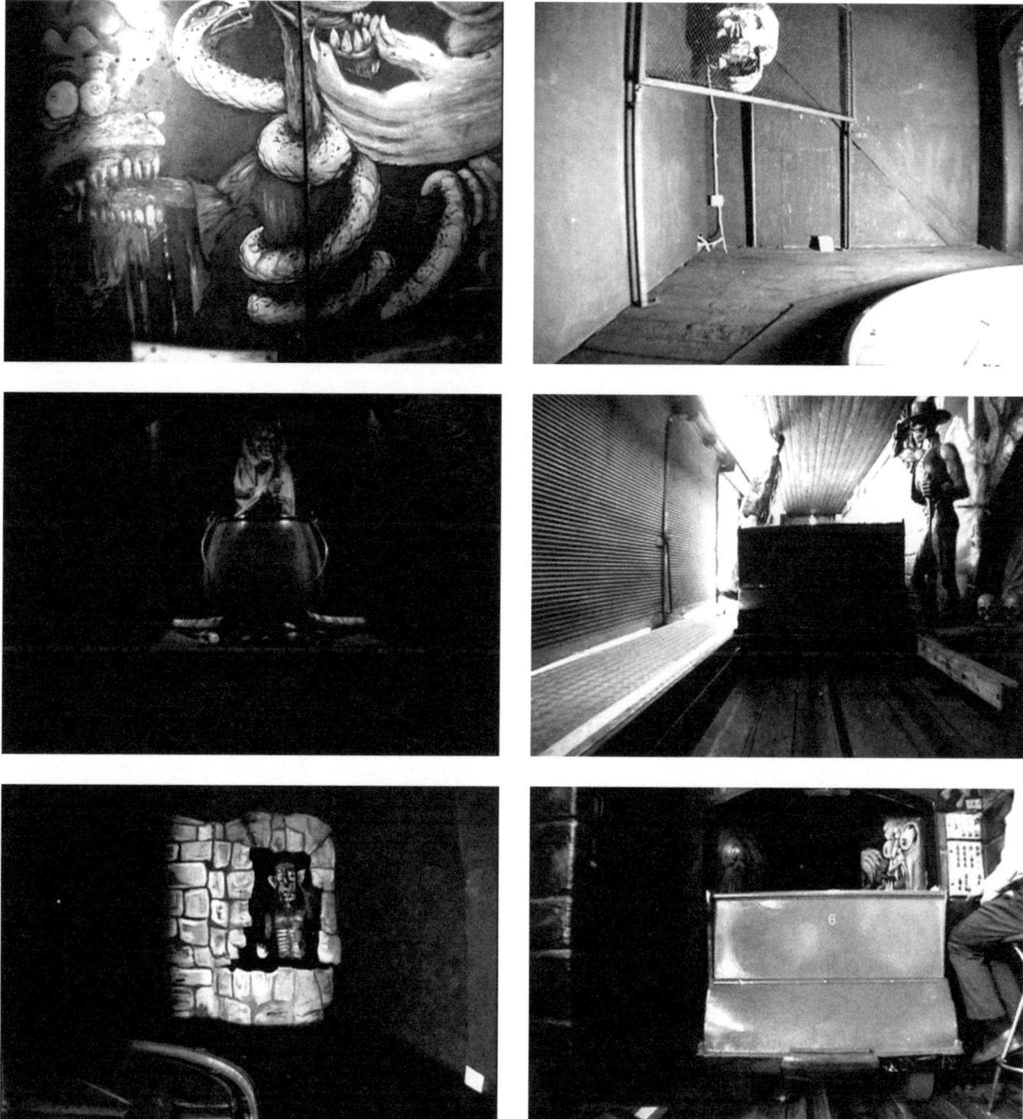

Bus Stop

1999

Following on from *Oświęcim, March 1997,* Almond produced *Bus Stop* by appropriating the bus shelters, as seen in the earlier film, from the Polish town formerly known as Auschwitz. The bus shelters were transported to the exhibition space and shown without any alteration. In these apparently ordinary pieces of street furniture, Almond finds a powerful symbol with which to bridge the gap between history and the present, and to connect to another place. Originally situated outside the Auschwitz-Birkenau Memorial and Museum, the shelters in *Bus Stop* were first shown in Berlin at Galerie Max Hetzler on Zimmerstrasse, a street that ran parallel to The Berlin Wall and bisected Checkpoint Charlie, gateway to the American sector and the West. In 2005, Almond presented another two shelters, which he entitled *Terminus,* but the project continued to develop and the final work in the series is also known as *Terminus,* 2007.

2 bus shelters, aluminium, glass, steel, wood, fibreglass, PVC
Each: 603 x 303 x 270 cm (237 ½ x 119 ¼ x 106 in)

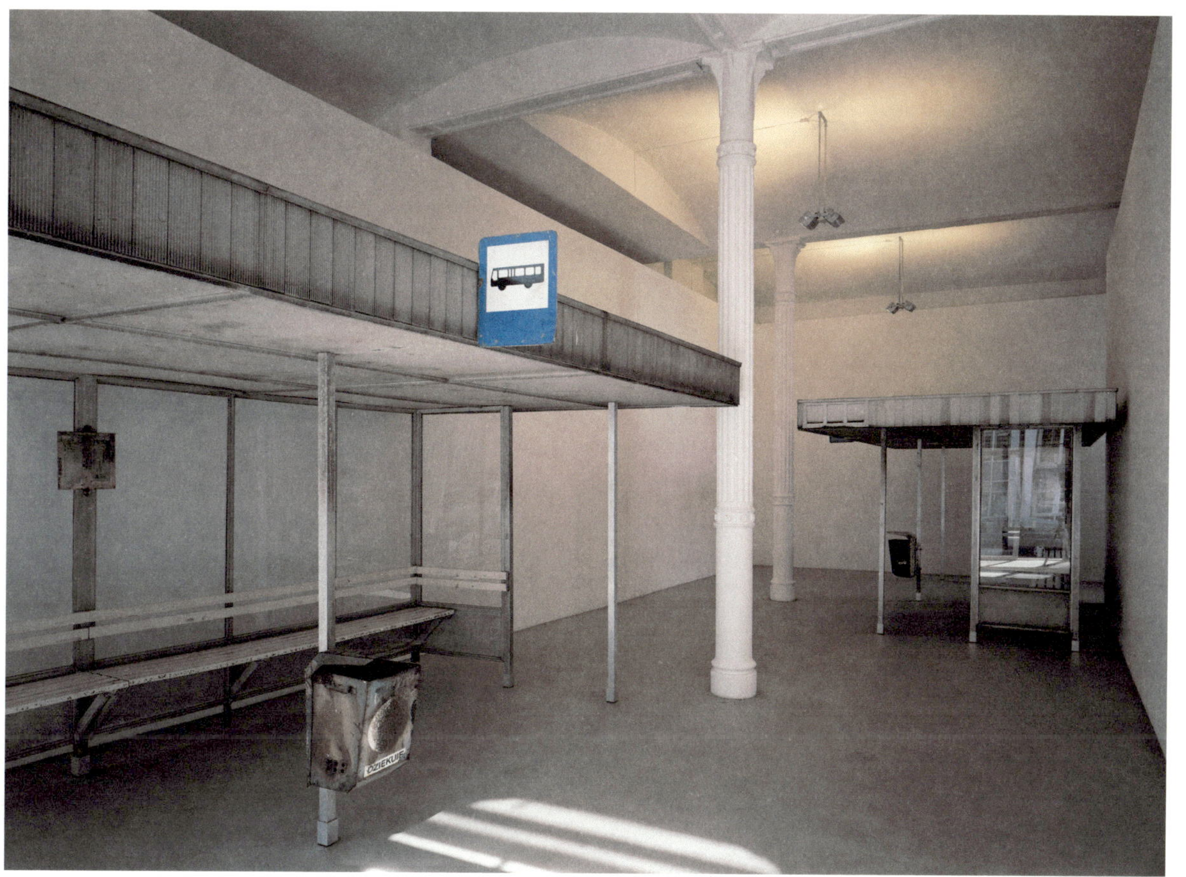

Fullmoons

Ongoing series begun 1999

Fullmoon@Rügen IV

2004

In 1999, Almond began a series of colour photographs, known as the *Fullmoons,* the first of which was his experimental *Fifteen Minute Moon.* He wanted to see what would result from photographing a moonlit landscape using an extended time exposure. He shot *Fifteen Minute Moon,* 2000, on a trip near Mont Sainte Victoire in Aix-en-Provence in the South of France, which was also the site of inspiration for much of Cézanne's painting. It remained in Almond's studio for a while and he continued to think about it. As he says, 'there is always a portion of the world in shadow', and for him the exercise of looking remains compelling. Almond continued the series by travelling to places that had inspired other artists, and literary figures, such as Turner (1775–1851) and Constable (1776–1837). To produce *Fullmoon@Rügen IV,* Almond followed in the footsteps of the Romantic landscape painter Caspar David Friedrich (1774–1840), who imbued his works with symbolism. Located in the Baltic Sea, Rügen is Germany's largest island. Friedrich often painted its famous chalk cliffs, and Almond has produced five photographic variations of the famous seascape. Almond has travelled the world photographing by the light of the full moon in America, Antarctica, Europe, Iceland, Japan, and in particular throughout the UK. The brilliance of moonlight and the colour-change in a landscape captured through extended time exposure continue to compel Almond to progress with his *Fifteen Minute Moon* experimentation.

C-print
121.2 x 121.2 cm (48 x 48 in)

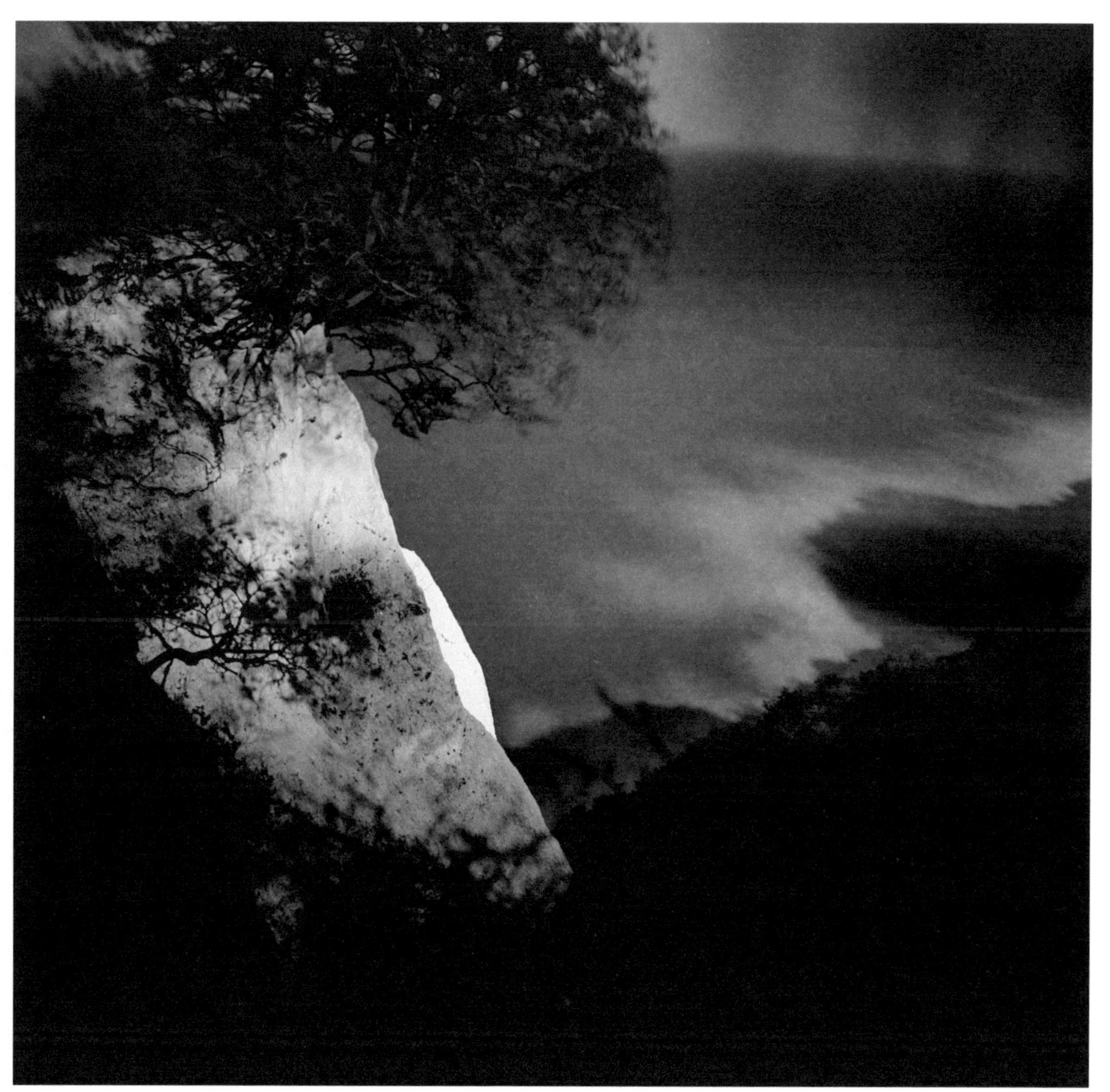

Traction

1999

First shown in 1999 at The Renaissance Society, University of Chicago, *Traction* is the only film by Almond to have a narrative dialogue. The main thread is Almond interviewing his father about the accidents and physical injuries the elder Almond had sustained, mostly as the result of industrial labour. The video installation is architecturally organized with the three screens arranged like an altarpiece. The black-and-white image of an excavator is shown as a central projection with two freestanding colour projections placed one on either side of it: one showing the interview with the artist's father, and the other his mother. She was filmed in the family home silently listening to her husband's interview, during which she periodically breaks into tears or laughter, then recomposes herself.

3-channel video installation
28 minutes
Dialogue
Dimensions variable. Ideally, heads are 180 cm high and the excavator 730 cm long

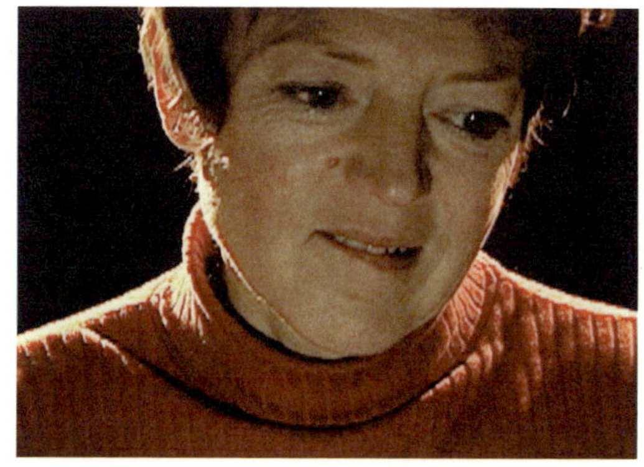
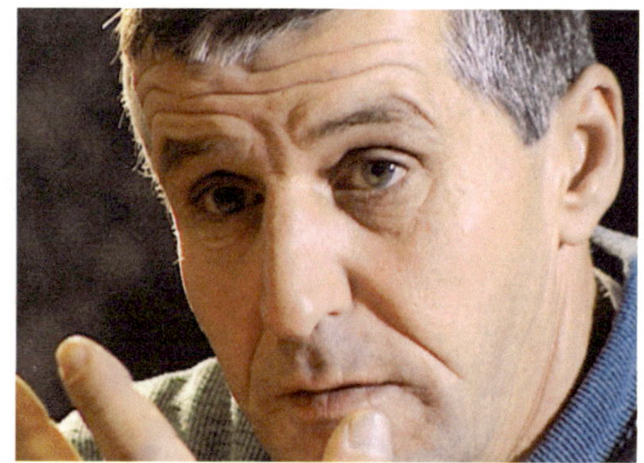

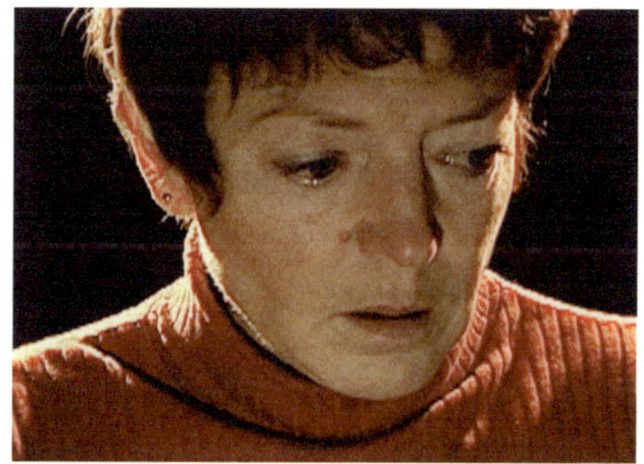
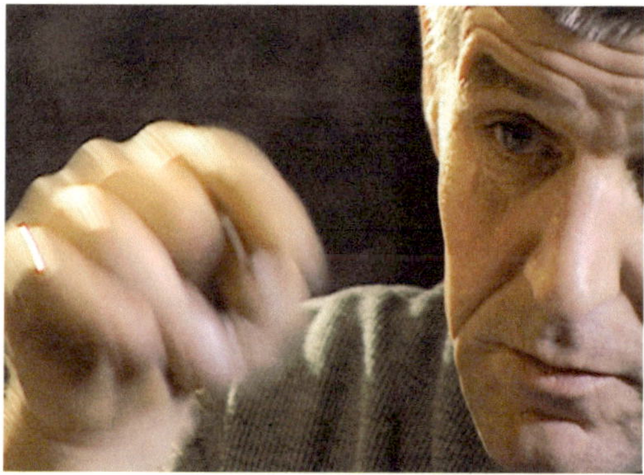

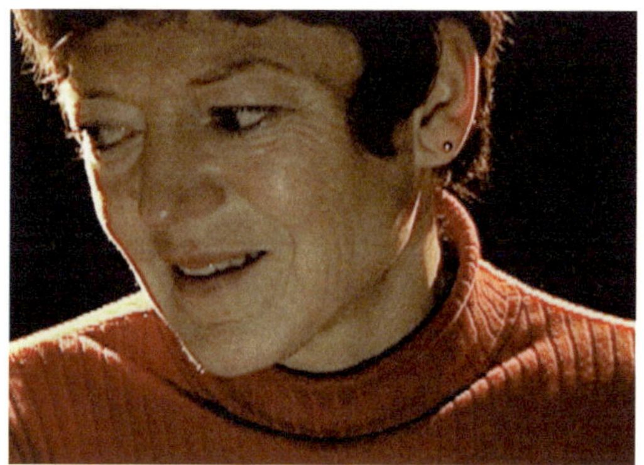
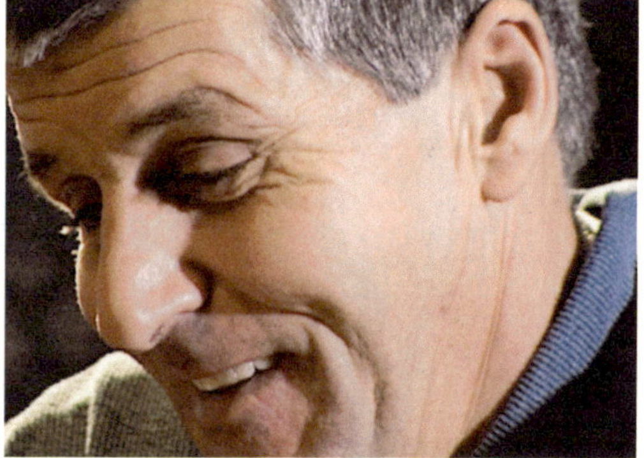

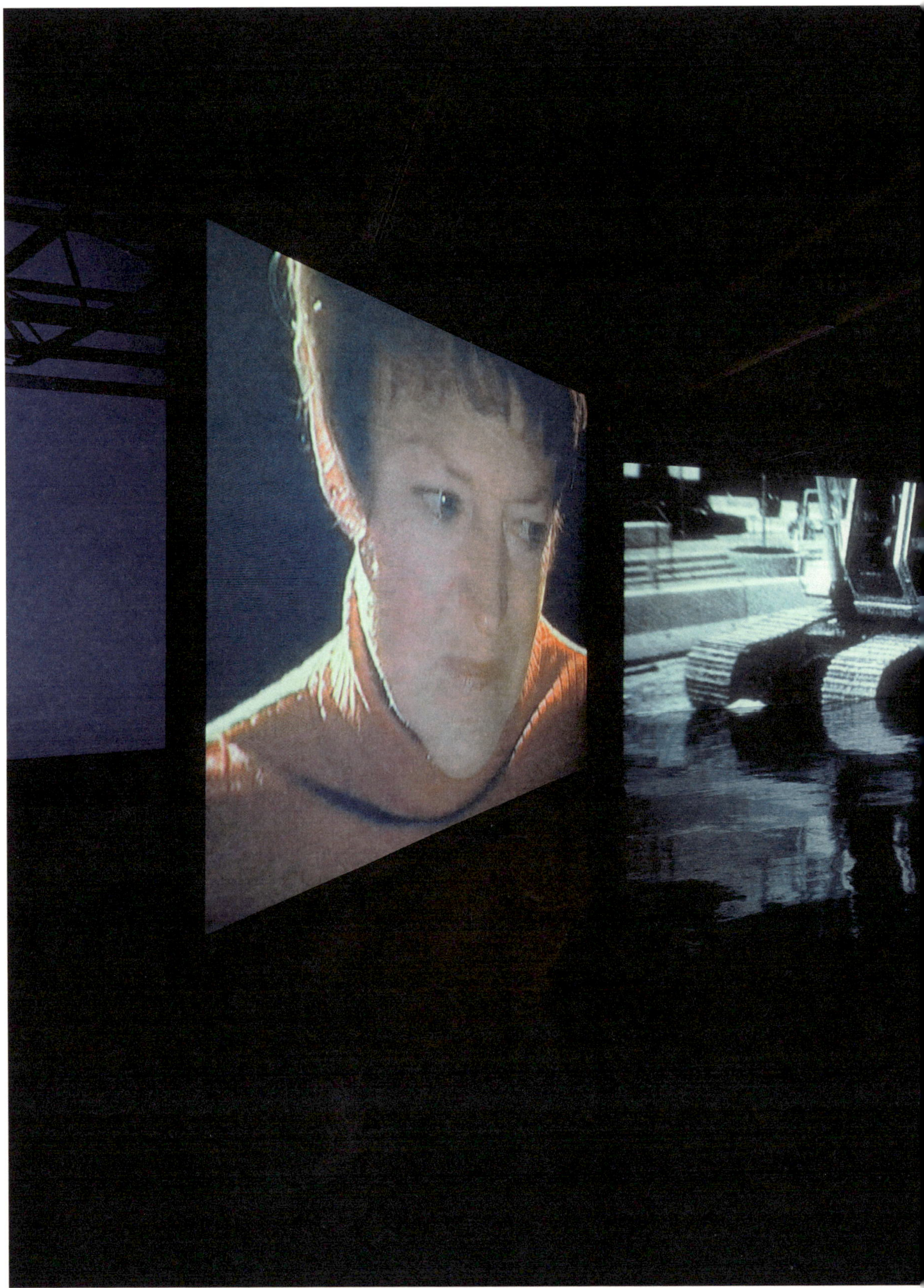

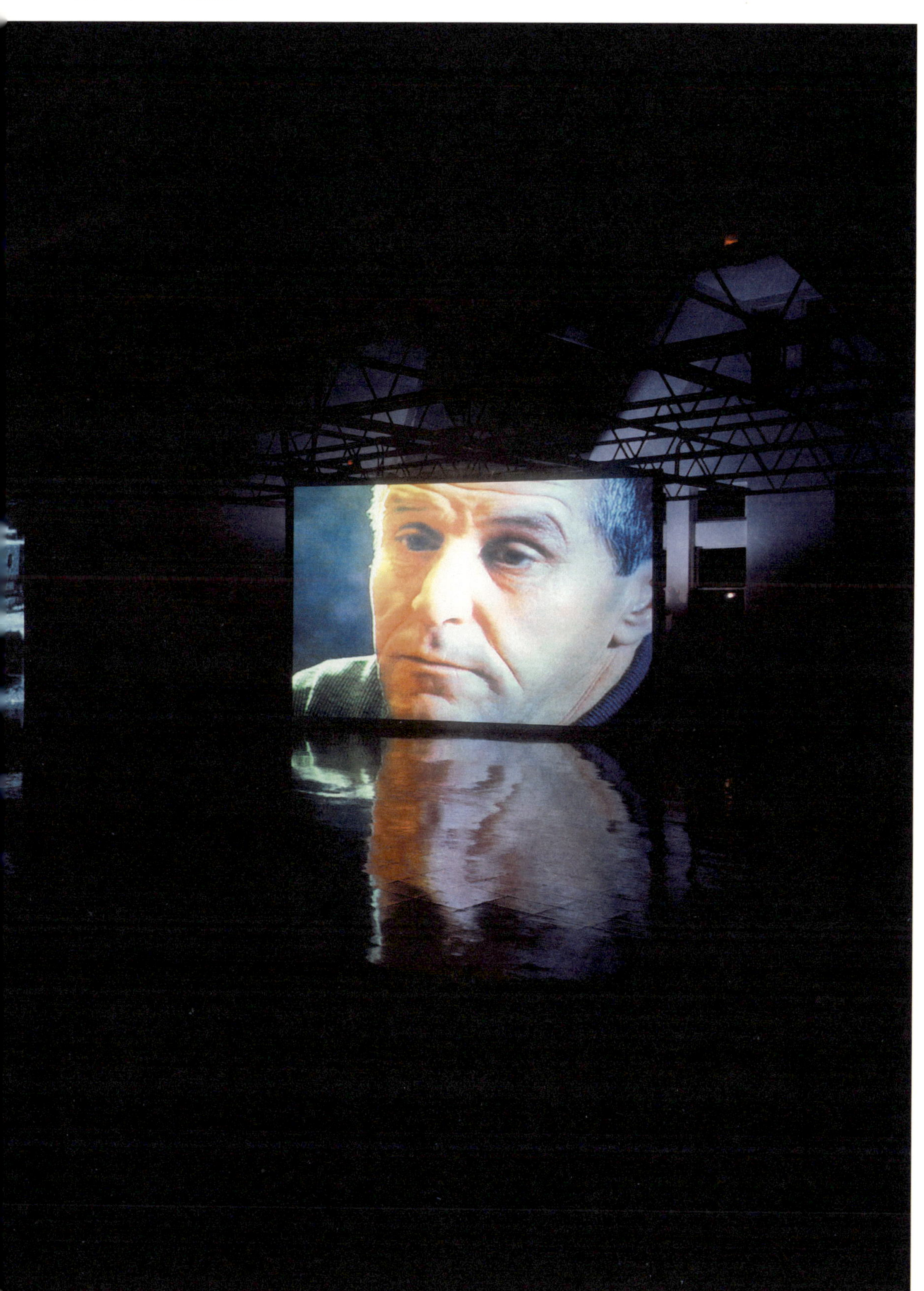

Meantime

2000

Meantime is a forty-foot orange digital clock set at Greenwich Mean Time and built into a shipping container. Almond transported and accompanied *Meantime* on its journey by cargo ship from London to New York following the arc of the Great Circle to mark his first solo exhibition in New York, at Matthew Marks Gallery. Later, *Meantime* continued to travel the world, including disembarkation at the Venice Biennale in 2003. Aboard-ship it has been used to measure longitudinal readings for navigational purposes. It keeps good time at sea, along rails, and on the road, and it is hoped *Meantime* will circumnavigate the globe. Built into a shipping container, *Meantime* references the international use of such containers as an accepted unit of value. *Meantime,* therefore, is like a singular unit of measure in what might be considered a floating stock exchange.

Steel shipping container, aluminium, polycarbonate, computerized electronic control system and components
289.6 x 243.8 x 1219.2 cm (114 x 96 x 480 in)

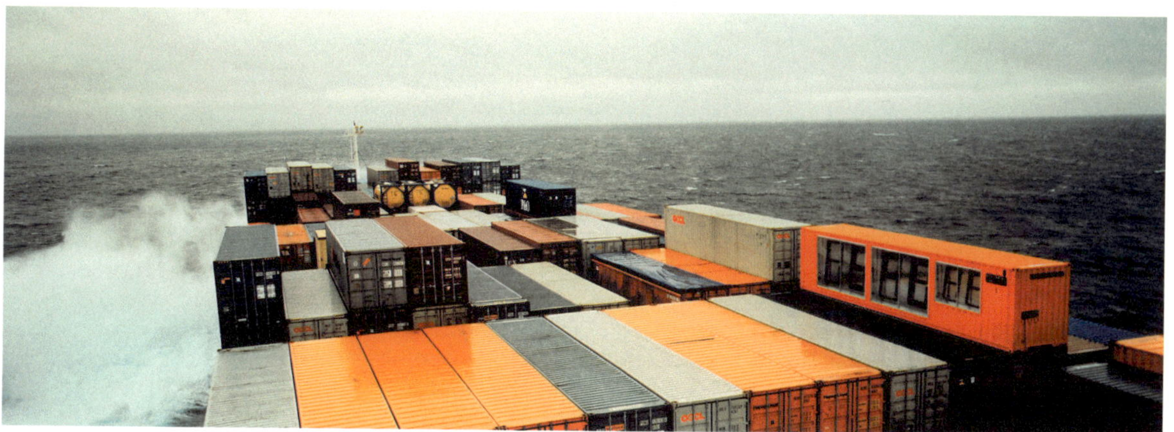

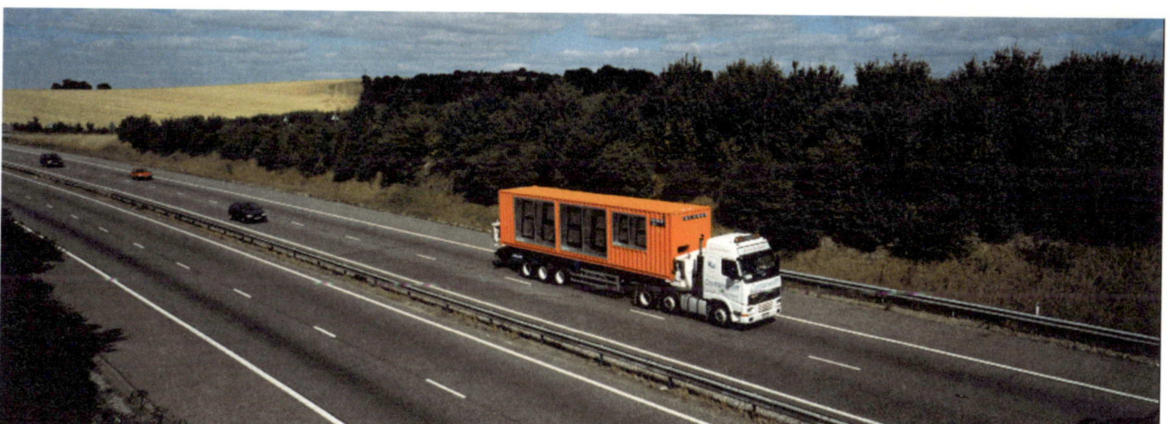

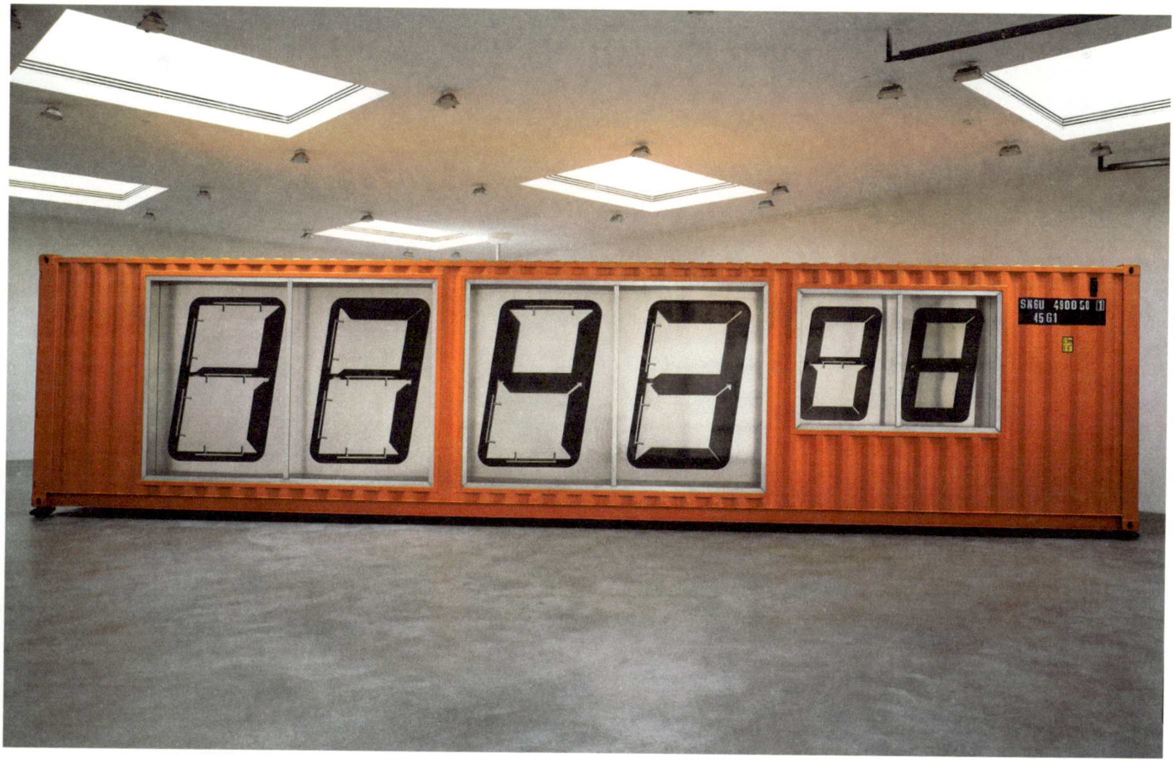

Schacta

2001

Schacta is Russian for 'mine', which is a relatively new term introduced during the Soviet era when mining and labour gained new significance. *Schacta* is shot in a coal mine in Kazakhstan. Workers are filmed in the changing room between shifts at dawn. One screen shows the men changing their clothes, while the other is a view of them descending on the suspended T-bar dragline down the mineshaft to the active seam of coal. This daily descent is the only time each miner is alone during the working day. The primitive conditions are similar to those Almond's grandfather experienced when he was a miner in Wigan, England. The workers (many of whom had lived through the Soviet era when surveillance was common) paid no attention to being observed. Almond consciously decided to use a long lens to avoid the film seeming to be voyeuristic. The image is slowed down so as to appear like a *ballet méchanique.* Since women never enter the mine, the female shaman's chant acknowledges a primal aspect of man's relationship to the land.

2-channel video installation
50-minute loop
Local shaman performing ritual chant
Dimensions variable. Ideally 640 x 910 cm (252 x 358 in)

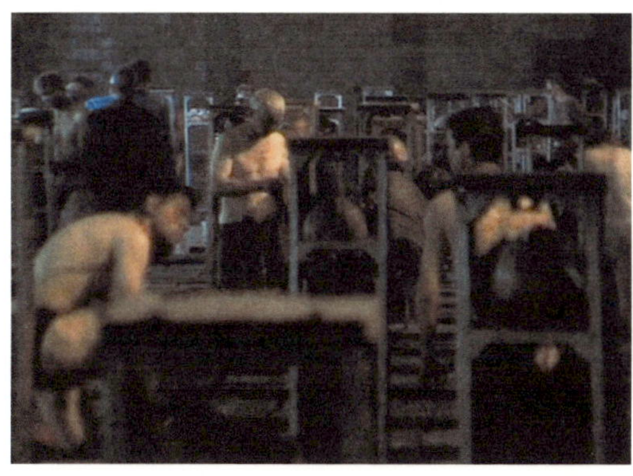 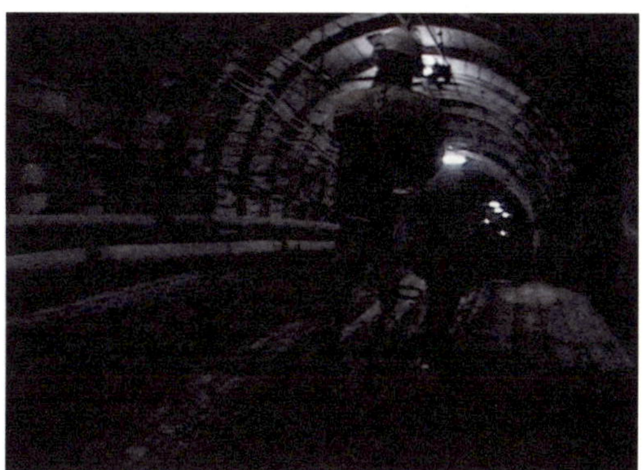

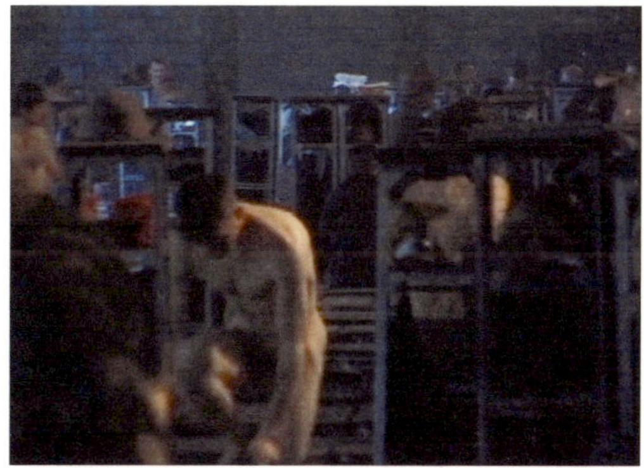 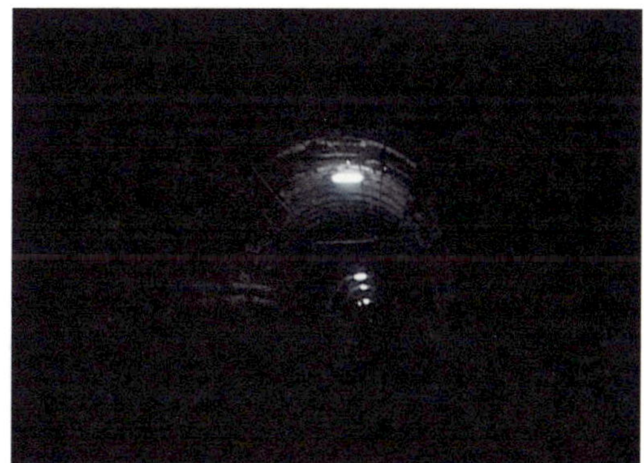

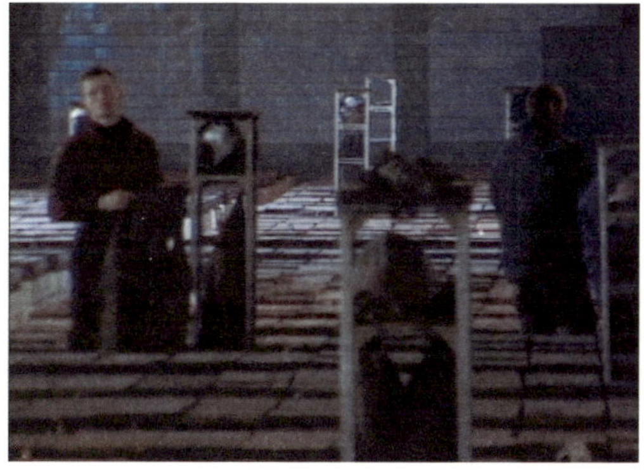 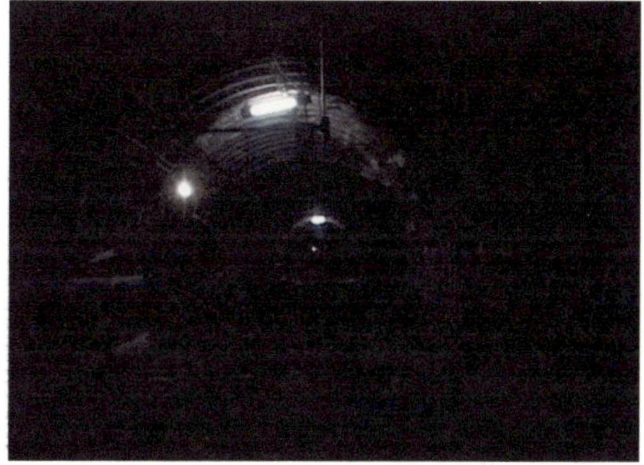

A

2002

Almond shot this trilogy of films during an artist's residency with Mission Antarctica. The first chapter of the trilogy documents the journey to Antarctica, the second depicts Antarctica itself with all the physical intensity of the ice, and the third addresses the disorientation and near hallucinatory state one experiences over a period of time spent in such a landscape. To further heighten the sense of disorientation the third chapter, known as *A-3,* is flipped upside-down (or is right-side-up relative to looking down on Antarctica from the Northern Hemisphere), which causes the reflections of sky on the ice and melted pools of water to appear to be the sky. The trilogy was publicly projected, with the three chapters in their entirety shown consecutively for one month on the Lyttelton Flytower of the National Theatre, on London's South Bank, and as a one-night screening in its Laurence Olivier Theatre.

Single-channel video trilogy
163   *A-1*
164   *A-2*
165   *A-3*
Each approximately 22 minutes
Score composed by Lyle Perkins using sound samplings recorded by Almond in Antarctica
Dimensions variable. Ideally 300 x 460 cm (118 x 181 in)

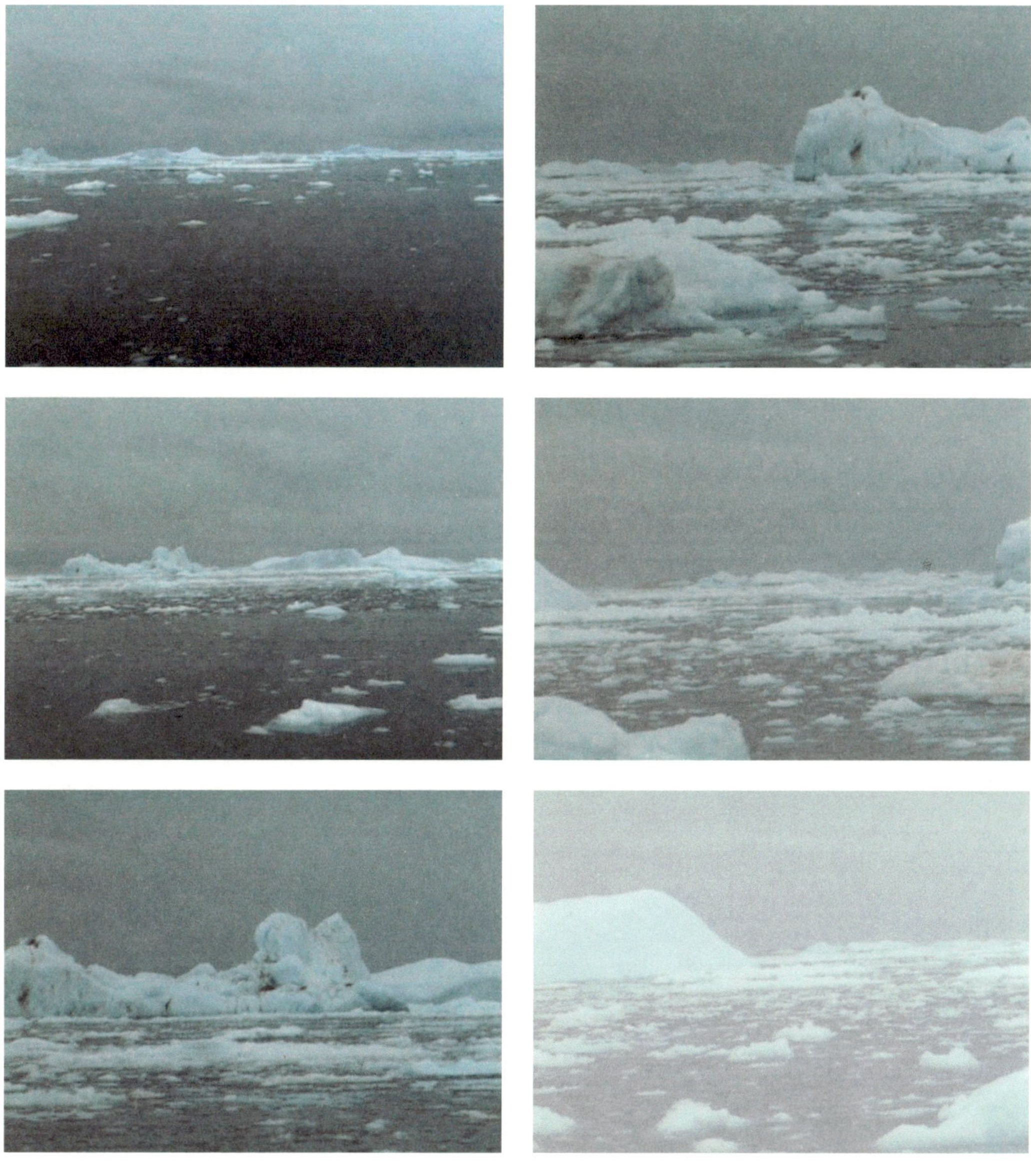

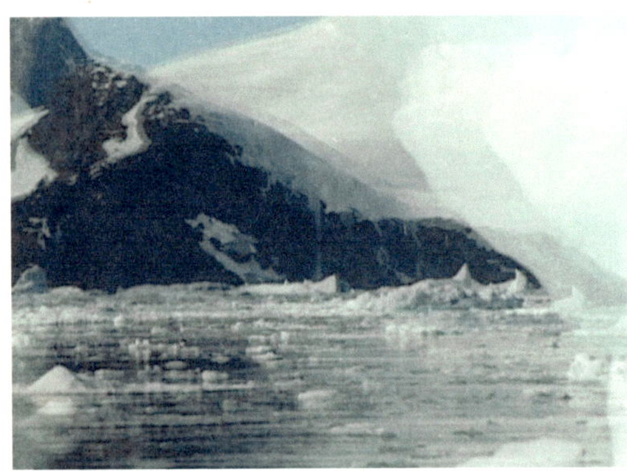
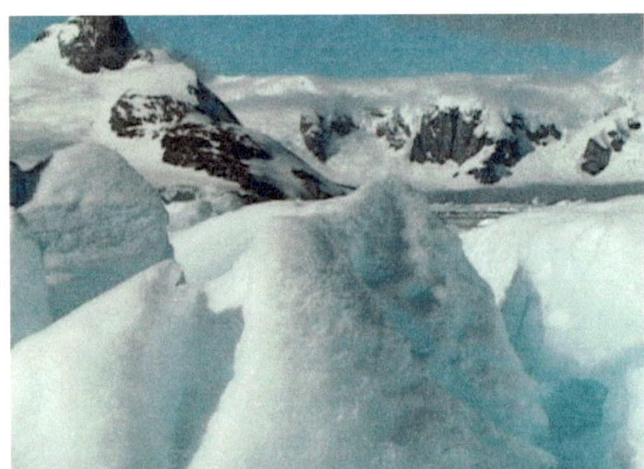
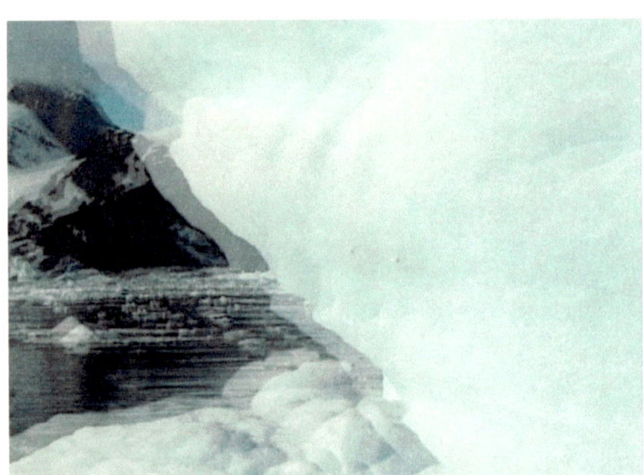
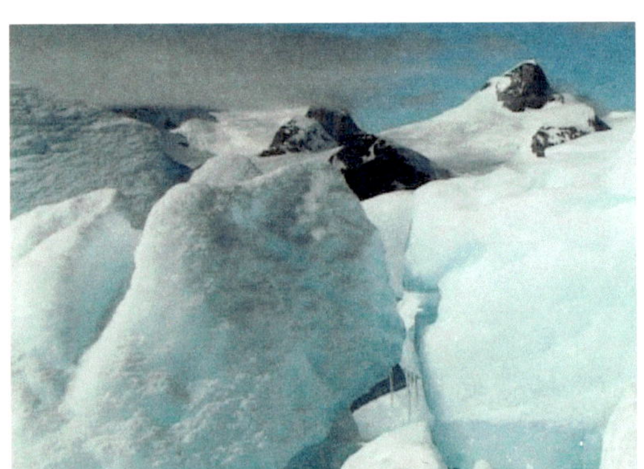
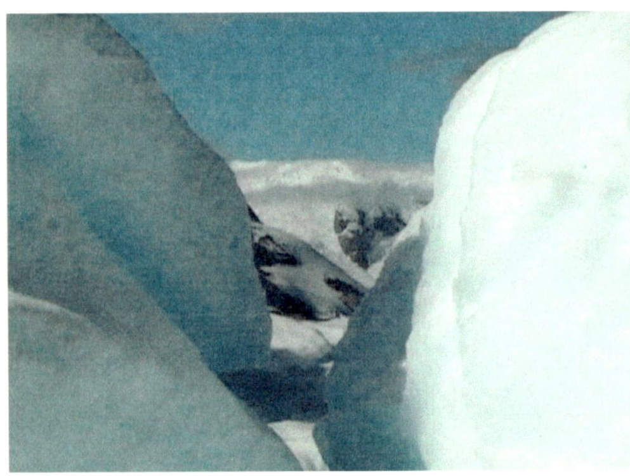
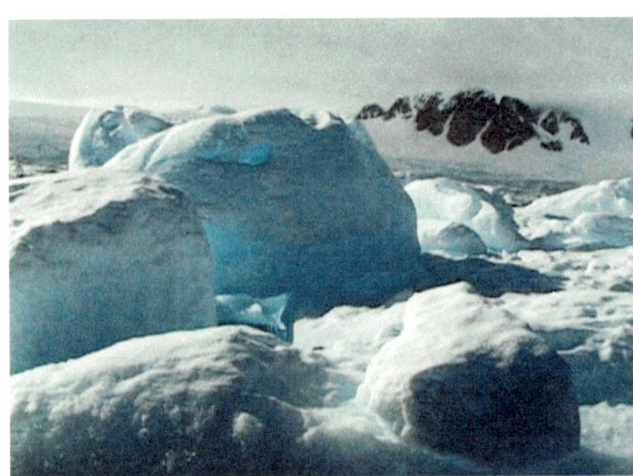

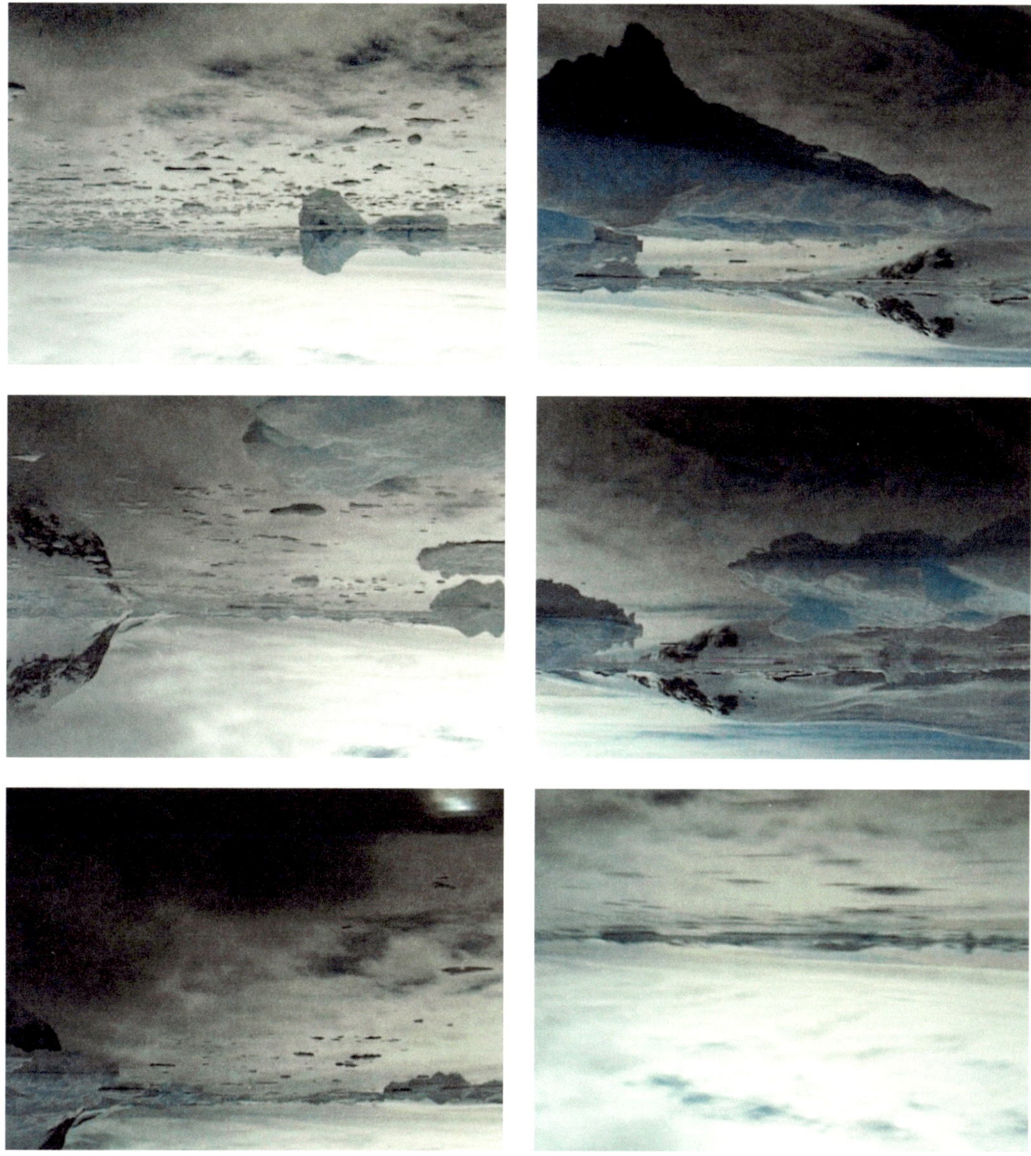

Arctic Pull

2003

Almond shot *Arctic Pull* in the Arctic Circle during his journey to Dudinka, Russia. He strapped his video camera to a sledge, and then secured himself to it with a long rope to pull it across the permafrost in the dark of night. As in much of Almond's video work, he uses acoustics to manipulate our perception of space and location. The sound of lashing winds and the grinding of the sledge heighten our sense of the extreme arctic conditions and the physical struggle of his journey. Shown on a suspended monitor in a pitch-black and soundproofed room, this installation produces a sense of disorientation and isolation in the viewer, a sense of spatial dislocation from their actual surroundings. Intermittently, the figure turns to look back at the camera and the light on his headgear is visible, like the ominous eye of Cyclops, plotting his course. Metaphorically, *Arctic Pull* is a portrait of the artist exploring unknown territory. References to Arctic adventurers and explorers are made in *Arctic Pull* by the proximity of the artist to the magnetic North Pole. *Arctic Pull* also references the *Fullmoon* photographs: in this instance, the pitch-black landscape does not result in a clear bucolic image, but rather the artist is seen to be fumbling along in the dark.

Single-channel infrared video
23 minutes
Wind static and the sounds of a sledge being pulled across the ice
50 x 60 cm (20 x 24 in) monitor

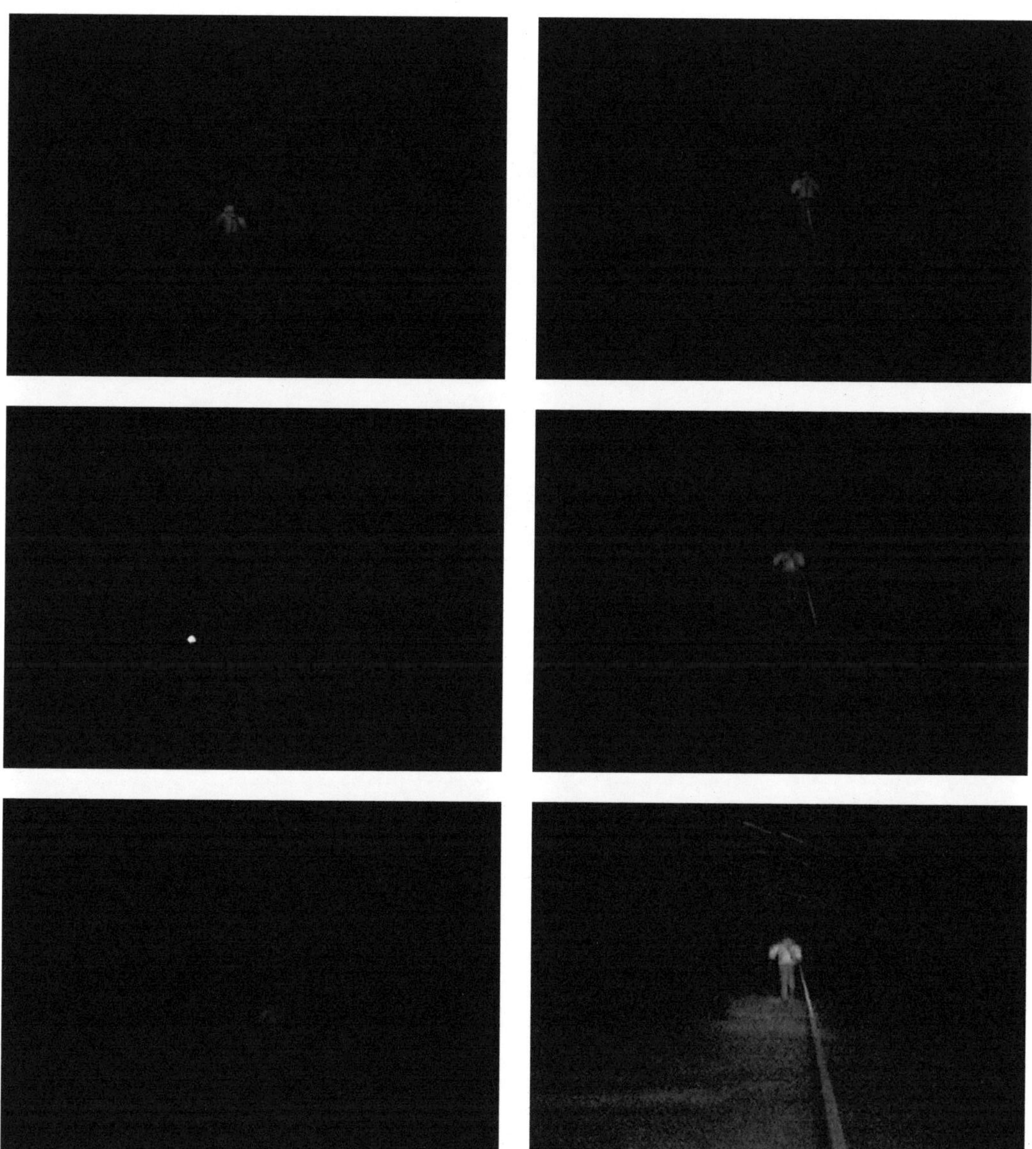

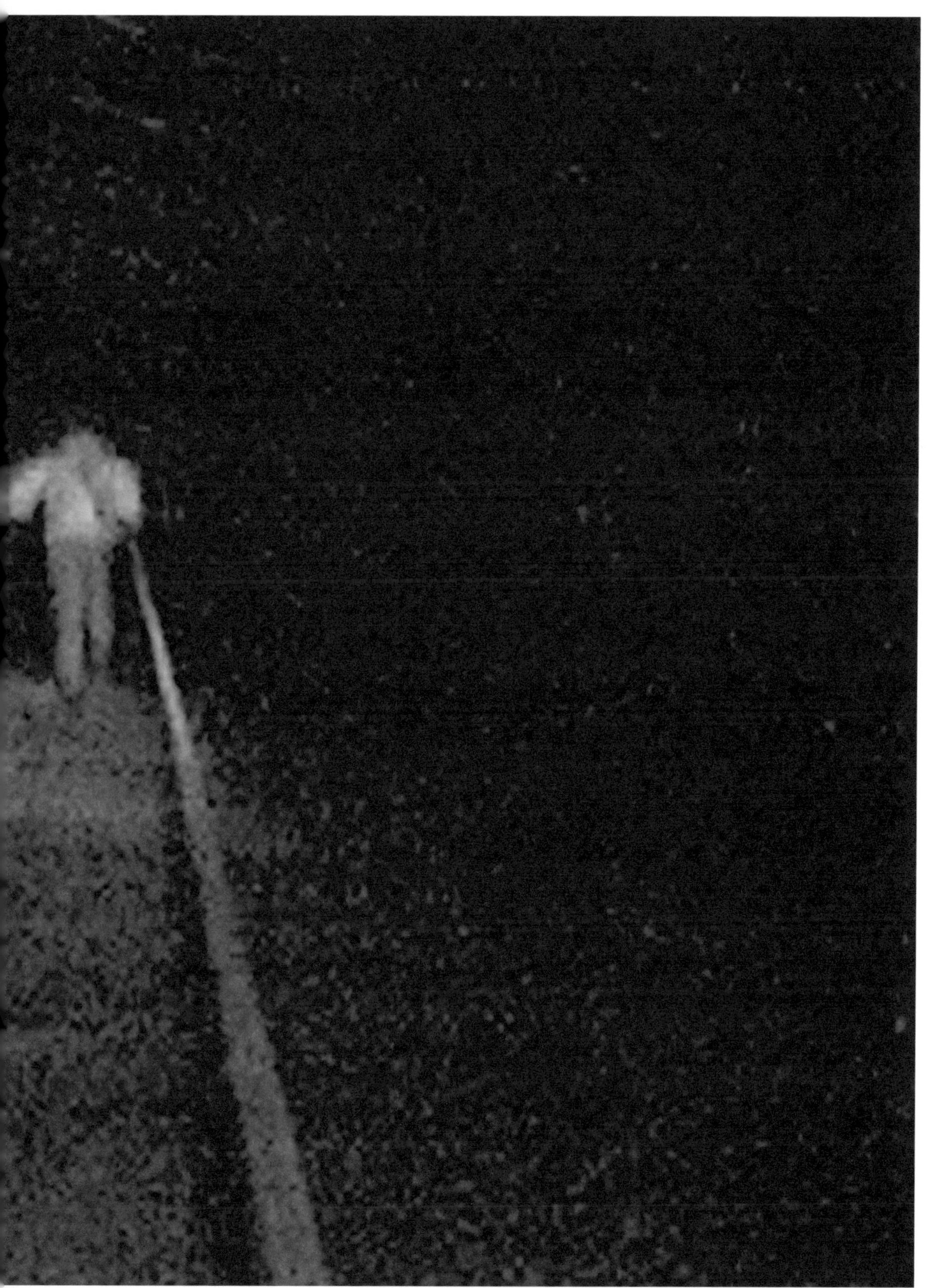

If I Had You

2003

The screens of *If I Had You* are monumental and their placement is determined by the fact that it was commissioned by the Fondazione Nicola Trussardi, Milan, to be exhibited at the Palazzo della Ragione in an elevated medieval storeroom. Shot in the seaside town of Blackpool, where Almond's grandparents honeymooned, his widowed grandmother reflects on her married life. *If I Had You* poignantly locates the theme of remembering in an overtly personal and intimate history by expressing emotional longing. Shot in saturated tones, it is nostalgically evocative of the past. This is the first instance of Almond playing with the frame rate within an installation by using different shutter speeds for the various projections. Richard James's melody *Avril 14*[th] is a sampled recording of James's own performance layered to create the sound of an out-of-tune instrument. *If I Had You* inspired a new piece of choreography by the Merce Cunningham Dance Company. They based the tempo of the dance on the variable frame rate and shutter speeds of If *I Had You,* and performed the piece at the Barbican, London, in June 2005.

4-channel video installation
Repeated piano melody from Richard James (Aphex Twin); the sound of leather-soled shoes dancing on a ballroom floor; the creaking noise of an illuminated windmill turning on the Blackpool Promenade
Dimensions variable. Ideally, each screen 640 x 910 cm (252 x 358 in)
Commissioned by the Fondazione Nicola Trussardi, Milan, Italy

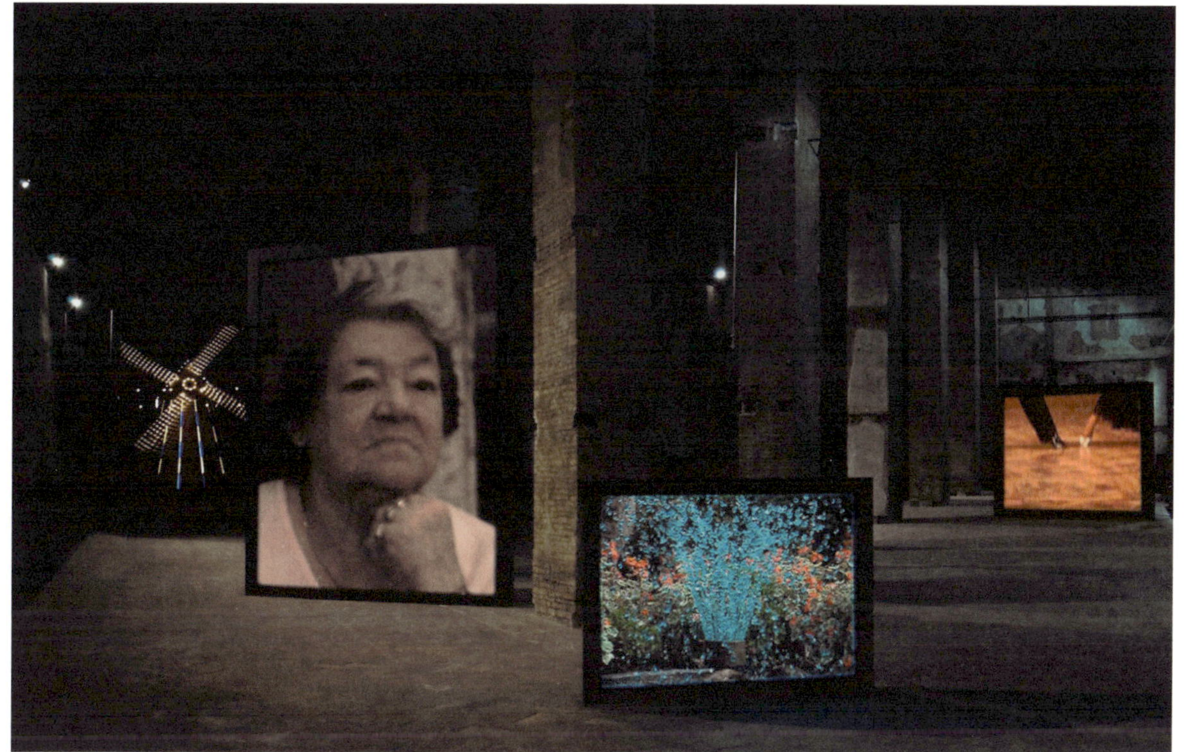

Mono / Chrono / Pneumatics

Ongoing series begun 2003

Mono / Chrono / Pneumatic Red

2007

A series of fully-functional pneumatic flip-clocks, the *Mono / Chrono / Pneumatics* often emphasize a particular aspect, or highlight a condition, of another work by Almond. For example, *Mono / Chrono / Pneumatic Black* was produced in 2003 to accompany the film trilogy *A* in a solo exhibition at White Cube, London. The clock emphasizes the countdown to the year 2041, when Antarctica will no longer be a protected territory but will be open for colonization and the exploitation of its natural resources. Each number on the clocks is controlled by exposed pneumatic mechanisms. In the red version, shown in 2007 at Matthew Marks Gallery, New York, with *In The Between,* the numbers of the clock are painted red, the dominant colour of the Chinese flag, while the pneumatic mechanisms that power the movement of the clock are coloured the yellow, white, red and blue of Tibetan prayer flags. Each passing minute produces a mighty noise, powered by the pneumatic mechanisms of the clock, and thereby accentuates the passing of time.

Aluminium, lacquer, pneumatic control systems
400 x 700 x 90 cm (157 x 276 x 35 in)

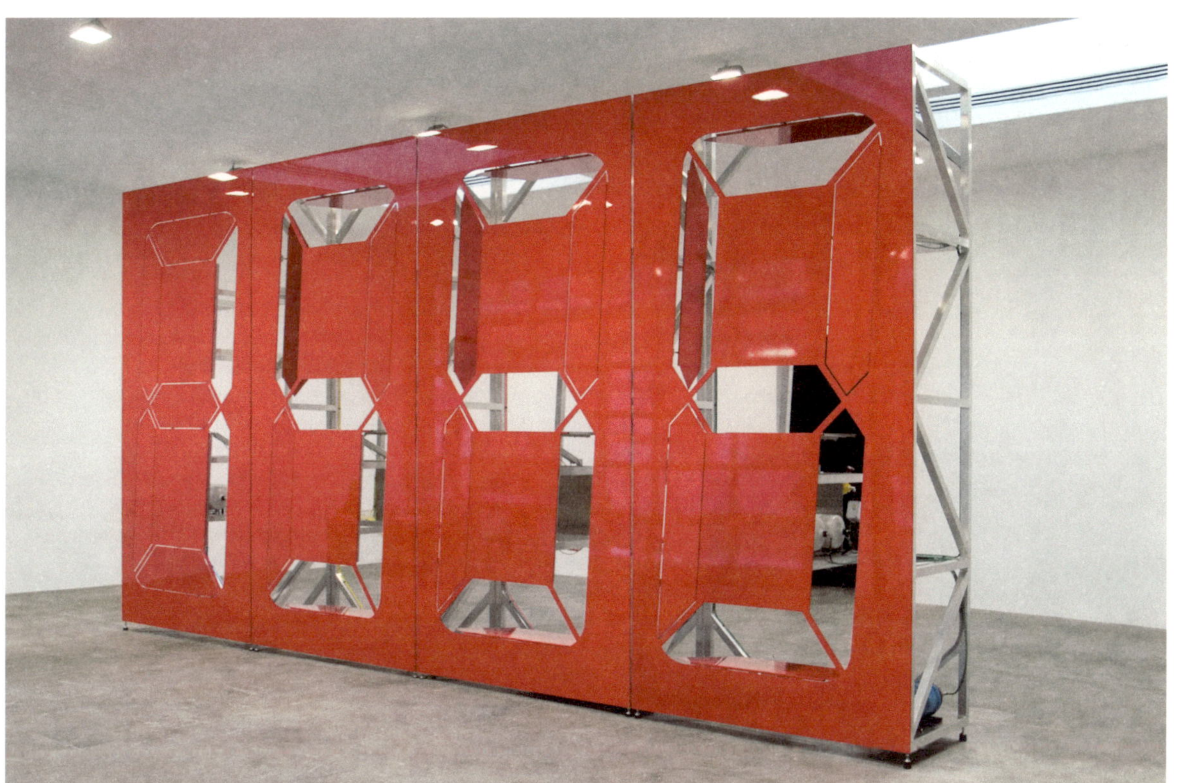

Terminus

2007

Terminus concludes Almond's decade-long investigation of the bus shelters from Oświęcim, formerly known as Auschwitz, in Poland. The 14 bus shelters are arranged in pairs and according to their state of physical dilapidation, the last pair being the most decrepit. The first two shelters are shown in isolation; one has the word MUZEUM written across it, directing travellers to the place from which it has been removed. This separation allows one to examine the shelters in detail – bus timetables, graffiti, cigarette burns, their general physical condition – before turning a corner to confront the remaining 12 shelters and the Trainplate reading TERMINUS, which was cast in salt mined in Oświęcim. The salt mine made Oświęcim the centre of transportation in Poland, which was a primary reason for Auschwitz being situated at this hub of mining activity and terminus for the transportation line. During the German occupation in World War II, prisoners from the labour camps at Auschwitz were put to work in the salt mine. Each pair of bus shelters face one another as if to represent arrival and departure. As an array, the shelters give physical form to the sense of being caught up in the congestion of a journey. Interested in the effect of time on objects, places, institutional systems and individuals, Almond puts the viewer at the centre of *Terminus*. Passing through the installation between the shelters allows viewers an opportunity for reflection, and leaves them to make the associations that transform a common-place urban object into a powerful work of art.

14 bus shelters: aluminium, steel, wood, fibreglass, PVC
1 salt-cast Trainplate
Each bus shelter 265 x 600 x 335 cm (104 x 236 x 132 in)
Plaque 25.5 x 179.5 x 2.5 cm (10 x 70½ x 1 in)

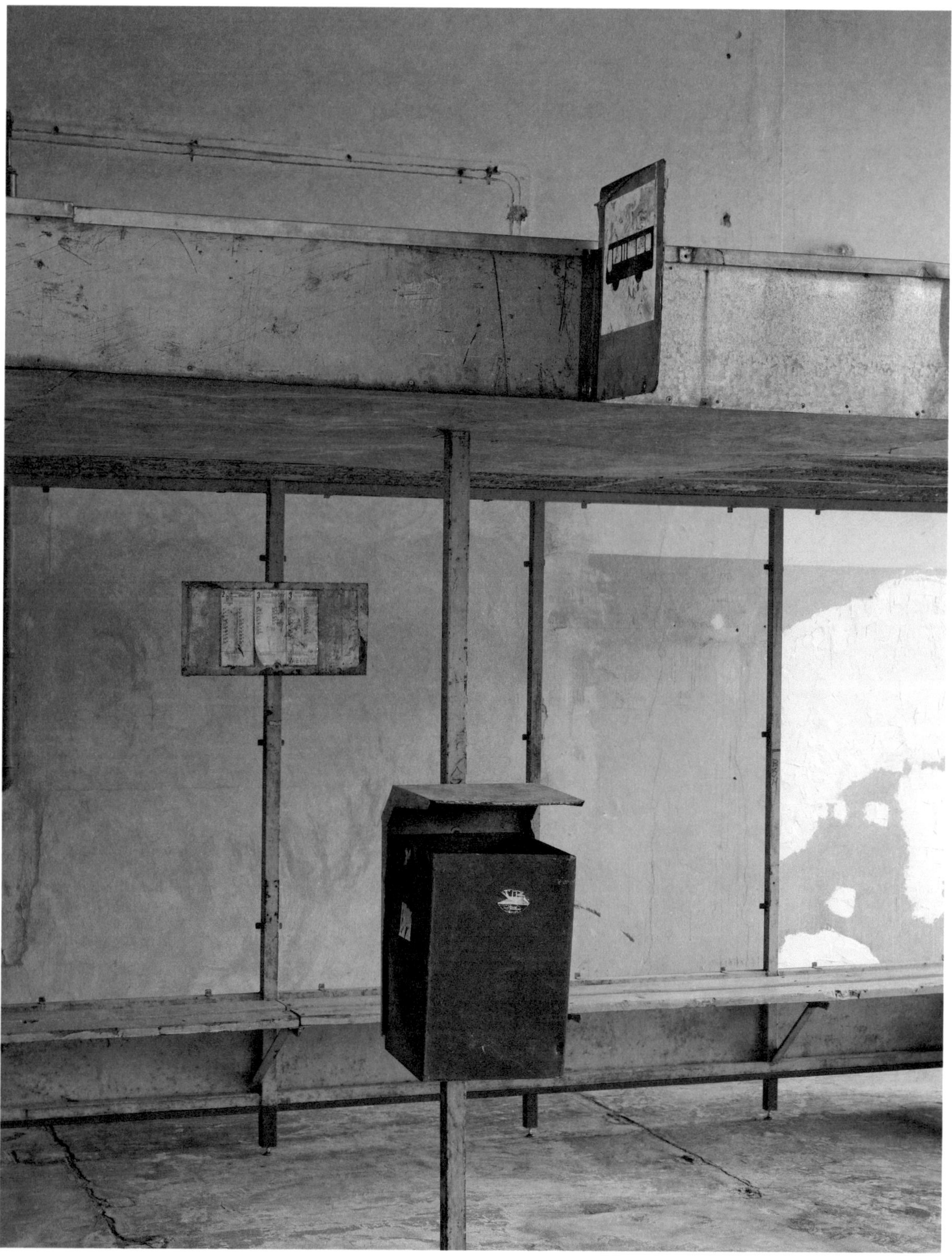

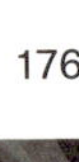

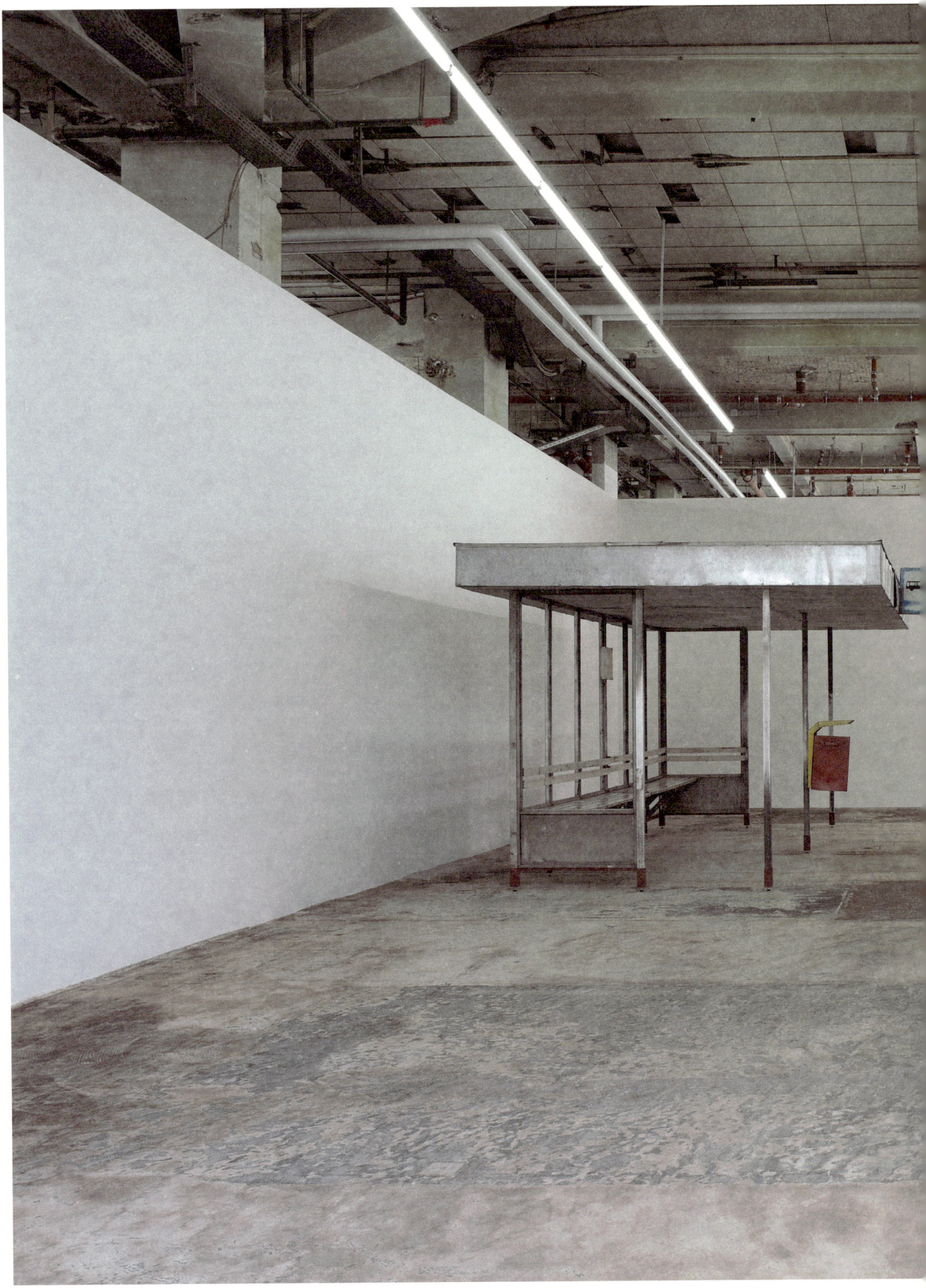

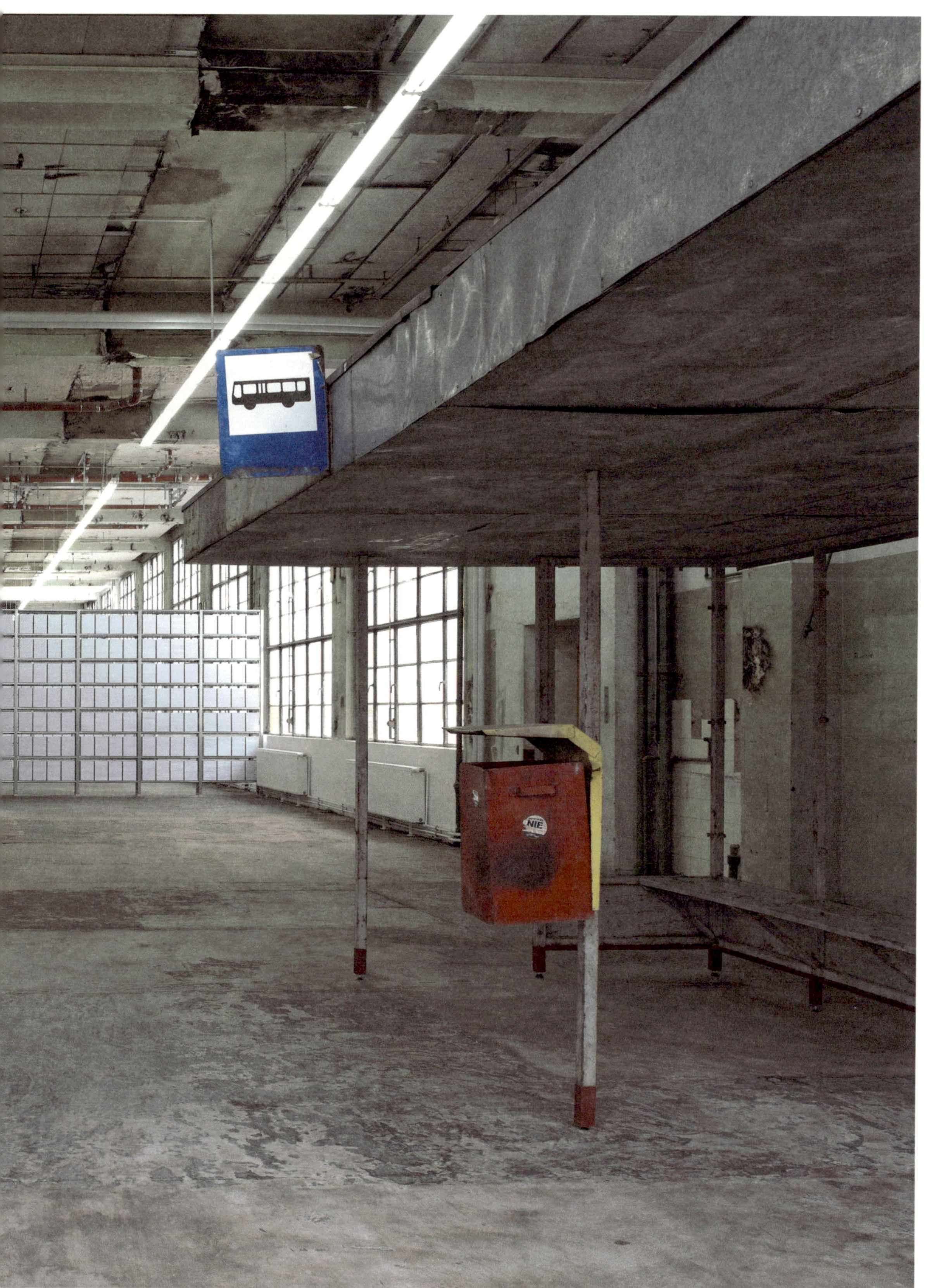
NIE

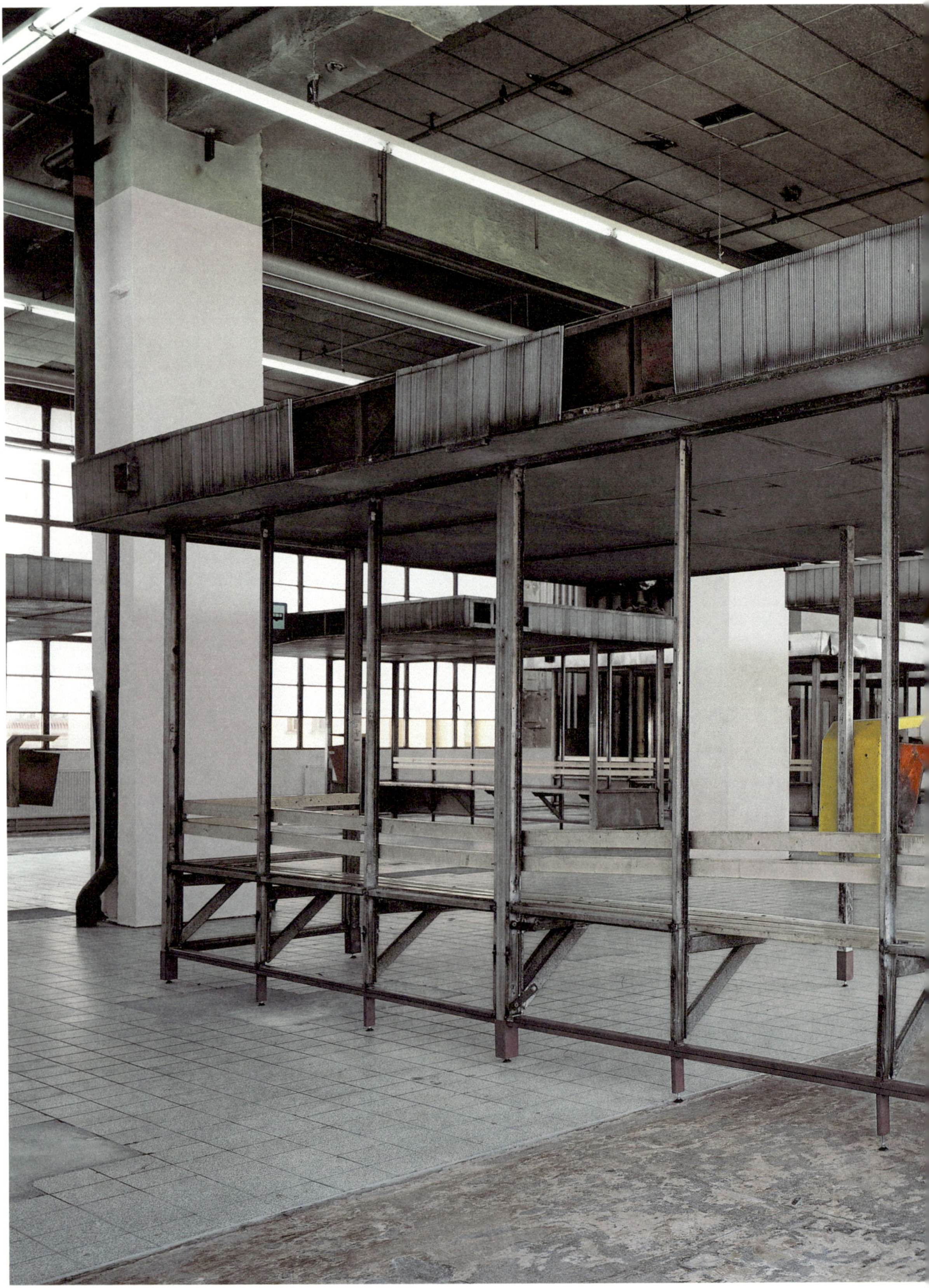

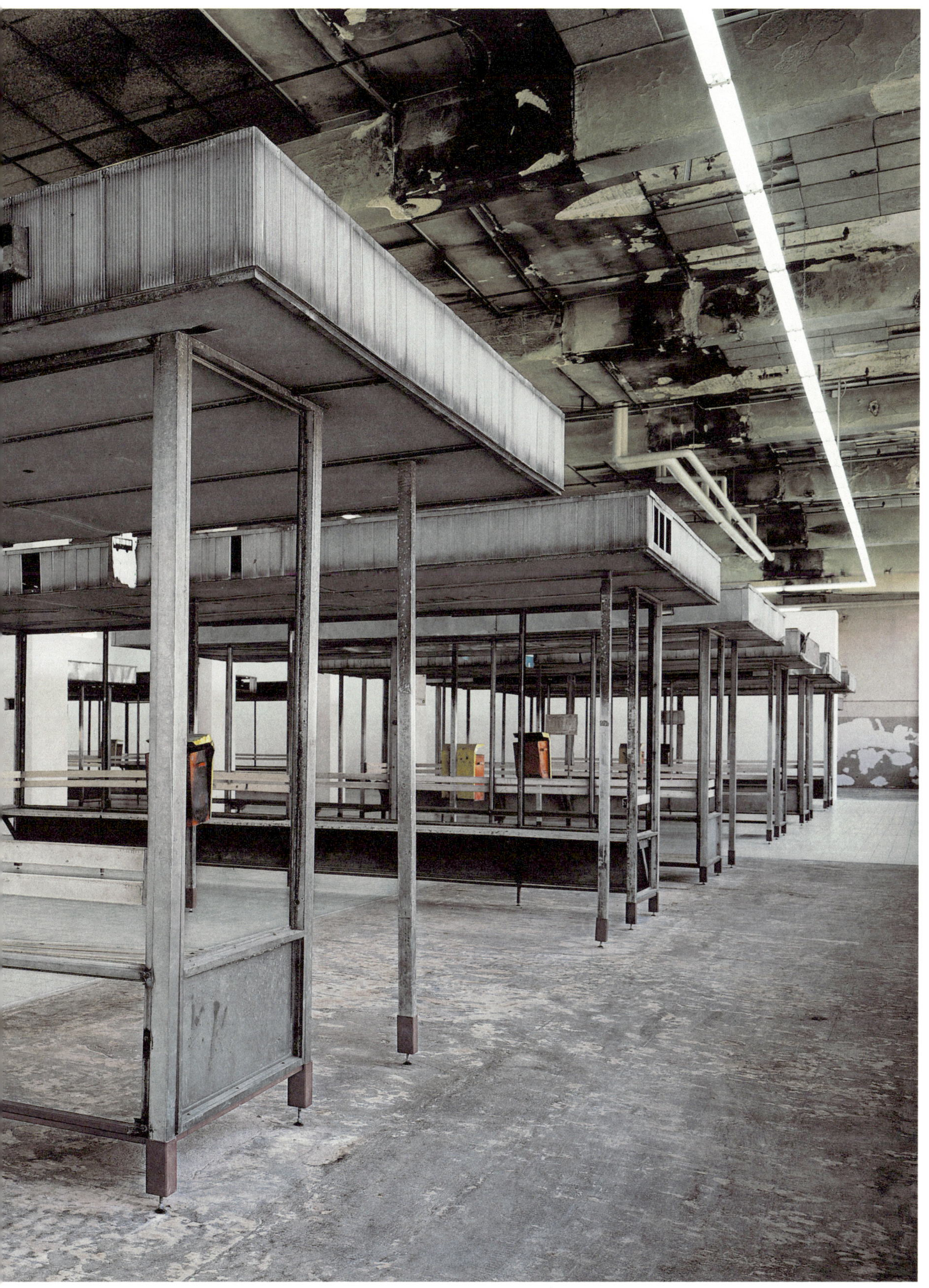

Archive

2007

Archive consists of 4,000,000 pieces of blank A4 paper arranged as if it is a bureaucratic hoard of (missing) information. The sheets of paper are neatly stacked and apparently well tended, but their content is invisible. The horseshoe-shaped galvanized steel shelves of the installation abut a wall to create an inaccessible space that excludes all spectators. This mass of documents, which may or may not represent an archive, leaves one with a sense of uncertainty.

Galvanized steel, paper
300 x 1536 x 1205 cm (118 x 605 x 474½ in)

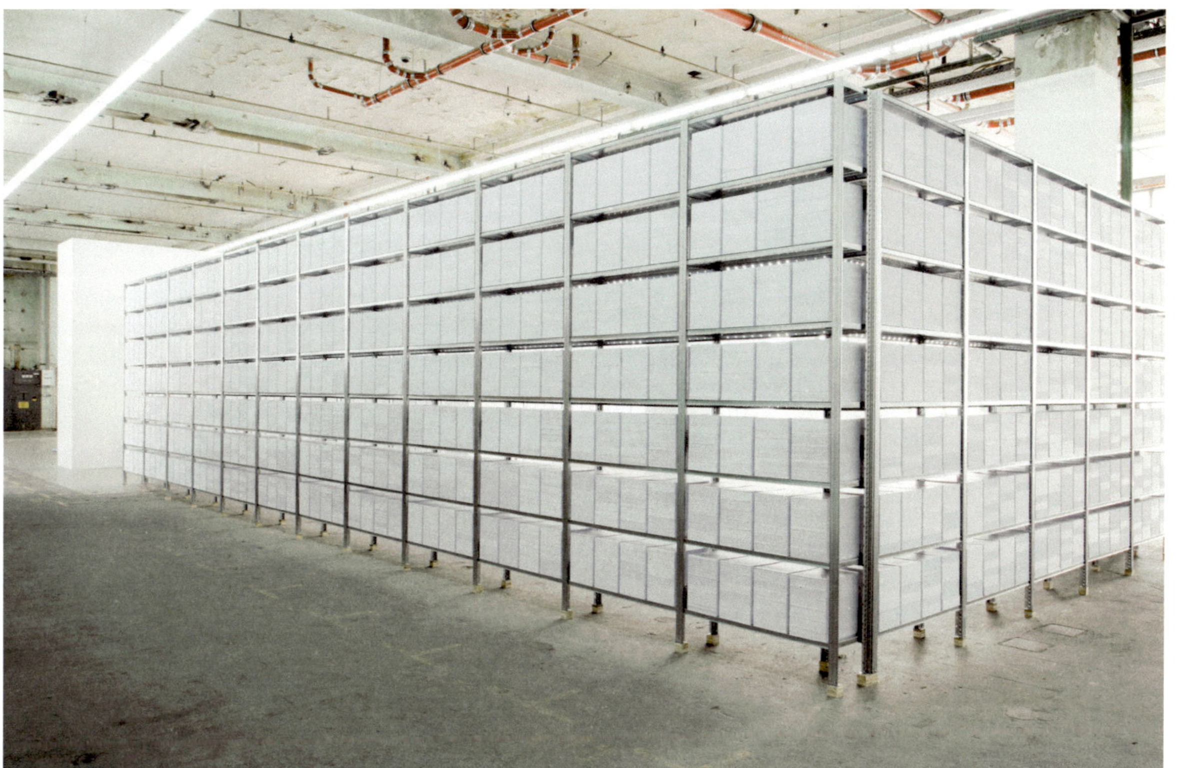

Infinite Betweens: Reality Between

2007

After filming *In The Between,* the last in his trilogy of train films, Almond returned to Tibet to shoot a series of Tibetan prayer flags under a full moon. These *Fullmoons* have been named for the essential Buddhist vision of relativity as followed by the Indian and Tibetan Adepts, who believe Buddha discovered this state. There are several subsections in this series of *Infinite Betweens: Death Point Between, Reality Between, Becoming Between, Life Between, Dream Between* and *Trance Between,* of which *Reality Between* is illustrated here. It was a particularly bright September moon when Almond photographed the *Infinite Betweens* and as dawn broke the moon was still up. The long exposure has revealed and heightened a sense of motion by recording the quivering of the flags in the night and in some of the *Infinite Betweens* double exposures appear. High up in the mountainous region of Tibet, prayer flags are strung along the ridges and peaks of the Himalayas to bless the surrounding countryside and sacred ground. Traditionally, the flags are woodblock-printed with texts and images, and Tibetans call these horizontal flags *lung ta* ('wind horse'). They are either square or rectangular and are connected by their top edge along a length of string. The flags come in five colours, each of which represents one of the elements and the Five Pure Lights: blue symbolizes sky and space; white symbolizes water; red, fire; green, wind and air; and yellow symbolizes the earth. Usually, five flags are flown together in a repeated pattern according to the Five Pure Lights.

C-prints
220 x 176 cm (87 x 69 in)

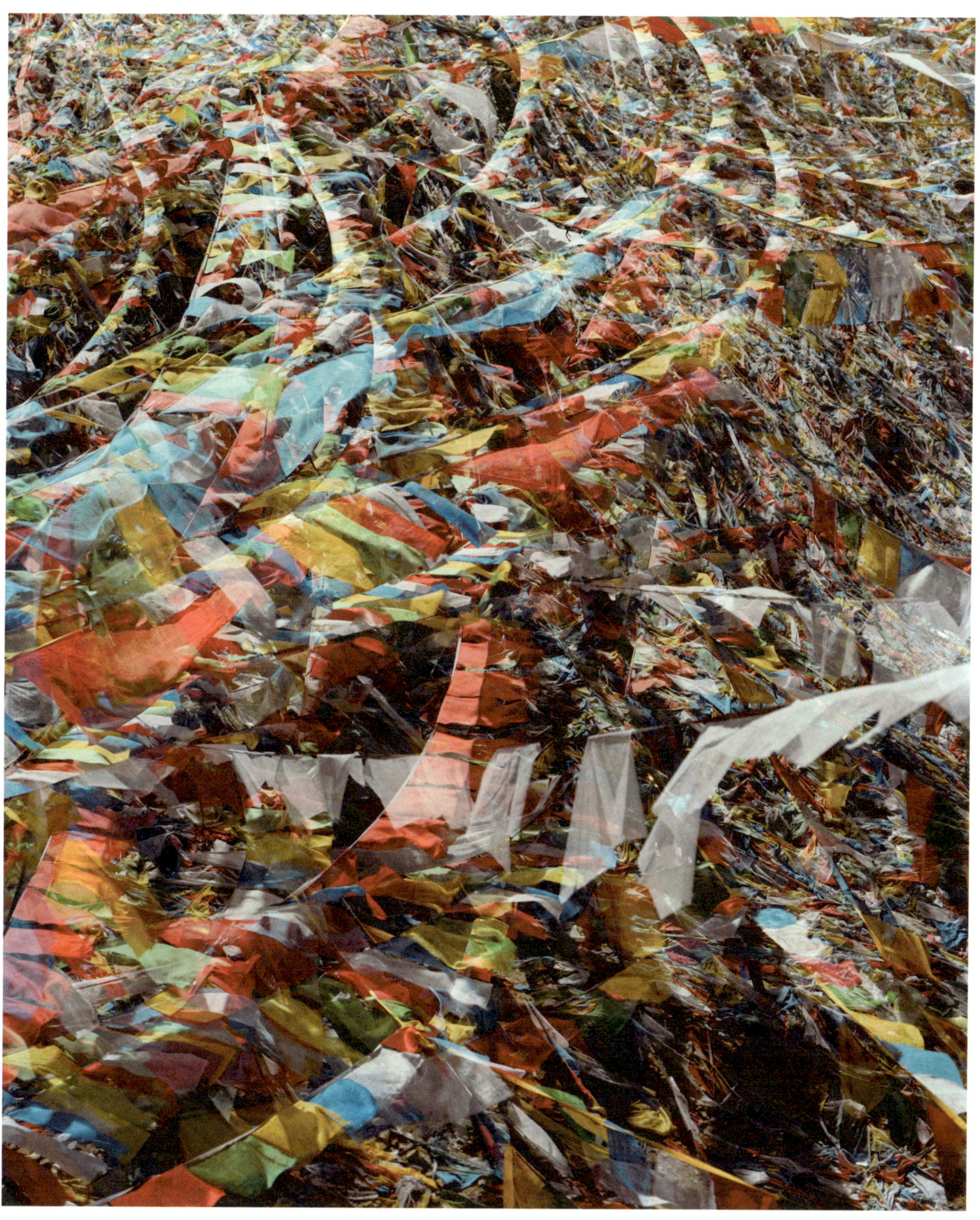

Darren Almond, born 1971, Wigan, United Kingdom
Graduated 1993, (BAFA) Winchester School of Art, United Kingdom
Lives and works in London, United Kingdom

Solo Exhibitions

2008   *Fire Under Snow: Darren Almond,* Parasol unit foundation for contemporary art, London, United Kingdom
Moons of the Iapetus Ocean, White Cube, London, United Kingdom

2007   *Darren Almond,* Alfonso Artiaco, Naples, Italy
Night + Fog, Galerie Max Hetzler, Berlin, Germany
In The Between, Musée d'art contemporain, Montreal, Canada
Day Return, Centre for Contemporary Art Ujazdowski Castle, Warsaw, Poland
Darren Almond, Matthew Marks Gallery, New York, United States
Darren Almond, SITE Santa Fe, Santa Fe, United States

2006   *Day Return,* Museum Folkwang, Essen, Germany
Take Me Home, DA2 – Domus Artium 2002, Salamanca, Spain

2005   *Darren Almond,* Alfonso Artiaco, Naples, Italy
Only Sound Needs Echo and Dreads its Lack, Galerie Chantal Crousel, Paris, France
Darren Almond, Matthew Marks Gallery, New York, United States
Isolation, K21 Kunstsammlung Nordrhein-Westfalen, Düsseldorf, Germany

2004   *Live Sentence,* Lentos Kunstmuseum Linz, Linz, Austria
If I Had You, Galerie Max Hetzler, St Johannes Evangelist Church, Berlin, Germany

2003   *If I Had You,* Fondazione Nicola Trussardi, Palazzo della Ragiona, Milan, Italy
Darren Almond, Galleri K, Oslo, Norway
11 Miles ... from Safety, White Cube, London, United Kingdom
Nightvision, Sommer Contemporary Art, Tel-Aviv, Israel
Darren Almond, Herzliya Museum of Art, Herzliya, Israel
A, Galerie Max Hetzler, Berlin, Germany

2002   *A,* National Theatre, Fourth Wall, South Bank, commissioned by Public Art Development Trust, London, United Kingdom

2001   *Night as Day,* Tate Britain, London, United Kingdom
Coming Up For Air, Matthew Marks Gallery, New York, United States
Darren Almond, Kunsthalle Zürich, Zürich, Switzerland
Darren Almond, De Appel Foundation Centre for Contemporary Art, Amsterdam, The Netherlands
Darren Almond, Galerie Max Hetzler, E-Werk, Abspannwerk Buchhändlerhof, Berlin, Germany

2000   *Transport Medium,* Matthew Marks Gallery, New York, United States
Geisterbahn, The Approach, London, United Kingdom
Traction, Chisenhale Gallery, London, United Kingdom

1999   *Darren Almond,* Galerie Max Hetzler, Berlin, Germany
Darren Almond, The Renaissance Society, University of Chicago, Chicago, United States

1997   *Darren Almond,* Institute of Contemporary Arts, commissioned by the ICA and Toshiba Art & Innovation, London, United Kingdom
Darren Almond, Jay Jopling / White Cube, London, United Kingdom

1995   *KN 120,* Great Western Studios, London, United Kingdom

1991   *Darren Almond,* Crawford Art College, Cork, Ireland

Group Exhibitions

2007   *Ensemble,* Institute of Contemporary Art, Philadelphia, United States
Her(his)story, Museum of Cycladic Art, Athens, Greece
Numerica, Palazzo delle Papesse Centro Arte Contemporanea, Siena, Italy
Shoot the Family, Canzani Center Gallery, Columbus College of Art & Design, Ohio, United States
Titled / Untitled: The Rubell and Devonshire Family Collections, Lismore Castle, Ireland
L'oeil écran ou la nouvelle image, Casino Luxembourg – Forum d'Art Contemporain, Luxembourg
Light, Winchester Cathedral, Winchester, United Kingdom
Full House – Faces of a Collection, Kunsthalle Mannheim, Mannheim, Germany
Going Staying: Movement, Body, Place in Contemporary Art, Kunstmuseum Bonn, Bonn, Germany
2nd Moscow Biennale of Contemporary Art, Former Lenin Museum, Moscow, Russia
Closed Circuit: Video and New Media, Metropolitan Museum of Art, New York, United States

2006   *Work, Rest and Play,* Laing Art Gallery, Newcastle, United Kingdom
Between a Rock and a Hard Place, Kenny Schachter Rove, London, United Kingdom
Darren Almond and Janice Kerbel: The Impossible Landscape, Horticultural Society of New York, New York, United States
Carbonic Anhydride, Galerie Max Hetzler, Berlin, Germany
Geisterbahn, 1999, Kino Arsenal, Berlin, Germany
Shoot the Family, Cranbrook Art Museum, Michigan; Knoxville Museum of Art, Tennessee; Western Gallery, Western Washington University, Bellingham, Washington, United States
Darren Almond / Albert Oehlen: Time 2 Kill, Galerie Max Hetzler, Berlin, Germany
Caspar David Friedrich, Museum Folkwang, Essen; Hamburger Kunsthalle, Hamburg, Germany

The Black Show, David Patton, Los Angeles, United States
37th Art Basel: Unlimited, Basel, Switzerland

2005   *Turner Prize 2005,* Tate Britain, London, United Kingdom
En Attente, Casino Luxembourg – Forum d'Art Contemporain, Luxembourg
20:Twenty: A Timeline of Cornerhouse Exhibitions 1985–2005, Cornerhouse,
Manchester, United Kingdom
World Without End, Australian Centre for the Moving Image, Melbourne, Australia
Land Marks, Galerie Chantal Crousel, Paris, France
Sequences, Q Arts Gallery, Derby, United Kingdom
Bidibidobidiboo, La Collezione Sandretto Re Rebaudengo, Palazzo Re Rebaudengo,
Piazza del Municipio, Guarene d'Alba, Fondazione Sandretto Re Rebaudengo,
Turin, Italy
Darren Almond / Albert Oehlen: Time 2 Kill, Galerie Max Hetzler, Berlin, Germany
The Mind is a Horse Part II, Bloomberg Space, London, United Kingdom
Getting Emotional, Institute of Contemporary Art, Boston, United States
Works on Paper, Galerie Max Hetzler, Berlin, Germany
Universal Experience: Art, Life, and the Tourist's Eye, Hayward Gallery, London,
United Kingdom; Museum of Contemporary Art Chicago, United States

2004   *Sequences,* Peterborough Digital Art, Peterborough, United Kingdom
Geisterbahn, 1999, 33rd Festival d'Automne, Passage du Désir – BETC, Paris,
France
ein-leuchten, Museum der Moderne, Salzburg, Austria
Eclipse: Towards the Edge of the Visible, White Cube, London, United Kingdom
Witness, Museum of Contemporary Art, Sydney, Australia
Die Neue Kunsthalle III: materiell – immateriell, Kunsthalle Mannheim, Mannheim,
Germany
Biennial of Pontevedra, Pazo da Cultura, Facultade de Belas Artes / Escola de
Restauración, Instituto Valle-Inclán, Pontevedra, Italy
After Images: Kunst als Soziales Gedächnis, Neues Museum Weserburg, Bremen,
Germany
Busan Biennale 2004, Busan Metropolitan City Hall and Art Museum, Busan, Korea
*Open Secrets: Something Old, Something New, Redefining the Boundaries of the
Art Collection,* Imperial War Museum, London, United Kingdom
Other Times: British Contemporary Art, City Art Gallery, Prague, Czech Republic

2003   *Heißkalt: Aktuelle Malerei aus der Sammlung Scharpff,* Staatsgalerie Stuttgart,
Stuttgart; Kunsthalle Hamburg, Hamburg, Germany
Video Time, Green on Red Gallery, Dublin, Ireland
The Spirit of White, Fondation Beyeler, Basel, Switzerland
Imagination: Perception in Art, Kunsthaus Graz am Landesmuseum Joanneum, Graz,
Austria
Outlook: International Art Exhibition Technopolis, Benaki Museum, Factory, Athens,
Greece
Game Over, Grimm / Rosenfeld, Munich, Germany
3rd Skulptur Biennale Münsterland, Stadtmuseum, Beckum, Germany

Hot Summer in the City, Sean Kelly Gallery, New York, United States
Dreams and Conflicts: The Dictatorship of the Viewer, 50th Biennale di Venezia,
Venice, Italy
Edén, La Colección Jumex, Antiguo Colegio de San Ildefonso, Mexico City, Mexico
Witness, The Curve, Barbican Art Gallery, London, United Kingdom
Breathing the Water, Galerie Hauser & Wirth & Presenhuber, Zürich, Zürich, Switzerland
The Guest, Schwebebahn, Hertzliya Museum, Tel-Aviv, Israel
*Sculpture: Darren Almond, Peter Fischli, David Weiss, Katharina Fritsch, Robert
Gober, Donald Judd, Ellsworth Kelly, Ugo Rondinone, Tony Smith,* Matthew Marks
Gallery, New York, United States
In Light: Video Projections by Eight Contemporary Artists, Art Gallery of Ontario,
Toronto, Canada

2002   *Video Acts – Single Channel Video Works from the Collections of Pamela and Richard
Kramlich and the New Art Trust,* Institute of Contemporary Arts, London, United
Kingdom; P.S.1 Contemporary Art Center, Long Island City, United States
Melodrama, Artim, Centre Museo Vasco de Arte Contemporáneo, Vitoria-Gasteiz;
Museo de Arte Contemporáneo de Vigo, Vigo; Centro José Guerrero / Palacio de los
Condes de Gabia, Granada, Spain
Happy Outsiders from London and Scotland, Pro Arte Institute, St Petersburg,
Russia; Katowice City Gallery, Poland; Zacheta Gallery, Warsaw, Poland
Video Zone – The First International Video-Art Biennial in Israel, Center for Contem-
porary Art, Tel Aviv, Israel
The Hate U Give Little Infants Fucks Everyone, SMART Project Space, Amsterdam,
The Netherlands
Contextualize, Kunstverein Hamburg, Germany
The Rowan Collection: Contemporary British & Irish Art, Irish Museum of Modern Art,
Dublin, Ireland
In the Freud Museum, Freud Museum, London, United Kingdom
At Speed, with Sarah Morris, Galerie Max Hetzler, Berlin, Germany

2001   *Tenth Anniversary Exhibition, 100 Drawings and Photographs,* Matthew Marks Gallery,
New York, United States
Open Plan P3 – The Marathon, Alphadelta Gallery, Artio Gallery, Athens, Greece
Presentness is Grace – Experiencing the Suspended Moment, Arnolfini Gallery, Bristol;
Spacex Gallery, Exeter, United Kingdom
Casino 2001, Stedelijk Museum voor Actuele Kunst and Bijlokenmuseum, Ghent, Belgium
Nature in Photography, Galerie Nachst St Stephan, Vienna, Austria
Berlin Biennale, Berlin, Germany
Tracking, Kent and Vicki Logan Gallery, California Collage of Arts and Crafts,
Oakland, California, United States
Unreal Time Video, Fine Art Center, Korean Culture & Arts Foundation, Seoul, Korea
Deliberate Living, Greene Naftali Gallery, New York, United States

2000   *British Short Film Festival,* UCI Cinema, Leicester Square, London, United Kingdom
Geographies (Darren Almond, Graham Gussin, Anri Sala), Galerie Chantal Crousel,
Paris, France

Apocalypse: Beauty and Horror in Contemporary Art, Royal Academy of the Arts, London, United Kingdom
Darren Almond, Mark Hosking, Kerstin Engholm Galerie, Vienna, Austria
Inverse Perspectives, Edsvik, Sollentuna, Sweden
Out There, White Cube², London, United Kingdom
Making Time: Considering Time as a Material in Contemporary Video and Film, Palm Beach Institute of Contemporary Art, Florida, United States
Diary, Cornerhouse, Manchester, United Kingdom

1999   *Sleeping Waters,* Galerie Chantal Crousel, Paris, France
Chronos and Kairos, Museum Fridericianum, Kassel, Germany
Seeing Time, San Francisco Museum of Modern Art, San Francisco, United States
So Far Away, So Close, Encore...Bruxelles, Espace Méridien, Brussels, Belgium
Concrete Ashtray, Friedrich Petzel Gallery, New York, United States
Common People, Fondazione Sandretto Re Rebaundengo, Turin, Italy

1998   *UK Maximum Diversity,* Galerie Krinzinger, Benger Fabrik Bregenz, Bregenz, Austria
View Four, Mary Boone Gallery, New York, United States
Hidden Desires And Images, Art Dynamics, Tayayo Lida, Tokyo, Japan
Art Crash, Århus Kunstmuseum, Århus, Denmark
Ray Rapp, Tz'Art & Co., New York, United States

1997   *A Print Portfolio from London, (Ridinghouse/Booth Clibborn Editions),* Atle Gerhardsen, Oslo, Norway
Delta, Musée d'Art Moderne de la Ville de Paris, Paris, France
Hospital, Galerie Max Hetzler, Berlin, Germany
Sensation: Young British Artists from the Saatchi Collection, Royal Academy of Arts, London; Hamburger Bahnhof, Museum für Gegenwart, Berlin, Germany

1996   *Art & Innovation Prize,* (winner), Institute of Contemporary Art, London, United Kingdom
Something Else, Exmouth Market, London, United Kingdom
A Small Shifting Sphere of Serious Culture, Institute of Contemporary Arts, London, United Kingdom

1993   Winchester Gallery, Winchester, United Kingdom

1992   Southampton Quays, Southampton, United Kingdom

The artist would like to thank:
Melanie Ahmed, Wolfram Aue, Ziba de Weck Ardalan, Alex Bradley, Russel Briant, Bridget Chew, John Cleur, Richard Dawson, Stephanie Dorsey, Sean Dower, Ute Elskidsen, Simon Ertz, Joanne Ferrone, Hartwig Fischer, Peter Friese, Daniella Gareh, Grayson Management Inc., Max Hetzler, Julian Heynen, the Hoover Institution, Husni, Jay Jopling, Katya Kosheleva, Connor Linskey, Steve McCloud, Keir McGuinness, Kathleen Madden, Matthew Marks, Richard Massey, Susan May, the Monks at Samyey Monastery, Cliodhna Murphy, Ahsen Nadeem, Anna Nesbit, Norilsk Nickel, Samia Saouma, Anya Stonelake, Robert Thurman, Greg Weir, Adam Withington, and Zainal Arifin (Vinny) of Bromo Tours.

Co-published by Parasol unit foundation for contemporary art and Koenig Books, London
on the occasion of the exhibition *Fire Under Snow:* Darren Almond, 18 January – 30 March 2008

Copyright © 2008 Parasol unit foundation for contemporary art, Koenig Books, the artist,
and the individual authors

Editor: Ziba de Weck Ardalan for Parasol unit foundation for contemporary art, London
Editing and copyediting: Helen Wire
Concept and design: Moiré, Marc Kappeler & Markus Reichenbach, Zurich
Photography: Courtesy Darren Almond Studio, White Cube, Galerie Max Hetzler and Matthew
Marks Gallery
Cover: Detail from *Night + Fog (Monchegorsk)(11),* 2007
Endpapers: Detail from *Night + Fog (Monchegorsk)(13),* 2007
Typeface: UnicaSB
Paper: F-Color, Lumisilk, Munken Print White, Munken Lynx
Printed and bound in Germany by Druckerei zu Altenburg, Altenburg

All works courtesy of the artist/Gallerie Max Hetzler, Berlin/Jay Jopling, White Cube, London/
Matthew Marks Gallery, New York

Parasol unit foundation for contemporary art
14 Wharf Road, London N1 7RW
T +44 (0)20 7490 7373, F +44 (0)20 7490 7775
E info@parasol-unit.org, www.parasol-unit.org

Koenig Books Ltd., at the Serpentine Gallery
Kensington Gardens, London W2 3XA
www.koenigbooks.co.uk

Distribution:
UK & Eire: Cornerhouse Publications, 70 Oxford Street, GB-Manchester M1 5NH
T +44 (0) 161 200 15 03, F +44 (0) 161 200 15 04, publications@cornerhouse.org
Germany: Buchhandlung Walther König, Ehrenstrasse 4, 50672 Köln
T +49 (0) 221 20 59 6-53, F +49 (0) 221 20 59 6-60, verlag@buchhandlung-walther-koenig.de
Switzerland: Buch 2000, c/o AVA Verlagsauslieferungen AG, Centralweg 16,
8910 Affoltern a. A., T +41 (0) 1 762 42 00, F +41 (0) 1 762 42 10, a.koll@ava.ch
Outside Europe: D.A.P./ Distributed Art Publishers, Inc., 155 6th Avenue, 2nd Floor
New York, NY 10013, T +1 212 627 1999, F +1 212 627 9484, eleshowitz@dapinc.com

First published by Koenig Books, London
ISBN 978-3-86560-376-0

STANLEY THOMAS
JOHNSON FOUNDATION

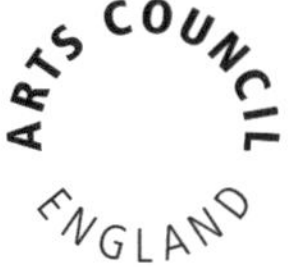